Ethics, Morality, and Insurance

The Indiana University Sesquicentennial Series on Insurance

ETHICS, MORALITY, AND INSURANCE

A Long-Range Outlook

John D. Long
Chairman and Professor of Insurance
Indiana University

Published by the Bureau of Business Research
Graduate School of Business / Indiana University

Library of Congress Catalog Card Number: 71-633786

Published by the
Bureau of Business Research,
Graduate School of Business,
Bloomington, Indiana 47401.
Printed in the United States of America.

To My Wife
HAZEL
And Her Optimism About The Future

CONTENTS

TABLES AND FIGURES

FOREWORD

The year 1970 marks the Sesquicentennial of Indiana University. This volume and the three companion volumes in the Sesquicentennial Series on Insurance stand as one of the contributions of the School of Business to this historic occasion.

A sesquicentennial afforded a peculiarly appropriate opportunity to consider concepts and events from the perspective of a long history and a long future. The idea of examining the institution of insurance within such a time dimension sprang in 1966 from the fertile imagination of Arthur M. Weimer, former dean of the Indiana University School of Business and now executive vice-president of the American Association of Collegiate Schools of Business. Professor John D. Long of Indiana University and several of his professorial colleagues in other institutions took up the idea shortly thereafter and in due course developed it into this series of volumes commemorating the Sesquicentennial. Mindful of the long history of insurance, the authors endeavored to speculate about numerous aspects of the long-range future of insurance. Their projections and anticipations extend at least into the beginning of the next century. I fully anticipate that in the years to come these volumes will be increasingly useful to planners and will clearly demonstrate the insight and vision of the authors. Whether time will corroborate their projections and prophesies is a matter that we will watch with fascination.

This particular volume deals with the connections between insurance and possible changes in ethical thought and moral behavior, a subject of deep and abiding interest to Dr. Long. Readers doubtless will be impressed (as I was upon reading this treatise) by the extent to which insurance depends upon the behavior of the people that the insurance serves. Professor Long's articulation of this relationship and his speculation about the long-range future are stimulating to the point of being disturbing. All those interested in the future of insurance, whether or not they agree with the tenets of this book, will find in it a common ground for discussion.

On behalf of Indiana University, I would like to express appreciation for several grants from insurance companies that permitted research to be undertaken for this series. In particular, we are indebted to Byron K. Elliott, chairman-emeritus of the John Hancock Mutual Life Insurance Company and long-time friend of Indiana University, who was personally responsible for raising the funds required for the project. We appreciate his friendship and thank him for his assistance in the financing of these studies.

The several authors in this series have worked independently, neither asking for nor receiving any substantive direction from the grantors, Mr. Elliott, or the several institutions at which the authors are based. Hence, all opinions, judgments, and recommendations found in these volumes are strictly the personal views and expressions of the respective authors. This statement does not imply that we would necessarily disagree, only that the authors had complete freedom to develop the substantive aspects of these studies.

Appreciation is expressed to the Indiana University Bureau of Business Research for undertaking the publication of these volumes. Congratulations and thanks are also extended to the several authors for accepting and completing their assignments with expertise and goodwill.

The author of this volume, Dr. John D. Long, is both a colleague in the Graduate School of Business and a long-time personal friend. Over the many years of our close working relationship, I have had many opportunities to bear witness to his high personal and professional standards. The success of the entire project was assured when Dr. Long accepted responsibility for the total effort including this volume. We are indebted to him for both his scholarship and leadership.

W. George Pinnell
Dean
Graduate School of Business
Indiana University

PREFACE

The subject matter of this volume has been annoying me for several years. As the project of which this volume is a part came into being, I knew that I would like to write about the long-range aspects of ethics and morality as they relate to insurance. At the same time I felt grossly incapable of giving this formidable topic the treatment it deserves. Finally, however, enthusiasm overcame discretion, and the present book was written.

Although ethics is hardly separable from theology, I have endeavored in the main to avoid the latter subject in my treatment of the topic. Similarly, even though many of the matters discussed in this book border on religion, I have endeavored to remain objective. I suspect, however, that my Christian heritage and evangelical faith in a triune personal God show through in numerous biases. If so, I offer no apology.

This book, like any other, is necessarily the work of many people. I am pleased to acknowledge and express my appreciation for the excellent editorial assistance provided by the Indiana University Bureau of Business Research. I am especially indebted to Robert W. Raichle, who, as an M.B.A. candidate and graduate assistant, helped me immensely in handling innumerable details and in readying the copy for submission to the publisher. I also thank Mrs. Deanna Collins, Mrs. Marilyn Barnett, and others for expertly typing several drafts of the manuscript.

A debt of a distinctly different type is owed to two of my colleagues, Professors Joseph M. Belth and Frederick G. Crane, who read and commented on the manuscript. More importantly, they listened with enviable forbearance to the exposition of my ideas and responded with lively and indispensable criticism. Out of fairness to them, I must report that they disagreed with my priorities, judgments, and conclusions more often than not. Nevertheless, their interest in my efforts was invaluable in improving the quality of my work. I also express appreciation to S. Travis Pritchett and Jerry Lee Shutt, who, as doctoral candidates in insurance in the Indiana University School of Business, read the manuscript and made helpful comments about it.

Every author who has a family also owes a debt to his family. My gratitude to Hazel, Douglas, Martha, and Elinor is large and overdue. They cheerfully bore a curtailment of usual activities to permit me to concentrate on this book, and I am grateful for their good nature.

Finally, I would like to thank Dean W. George Pinnell for consistently demonstrating his confidence in this project and for helping me find the time to complete it.

John D. Long

Bloomington, Indiana
July, 1970

1

INTRODUCTION

To one interested in insurance the train of events in recent years raises provocative questions: Have the recent changes in what people in the United States do and think been superficial or fundamental? What additional changes in attitudes and behavior are in store? Is the institution of insurance flexible enough to adjust to a changing environment? Is social behavior changing for the better or the worse, and what standards of good and bad are to be used in answering such a question? As society changes, will children of later generations feel that they can significantly shape their own future? Will they be genuinely interested in preparing for it? In a new and perhaps grossly different world how will their philosophies affect the sphere of insurance?

To what extent will violence become a way of life? How much violence can insurance, the major vehicle for sharing society's losses, absorb? Is insurance ultimately compatible with the concept of civil disobedience, whatever the motives and tactics of the latter? Will theft penetrate the outer limits of insurability? How much arson can the insurance system tolerate? Can expanding government and private insurance coexist indefinitely?

Does insurance require acceptance of a specific concept of right and wrong? Does the future really hold the promise of widespread

1

material profusion? If so, what prevailing attitudes toward right and wrong will this profusion be likely to produce? Is insurance on the threshold of a golden era, on the brink of great travail, or in neither position?

These and a host of complementary questions have prompted this book. The author makes no promise to answer all of the questions listed here. Some answers will be suggested, but the reader may find that even these do not satisfy him. The answers to some of the questions posed require facts that are difficult to obtain; others require value judgments that are debatable; and most bear on the future. We must all agree that the details of the future, if not its general outline, are impossible to fathom. The future guards its secrets well, and the progression of time has a way of summarily discrediting even the best predictions. As one professor is reputed to have told his class while discussing the hazards of speculation, "History sometimes plays jokes upon us which are not always in good taste."[1] This book has been written with the conviction that good can come from seeking facts, from offering value judgments, and from speculating about what may come to pass, even though readers may disagree as to what is best and time may prove the speculations entirely wrong.

THE CONCEPTS OF ETHICS AND MORALITY

The questions previously posed relate to the general subjects of ethics and morality. Since these concepts have received quite diverse treatments over the centuries, we should hasten to clarify the sense in which they are used in this book. Otherwise, we could soon find ourselves in a terminological quagmire.

A convenient starting point is to consider the word "ethics." The Swiss theologian, Heinrich Emil Brunner, has stated that the central ethical question is, "What ought we to do?"[2] Henry Sidgwick reached much the same meaning by describing ethics as the study

---

[1]Joseph A. Schumpeter, as related in Spencer D. Pollard, *How Capitalism Can Succeed* (Harrisburg, Pa.: The Stackpole Company, 1966), pp. 65-66, used by permission.

[2]Heinrich Emil Brunner, *The Divine Imperative: A Study in Christian Ethics* (Philadelphia: The Westminster Press, 1947), p. 90.

"of what individual human beings 'ought'—or what it is 'right' for them—to do, or to seek to realize by voluntary action." He added:

> By using the word "individual" I provisionally distinguish the study of Ethics from that of Politics, which seeks to determine the constitution and the right public conduct of governed societies: both Ethics and Politics being, in my view, distinguished from positive sciences by having as their special and primary object to determine what ought to be, and not to ascertain what merely is, has been, or will be.[3]

This concept of ethics does not indicate whether the question of "ought"—as posed by Brunner, Sidgwick, and earlier thinkers—has one answer or many. For centuries learned men and women have been debating absolutism versus relativism in matters of right and wrong. Even absolutists themselves cannot agree whether or not the standard as to what men ought to do has been prescribed by the Creator of the universe unequivocally to all men in all circumstances. One absolutist view is that the answer, while not a matter of specific divine revelation, is nevertheless innate in the state of things, immutable, and universal. Relativists, on the other hand, see the answer to the "ought" question as depending on the person, the timing, and many other variables. What is good and proper in one circumstance, according to this view, may be bad and totally improper in another circumstance. While little can be added in this book to the continuing debate, the issue is especially pertinent to Chapter 8 and is treated there at some length as it pertains to insurance.

Leaving this absolute-versus-relative issue for now, let us clarify some terminology about morality. Accepting the idea that ethics refers to what men ought to do, we can with some logic regard morality as the behavior of a person or group, insofar as the behavior is relevant to and measured against the ethics. In this classification ethics is normative (the standard) and morality is empirical (the actual behavior as related to the standard). Another way to put the distinction is that morality is the practice of ethics.[4] The practice may be close to or wide of the mark.

---

[3] Henry Sidgwick, *The Method of Ethics* (7th ed.; Chicago: The University of Chicago Press, 1907), p. 1.

[4] For a discussion of the detailed rationale for following this terminology, see Edgar Sheffield Brightman, *Moral Laws* (New York: The Abingdon Press, 1933), pp. 11-32, 55-80.

In this usage of the terms, good morals are relatively close to the ethical norm, and bad morals are relatively far removed. Some conduct perhaps is amoral or unmoral (but not immoral) by being irrelevant to the norm because of its neutral character. "Moral law" is a useful expression often employed either to describe the behavior constituting the ethical norm or to point up the consequences of violating this behavior. Probably no facet of the debate over absolutism and relativism creates more interest and more acrimony than the disagreement over whether moral law is absolute or relative.[5]

A few other comments about our understanding of the meaning of ethics and morality may help to clarify the subject. As we have seen, we can refer to good or bad morals within the framework of a single ethics, making our judgment on the basis of the disparity between the ethics and the behavior. However, we cannot similarly speak of good or bad ethics while remaining within the ethical system on which we are passing judgment, since the ethics is the norm for what is good. This constraint does not imply that we are bound to accept any ethics foisted upon us without objection. In a free society a highly important option—perhaps the most important—is the choice of one's ethics, a choice that must be made with the utmost care. Furthermore, the citizen is behooved to urge his ethics upon others who, in turn, are free to accept or reject his importunities. In defining morality, therefore, we should remember that any meaningful discussion of the term must be considered in the framework of a particular ethics.

Chapter 2 sets forth the general pattern of ethics on which the author regards the long-range availability and use of insurance to depend. Since insurance probably can function within a fairly wide range of ethics, Chapter 2 does not actually suggest how much or how little of a particular attitude or belief is necessary for insurance to be available and to be wanted. In fact, the point is stressed that quantitative considerations are impractical or perhaps even impos-

---

[5]For a tightly argued hypothetical dialogue between teacher and student, see Mortimer J. Adler, *A Dialectic of Morals* (Notre Dame, Ind.: University of Notre Dame, 1941). The teacher argues for a moral law applicable to all men in the same way. The student, a moral skeptic, insists that there is no natural moral law but, rather, that what is good is subjective depending on the events, the time, and the place. We give more attention to this issue in Chapter 8.

sible. For example, as explained in Chapter 2, the insuring process presumes honesty, a relative phenomenon. One can hardly measure the minimum degree of honesty essential to insurance. Chapter 2 is merely an attempt to identify the various elements of an ethics that will encourage and reinforce widespread availability and use of insurance.

Because much attention is given in later chapters to possible future changes in morality (the practice of ethics), we need to be as specific as possible about the kinds of behavioral changes subject to our speculations. Two patterns are especially important. Whether they involve fundamentally different types of morality changes depends upon whether one is an absolutist or a relativist in matters of ethics and morality. The distinction between the patterns, however, will be useful in later chapters and therefore shall be drawn here. One pattern is apparent from the fact that a person can change his behavior without changing his ethics. The result may be to widen the gap between what he believes he ought to do (his ethics) and what he does (his morality). Suppose that Mr. A, never having committed act "y" and believing it to be contrary to his ethics, nevertheless commits act "y." His action, for example a theft, may have been the result of severe economic pressure or may simply have revealed his own frailty of character. Whatever the reason, his morality changed in the process, and the spread between his ethics and his behavior widened. In subsequent chapters we shall speculate about numerous possible changes in the morality of individuals.

The second pattern involves a different kind of change in morality. A person can alter his professed ethics to accommodate a form of behavior previously repugnant to his old ethics or to repudiate an act which was compatible with his former ethics. Mr. A is prevailed upon to accept a new ethics, "E^2," as a replacement for his former ethics, "E^1." Suppose that an act "w," repugnant to his old ethics "E^1" is tolerable or, even under certain circumstances, commendable under his new ethics "E^2." Suppose further that Mr. A, after embracing "E^2," begins to practice act "w." In this circumstance, his morality has changed absolutely in the sense that he now commits act "w," whereas under his former ethics "E^1" he did not. Because of his switch in ethics, however, his morality in a relative sense may not have changed; the relationship between his new behavior (including act "w") and his new ethics "E^2" is not necessarily different from that between his former behavior (excluding act "w") and his former ethics ("E[1]").[6] In later chapters we speculate about possible future behavioral changes of this type that could be fundamentally important to insurance.

In some circumstances changing practices by large segments of the population can cause commensurate changes, after due time lags, in the prevailing social sentiments as to what is right and wrong. If increasing numbers of people join Mr. A in committing act "w," the prevailing reaction by society might also change over time. Behavior in this sense, then, could alter ethics. In other circumstances a few leaders of ethical thought, through their exhortation and example, could in time produce significant and widespread changes in the behavior of the society. In this sense, ethics alters behavior. When Mr. A, in our previous example, switched his ethics from "E[1]" to "E[2]," he might have been the beneficiary—or the victim—of just such a process.

Although the words "ethics," "morality," and "insurance" may appear an unseemly combination to use in a book title, the words go together quite well for the purpose envisioned here. Ethics, with its relationship to morality, provides a convenient and meaningful umbrella under which to gather numerous behavioral considerations bearing on insurance and to speculate about their importance to insurance in the future.

THE APPROACH USED IN THIS STUDY

This book summarizes the results of efforts on the part of the author to identify changes in ethics and morality that may influence the availability of and demand for insurance. The time dimensions for this evaluation extend to the turn of the century (although the implications, of course, are not limited to this period). The end of one millenium and the beginning of another is a dramatic instant of time and a natural benchmark in the affairs of men. Despite the prospect of the year 2000 becoming a faddishly popular topic of

---

[6]Absolutists might insist that Mr. A is deluding himself in thinking that he can change his ethics. They might feel that behavior is necessarily measured against unchanging absolute ethics, and that if act "w" is contrary to the immutable ethics, it is wrong despite any futile machinations on Mr. A's part to escape from the consequences of natural law. Absolutists might feel that the answer to the question "What ought we to do?" is not susceptible to Mr. A's changing whims and not in the least altered by his ostensibly shifting from "E[1]" to "E[2]."

study, the change of millenia remains a legitimate and inviting point of reference against which to appraise insurance or virtually anything else.

As previously mentioned, the ethical foundations of insurance are described in Chapter 2. The remainder of the book is devoted to speculations about major changes that might affect insurance over the long-range future either by altering the gap between moral behavior and the prevailing ethics or by altering the prevailing ethics and, in turn, the moral behavior relevant to insurance.

The current size of the institution of insurance in this country is ample evidence that the ethical foundation of insurance, whatever its characteristics may be, is solid enough to support a thriving and growing insurance system. Consequently, a logical way to speculate in long-range fashion about insurance is to look for possible erosion of the ethical foundation or for possibilities of a moral behavior increasingly at variance with the ethics. This approach means that the present book relates primarily to the possible major changes that could interfere seriously with the insuring process; thus, the objective is to anticipate possible dangers and ways of avoiding them. Incidental attention is also given to the possibility that some of the future changes in ethics and morality may strengthen the institution of insurance.

Chapter 3 is devoted to an appraisal of population history and prospects on the presumption that population growth may be the most probable cause of changes in ethics and morality as they relate to insurance. Chapter 4 discusses the consequences for insurance of possible changes in ethical thought and moral behavior produced by population growth. Chapter 5 deals with the implications of possible changes in ethical thought and moral behavior produced by inflation. Chapters 6 and 7 pertain to changes in ethics and morality and their implications for insurance that may result from advances in certain technologies. Chapter 8 treats various consequences of relativism in ethical thought, particularly the possible development of the "new morality" to which increasing attention has recently been given. Chapter 9 suggests some actions that might be taken within the institution of insurance to forestall or encourage various developments.

The reader can quickly see that the organizational demarcations are somewhat artificial in that the topic of each chapter spills over into the topics of the others. Population growth, for example, may strongly influence inflation. A progressively complex technology coupled with an expanding population, as another example, may be quite influential in shaping a new morality, if indeed there can be any such thing. Even so, the chapter divisions afford some semblance of order for the ensuing discussions.

A possible pitfall warrants comment at this point. One glaring uncertainty involves what the relative importance of private as compared with public insurance will be by the turn of the century. For purposes of this discourse, however, no attempt is made to distinguish between private and public insurance. Insurance is essentially the same, regardless of the private or public nature of its organization, and the ethical foundation upon which the insuring process depends does not necessarily vary with the private or public quality of the management. Hence, the ethical requisites of a successful, long-range use of insurance can be identified whether the management is private or public. Similarly, possible changes in ethics or morality may be as helpful or as detrimental to a public insurance program as to a private one. Numerous references are made in this book to private and public insurance and to possible future changes in the private-public insurance mix. These are incidental, however, to the principal consideration of insurance as an entity in itself. We would do well, also, to remember that not every process passing under the name of insurance is, in fact, insurance. Numerous activities in the private and governmental sectors take the name of insurance unwarrantedly. This book is not concerned with private guarantees or public assistance programs.

THE DILEMMA OF THE FUTURIST

A study which deals with the future is fraught with possibilities of error. The topic calls for a knowledge of the future; yet the future is unknowable. However keen one's knowledge of the past and insight into the present may be, one is forced to resort to guesswork in order to pursue the topic at all. Still, our urgent need to be prepared for the future as best we can justifies to some extent our use of guesswork.

As we begin to speculate about the future, we could easily grow confused by the nuances in the meaning of such words as forecasting, previsioning, predicting, and the like. Fashion and common sense encourage the futurist to couch his statements in carefully qualified terms to protect himself from embarrassment should events prove him wrong. Possessing this understandable apprehension, futurists normally work with projections as opposed to predictions. The projections, they take pains to note, are dependent on one or more precisely stated assumptions. Whether or not the future bears out the projections depends in large measure upon the accuracy of the assumptions, and the reader is normally free to accept or reject these assumptions. Projectionists may go so far as to include several sets of projections from among which users can choose. Some projectionists are more courageous (or foolhardy) and indicate which of the projections they regard as most probable. Normally, however, even these projectionists are careful to recognize that the probabilities can change as individuals take steps either to fulfill or defeat the prophesies implied in the projections.[7] Users normally welcome indications of which projections are most probable because they want to learn what the futurist believes is going to happen. A large set of projections from which the user must make his own choice is hardly satisfying.

On the other hand, a futurist has to be wary lest the unsuspecting user impute to the projections a finality or a credulity that the projectionist himself would never dream of attaching to them. Bertrand de Jouvenel cautions that the futurist "must fear skepticism far less than credulity" because of the readiness with which others may accept his surmises as gospel.[8] Moreover, the futurist must never forget that even the most probable outcome is subject to change. The very act of projecting may cause things to be different than they would have been had the projective effort not been undertaken in the first place. This idea is the same as that of Von Heisenberg and others who admitted to the "principle of uncertainty" in their efforts to ascertain the position and velocity of particles. The act of measurement, they concluded, was itself disturbing. Percy W. Bridgman put the thought quaintly many years ago when he said

[7]See for example the fascinating and expert work of Herman Kahn and Anthony J. Wiener, *The Year 2000: A Framework for Speculation on the Next Thirty-Three Years* (New York: The Macmillan Company, 1967). We might also notice in passing that the national economic projections of the National Planning Association sometimes emerge as "judgment" projections, representing what the projectionists regard as the most probable outcome. An example is *National Economic Projections to 1975/76* (Washington, D.C.: National Planning Association, 1965).

[8]Bertrand de Jouvenel, *The Art of Conjecture*, translated by Nikita Lary (New York: Basic Books, Inc., 1967), pp. 16-17.

that the fact that "a cat looks at a king" may cause things in the kingdom to proceed on a different course thereafter.[9] The simple act of
projection, even though diminuitive in comparison to total events,
creates an alteration, however slight it may be.

These remarks do not imply that this small book will perceptibly
influence the long-range nature of ethics and morality in the United
States. There is an implication, however, that increasing attention
by a large number of persons can and will alter the future course
of events. De Jouvenel comments on this point as follows:

Man is fortunate when the desirable and the probable coincide! The case is
often otherwise, and thus we find ourselves trying to bend the course of
events in a way which will bring the probable closer to the desirable. And
this is the real reason why we study the future.[10]

The possibility of bending the future so as to bring the probable
closer to the desirable poses still another difficult problem for the
futurist. Ideally, the futurist, in arriving at what he regards as the
most probable outcome, takes into account the bending of events that
will bring the probable closer to the desirable. In practice, few futurists can be so sophisticated, and even if they could, they might
still have a problem. If futurists generally did take an expected
bending into account and did project thereby a certain desirable
outcome as the most probable, they might find that others, upon
seeing the "most probable" projection, would be less inclined to effect the necessary bending of events that would render that projection truly the most probable. Thus, the futurist normally makes
some projections about the future that he fervently hopes will be
self-defeating because of the resistance and the consequent bending
that the projections will elicit. Such is the nature of much of the
speculation about the future that is summarized in this book.

DISCERNING THE TRENDS

The main way to contemplate future behavioral changes that might
be morally incompatible with insurance is to search for such
changes on the assumption that current trends will continue. This

---

[9]Percy W. Bridgman, "The New Vision of Science," *Harper's Magazine*, vol. 158
(March, 1929), p. 448.

[10]De Jouvenel, *The Art of Conjecture*, p. 19, used by permission.

method is faulty because mass moral behavior could change almost overnight to strengthen or weaken the existing system of insurance. Abrupt and unexpected change, however, by its very nature can never be predicted, and all projective efforts are in danger of running afoul of such imponderables.

Fortunately for most projectionists, most changes come about slowly and deliberately, especially those changes concerned with mass behavior. By assuming that the same holds true for the future, it follows that many of the moral behavior changes that may occur during the next 30 years or so will result from forces already at work. Thus, searching for relevant trends and speculating about the continuation of such trends were the principal activities in preparing this book. However, all of the searching and speculating may have been done at the expense of completely overlooking events or processes that may cause the trends discussed here to be halted or even reversed. Such are the dangers of speculating about the future.[11]

One of the most problematic aspects of the speculations summarized later in this book is whether certain recent and disconcerting changes in human behavior are (1) mere irregularities in a centuries-old swell of kindness, compassion, gentleness, and similar attributes or (2) an actual reversion toward former lower levels. This question appears throughout this manuscript. Have we temporarily slipped in recent years on our upward climb on the "curve of gentility," or have we peaked and begun a retrogression?

Burnham Putnam Beckwith in a recent book would have us believe that we are still riding, and will continue indefinitely to ride, the trend of the "rise of humanitarianism." He writes:

> The rise and spread of humanitarianism has been a major social trend for over 500 years and will continue for another 500. It includes all phases of the movement from cruelty and brutality toward consideration and tenderness in the treatment of human beings. This general trend has been obvious in the ever more humane treatment of defeated nations, prisoners of war, heretics and dissenters, juvenile and adult delinquents, children, wives, the feeble-minded and insane, the poor, the sick, and all other potential victims of brutality.[12]

---

[11]A considerably more detailed and erudite discussion about the techniques and reasons for conjecturing about the future can be found in the first chapter of a forthcoming book by Robert I. Mehr and Seev Neumann, "Inflation, Technology and Growth: Possible Implications for Insurance" (to be published by the Bureau of Business Research, Graduate School of Business, Indiana University).

[12]Burnham Putnam Beckwith, *The Next 500 Years* (New York: Exposition Press, 1967), p. 32, used by permission.

When one reflects on behavior in antiquity, in the medieval centuries, or even in more recent times, one can have little disagreement with Beckwith. Clearly, we have been improving over the centuries. Man has come a long way in terms of the concern he displays for others, especially in the United States and certain other parts of the world. Old people and infants are no longer routinely left in the elements to die. Debtors' prisons are no longer a way of life. Even though war is potentially more devastating, treatment of prisoners, the wounded, and civilian victims of war generally is much more humane. Few people, at least in this country, are left to starve. Through private and public charity, those in physical need are aided on an elaborate scale. Society attempts to restrain individuals from inflicting bodily harm on one another. Private and public social control attempts to protect citizens from being harmed through what they eat, drink, wear, ride, or otherwise use. Safety is emphasized. The law in the main is protective and beneficent and is not antagonistic to rehabilitation. While modern personal competition is fierce, it is not often barbaric.

Despite these encouragements, however, a strange disquiet is evident. The social upheavals of the 1960s have left their mark. We cannot help but wonder if they portend major deterioration to come. The hatreds, the disenchantments, the destruction, the gross ill will may be but the relatively minor growing pains of a world society destined in the long run to possess a degree of humanitarianism much greater than has ever been realized previously. Still, we are distressed by the increase in various social indexes such as crime rates. If these ills are merely growing pains, they are nonetheless acute. If they are harbingers of change in the directions of the present trends, they are extremely serious messages. At this stage we can only guess what they are.

The view that humanitarianism in a prosperous society after many generations of development can reach the point of turning upon itself may be valid. An ugly possibility is that the population growth can become so rapid that it will interfere with the orderly progression of humanitarianism. The related difficulties of inflation and changing technology mentioned earlier fan the fires of uncertainty. The critical issue for us will be whether this nation can maintain its moral momentum during the next several decades or whether a reversal will delay or even destroy our ascent into the golden age to which we aspire.

2

THE ETHICAL
FOUNDATION
OF INSURANCE

To speculate about the long-range influence of ethics and morality on insurance, we need a frame of reference. Chapter 2 is a brief articulation of the ethical foundation of insurance. A brief treatment of four preliminary matters will simplify the discussion of insurance ethics. These preliminaries concern (1) the redistributive nature of insurance, (2) the relationship between national income and national purchases of insurance, (3) the essential steps in the insuring process, and (4) the institutional apparatus essential to the insuring process. A review of each of these four conceptual aspects of insurance should contribute to a better understanding of the ethical foundation of insurance.

INSURANCE IS REDISTRIBUTIVE

Before contemplating the ethical underpinnings of insurance, we should remind ourselves of the nature of insurance. This reminder is timely because our study concerns only insurance and not other ways of treating loss. Aside from being a possible means of saving—and the savings can be quite substantial in certain types of insurance—insurance is essentially a device for redistributing resources. In many respects voluntary redistribution through insurance may be more pleasant and efficient than the redistribution that occurs through taxation and public spending, although redistribution through insurance is small-scale by comparison.[1]

In essence, monies are collected; some of the monies are held or invested; and eventually disbursements are made for expenses, claims, refunds, rewards to suppliers of capital, and other purposes. Individuals or organizations experiencing certain contingencies are compensated by a stipulated amount or an amount measurable in some manner relative to the contingency. Occasionally the compensation is made in kind instead of in money. The amount of compensation to the claimant may bear little discernible relationship to the amount the insured paid the insurer. With relatively few of the individuals or organizations engaged in the arrangement normally experiencing the contingencies that evoke the payments (except in respect to whole life insurance), a relatively large number of those who are insured pay but do not receive money.[2]

Thus, whatever else it is, insurance is basically a redistribution. The stress on redistribution, however, is not intended to deprecate the important by-products that flow from the use of insurance. The overworked metaphor about insurance being the handmaiden of commerce is still appropriate. If it is weak at all, the weakness stems from understatement. "Commerce" is perhaps too narrow a term. "Business enterprise" or "economic activity" might be used to improve the metaphor. In a sophisticated economy, insurance assumes many roles. Despite all the trappings, however, and in the

---

[1]Redistribution through private insurance is distinctly limited compared to redistribution through acts of government. Private insurance premiums in the United States in 1968 were perhaps about $65 billion (a figure determined by taking premiums, including subscriptions to private hospital plans, as reported in the several fact books and eliminating the estimated duplication, especially with respect to health insurance premiums). These premiums were about 7 percent of 1968 GNP. Taxation by all levels of government in this country for the same year probably was at least $215 billion (although this figure may be very rough), or about 25 percent of GNP. Premiums and taxes were estimated from data in the following: *Insurance Facts* (New York: Insurance Information Institute, 1969), p. 9; *Life Insurance Fact Book* (New York: Institute of Life Insurance, 1969), p. 53; *Source Book of Health Insurance Data* (New York: Health Insurance Institute, 1969), pp. 43-44; U.S. Department of Commerce, Bureau of the Census, *Statistical Abstract of the United States,* 1969 (90th ed.; Washington, D.C.: U.S. Govt. Printing Office, 1969), pp. 385, 408; *Survey of Current Business,* vol. 50 (April, 1970), p. S-1, is the source for the GNP figure. The taxation figure apparently does not include taxes for social security and medicare.

[2]This is not to say that they do not receive a value for their payments to the insurer. They purchase the benefit of protection.

face of all the activities that insurance facilitates, insurance (except when it is a means of saving) is still essentially a redistribution. This point is useful to remember.

USE NOT SOLELY A FUNCTION OF INCOME

Another matter deserving preliminary attention in this chapter is the influence of income on the use of insurance. The point is relevant because a casual observer might feel intuitively that use of insurance depends completely on the level of income and is not related in any significant way to ethics and morality. He might expect an individual or a society with relatively low income to buy commensurately less insurance. While no data are presented relating income levels to insurance purchases by individuals, some figures are presented in this section to suggest that use of insurance among the several nations is not completely explained by the respective levels of national income. Hence, the availability and use of insurance in a society must depend in part on other variables, which may include the ethics and morality of the society.

The figures summarized in this section are based on worldwide national income and insurance premium data. Both sets of data are of dubious accuracy, the latter even more than the former. Still, the accuracies probably are close enough to justify the generalization that the ethical and moral climate of a society may influence the use of insurance.

To the author's knowledge, the best source of data on the magnitude of insurance premium volume for numerous nations of the world is the Swiss Reinsurance Company.[3] Similarly, the company is also a convenient source of data about absolute or relative national income for various nations of the world. Numerous data may

---

[3]In 1964 Swiss Reinsurance Company, on the occasion of its 100th anniversary, published *Insurance Markets of the World*. This volume contains sketchy but (as of the time of this writing) the best available data on the magnitude of private insurance premiums in the several nations of the world. The premium data are presented in local currencies. The exchange rates for converting the various monetary units into U.S. dollars are also included. For most of the nations the respective conversion rates are for 1960. For a few nations the conversion time is a bit earlier or later. The publication does not indicate the time during a particular year when the rate applies. Presumably it is as of the end of the year. With all their shortcomings, the data are extremely useful.

be found in the company's *Experiodica* and *Sigma,* occasional publications having to do with international insurance.

Table 1, based on *Insurance Markets of the World* and several other sources, summarizes the private insurance premium volume of major sections of the world. The data pertain mainly to 1960. Several caveats are essential in the use of this table. First, premium data pertaining to countries other than the United States were extracted from *Insurance Markets of the World* in the respective local currencies and then converted into U.S. dollars according to the conversion rates listed in the publication. Second, available premium information about the respective nations was supplied to *Insurance Markets of the World* by contributing authors, each of whom was familiar with insurance in the nation for which he was reporting. Third, while the premium data generally apply to 1960, some discrepancies exist. Some figures are noted as pertaining to different years; other discrepancies in the figures may have passed unnoted. Fourth, U.S. premium data, which were not reported for 1960 in *Insurance Markets of the World,* were taken from other sources as indicated. The U.S. figures, therefore, may be inconsistent with the others.

Fifth, the treatment of voluntary insurance premiums paid to governmental insurers in collectivized nations and the treatment of voluntary and compulsory premiums paid to governmental insurers in nations with large private insurance sectors complicate the summary. *Insurance Markets of the World* reports at least some of the premiums collected by Gosstrakh (the insurance facility of the Soviet government) and some of the premiums collected by some, but not all, of the other socialist governments. No data, for example, are included for Red China or Bulgaria. The data for the United States do not include governmental insurance. Insurance premiums paid to insuring instrumentalities of the U.S. government or state governments are relatively small except for the payments into the federal Old Age, Survivors, Disability, and Health Insurance Program. Since the counterparts to these payments in the socialized countries are not included in the figures,[4] such payments have been omitted from the U.S. figures in an effort to achieve a consistent comparison.

---

[4]Perhaps in the socialized countries these payments in money or kind are not regarded as insurance at all. In a sense collectivism is a sort of loss-sharing arrangement, albeit often of a dismal variety.

TABLE 1

Private* Insurance Premiums by World Geographic Areas, 1960
(converted to U.S. dollars)

	Dollars (billions)	Percent of Total
North America	$36.1	65.4%
United States	34.4+	62.3
Canada (1961)	1.7	3.1
Latin America‡	0.7	1.3
Europe	15.6	28.3
Western Europe	13.0	23.6
Satellite countries	1.1	2.0
USSR	1.5	2.7
Africa	0.5	0.9
Asia	1.4	2.5
Japan	1.0	1.7§
India	0.2	0.4
Others	0.2	0.4
Oceania	0.9	1.6
Australia	0.7	1.2
All others	0.2	0.4
Total	*$55.2*	*100.0%*

*"Private" is not fully descriptive as a part of the table title. Certain voluntary premiums paid to government insurers are included for some of the collectivist nations but not for the United States. Neither does the U.S. figure include payments into the social security programs.

+An effort was made to estimate and eliminate from the U.S. total the duplication, particularly with regard to health insurance premiums, found in the fact book figures.

‡Central and South America.

§Rounding inaccuracies were necessary to bring the total to 100.

Sources: All premium data other than those for the United States came from *Insurance Markets of the World* (Zurich: Swiss Reinsurance Company, 1964). All premium data were converted to U.S. dollars at the respective conversion rates shown on the several pages of this publication. U.S. premium data came from *Best's Insurance Reports, 1965* (New York: Alfred M. Best Company, Inc.), p. n; *Best's Insurance Reports, Fire and Casualty, 1965* (New York: Alfred M. Best Company, Inc.), p. x; *Source Book of Health Insurance Data* (New York: Health Insurance Institute, 1968), pp. 44-45; *Life Insurance Fact Book* (New York: Institute of Life Insurance, 1968), p. 51; and *Insurance Facts* (New York: Insurance Information Institute, 1968), p. 17.

Finally, the data are old. The current absolute figures doubtless are different now. They probably are larger for virtually every reporting nation. The numerical relationships between national income and insurance premiums may also have changed substantially. Nevertheless, with all of their possible weaknesses, the figures show a tremendous concentration of private insurance premiums in North America and Europe. Such concentration is to be expected because North America and Western Europe are the sites of most of the free world's income.

TABLE 2

World Population, GNP, Insurance Premium Volume, and Ratio of Premiums to GNP by World Geographic Areas, 1963

	Population		Gross National Product		Insurance Premium Volume		
	Millions	% of World Total	Dollars* (in billions)	% of World Total	Dollars* (in billions)	% of World Total	Ratio of Premiums to GNP
North America	208	7%	$629	36%	$40.3	64%	6.4
United States	189	6	589	34	38.3	61	6.5
Canada	19	1	40	2	2.0	3	5.0
Latin America+	231	7	67	4	0.8	1	1.2
Western Europe	314	10	415	24	15.1	24	3.6
European Economic Community	175	6	250	14	7.0	11	2.8
European Free Trade Area	92	3	137	8	7.6	12	5.5
Others	47	1	28	2	0.5	1	1.8
Eastern Bloc	1,085	34	425	24	2.8	4	0.7
China	740	23	106	6	0.2	—	0.2
USSR	225	7	247	14	1.9	3	0.8
Eastern Europe	120	4	72	4	0.7	1	1.0
Africa	294	9	41	2	0.7	1	1.7
Asia‡	1,008	32	152	9	2.3	4	1.5
Oceania	17	1	22	1	1.1	2	5.0
Total	3,157	100%	$1,751	100%	$63.1	100%	3.6

*Converted to U.S. dollars.
+Central and South America.
‡Excluding Communist China.
Source: Experiodica, vol. 3, no. 4 (no date), p. 3.

Table 2, constructed from data appearing in the Swiss Reinsurance Company's *Experiodica,* indicates population distribution, gross national product, insurance premium volume, and ratio of premiums to GNP by geographic region for 1963. The heavy concentrations of premium volume in North America and Western Europe are still observable. For most nations or blocs of nations, however, the ratios of premium volume to GNP vary noticeably, and the differences seem large enough to be significant. The low percentages for the collectivized nations or blocs are easy enough to understand; insurance premiums simply do not serve the function in those countries that they do in others. The spread in the percentages among the other nations, however, is not as easily explained and is the subject of our particular interest.

Since the comparisons are subject to many possible errors, the discrepancy between a nation's share of world income and its share of world premium volume may be due to errors in reporting or to inconsistencies in processing the data. One could argue convincingly, however, that the range of the ratios given in Table 2 is too large to be dismissed summarily. Another possible explanation is that all or a substantial part of the range in the ratios may be due to differences in the cost of insurance from one nation to another rather than to differences in the real use of insurance. The differences in cost may reflect differences in loss frequency, loss severity, operating efficiency of the insurers, or other characteristics of the insurance system. Here again, however, the variation is a bit too large for easy acceptance of this explanation.

Any of these factors or some combination of countless others may account for the range in percentages. The figures are presented simply to suggest that, while income level seems to be a highly important influence in the use of insurance in a nation or bloc of nations within the free world, it does not appear to be the sole determinant. Some additional clarification is needed.

Among the possible explanations is the thesis that differences among nations in the use of insurance (relative to national income) are partially attributable to differences in the ethical and moral characteristics of the several nations. The idea to be discussed later in this chapter is that the availability and the use of insurance depend on a certain type of ethics. No effort is made in the chapter to prove any empirical and quantitative relationship between a particular national ethics and the national spending on insurance (relative to national income). Since quantification of ethics and morality is difficult, if not impossible, such an effort probably would be doomed to frustration from the beginning. The discussion is directed, instead, toward identifying and describing the ethics believed to be most conducive to widespread and sustained availability and use of insurance in any society. Even this more modest undertaking is tenuous at best.

THE INSURING PROCESS

Insurance literature is replete with detailed descriptions of the nature of insurance, how it is created and used, the requisites of an insurable condition, the use of probability theory in insurance, and the uses and limitations of insurance.[5] Much of this material is not pertinent to our discussion. We do need to understand, however, the process through which insurance is made available and accepted for use. The fundamental process can be synopsized as follows:

1.   One or more individuals create an organization, simple or complex, through which promises are to be made to pay fixed or determinable amounts to persons or to other organizations (or to their beneficiaries) who, having paid or promised to pay money or other resources into the organization or having otherwise served or promised to serve the organization, experience a specified type of contingency such as loss of life, loss of property, disability, or incurrence of an obligation.[6]

2.   The newly created organization accumulates resources, normally in money but conceivably in kind, through the sale of some sort of proprietary interest or participatory claim against the resources so accumulated.

3.   The organization holds these resources in a custodial confidence to the extent that they are not used in creating and maintaining the organization. The custodial arrangement normally permits an investment of the monies or use of other property in such a way as to yield an increment to the resources so held. It also normally permits within a narrow range of possibilities a change of the resources from one form to another.

---

[5]For readings representative of the ways in which these subjects are treated in insurance literature see Herbert S. Denenberg and others, *Risk and Insurance* (Englewood Cliffs, N.J.: Prentice-Hall, Inc., 1964), pp. 141-51, 167-93, 379-408; Mark R. Greene, *Risk and Insurance* (2nd ed.; Cincinnati: South-Western Publishing Company, 1968), pp. 1-76, 747-90; J. D. Hammond, ed., *Essays in the Theory of Risk and Insurance* (Glenview, Ill.: Scott, Foresman and Company, 1968), particularly Part III, pp. 149-257; Allen L. Mayerson, *Introduction to Insurance* (New York: The Macmillan Company, 1962), pp. 1-19; Robert I. Mehr and Emerson Cammack, *Principles of Insurance* (4th ed.; Homewood, Ill.: Richard D. Irwin, Inc., 1966), pp. 3-43, 758-825; Irving Pfeffer, *Insurance and Economic Theory* (Homewood, Ill.: Richard D. Irwin, Inc. for the S. S. Huebner Foundation for Insurance Education, 1956), pp. 5-8, 15-69; Robert Riegel and Jerome S. Miller, *Insurance Principles and Practices* (5th ed.; Englewood Cliffs, N.J.: Prentice-Hall, Inc., 1966), pp. 1-39, 565-95; C. Arthur Williams, Jr. and Richard M. Heins, *Risk Management and Insurance* (New York: McGraw-Hill Book Company, 1964), pp. 47-55, 478-504.

[6]In certain arrangements, for example a Lloyd's type of association, one or more individuals make the promises, hold and use the resources, pay the claims, and perform all the other acts. In a reciprocal the promises technically are made by each insured also being an insurer. In practical terms, the reciprocal itself does the promising and engages in the other necessary acts, especially if it is large. In all other arrangements a distinct organization is created.

4.   One or more individuals on behalf of the insuring organization prescribe the contingent circumstances in which and the
types of individuals or organizations to whom the insuring organization is willing to pay money or to perform specific tasks.

5.   One or more individuals on behalf of the insuring organization articulate precisely the promises which the organization is to
make. Almost invariably the promises are eventually reduced to
printed or written form.

6.   One or more individuals on behalf of the insuring organization decide the nature and magnitude of the consideration which
the organization must receive from each promisee in order to be in
a position to fulfill its promises. This decision may be made as the
result of simple or complex assumptions and calculations that are
normally quite sophisticated and highly mathematical.

7.   One or more individuals on behalf of the insuring organization solicit expressions of willingness of other individuals or
organizations to do whatever is prescribed so as to qualify, in the
event of a given contingency, for the benefits specified in the promises.

8.   One or more individuals on behalf of the insuring organization decide how to respond and then respond accordingly to each
solicited or unsolicited expression of interest in the promises. The
decision making in this step may be heuristic or highly systematized.

9.   One or more individuals on behalf of the insuring organization collect from each promisee the money or other valuables required. Normally, but not necessarily, the collection is made periodically with one or more installments to be received before the occurrence of the contingency to which the promise pertains.

10.   Upon being notified that an individual or organization
conditionally subject to a promise of payment or specific performance has experienced a specified contingency, one or more individuals on behalf of the insuring organization verify the authenticity
of the contingency, verify the eligibility of the recipients to receive
money or specific performance, ascertain the magnitude of payment
or the nature of any other performance to which each recipient is
entitled, and do what is necessary to fulfill each promise.

11.   Depending on the results of earlier activities, one or more
individuals on behalf of the insuring organization decide how to dis-
pose of excess resources and/or how to acquire additional pro-
prietory or participatory resources and act accordingly. Normally,
any excess is distributed periodically and proportionately to owners

and/or promisees and any additionally needed resources are acquired as in step two.

12.   With time limits on certain of the promises and with consummation of certain of the others, steps four through eleven are repeated indefinitely and in varying frequency.[7] Growth or other circumstances may call for repetition of step one so as to create a different organization.

13.   One or more individuals on behalf of the insuring organization may engage regularly or intermittently in one or more repetitive or ad hoc ancillary activities such as encouragement of loss prevention. The ancillary activities, while varied and important, are not central to the *raison d' être* of the insuring organization.

Throughout this process the insuring organization normally is subject to detailed public control extending to approval of the nature and size of the accumulated resources; the uses to which the resources can be put; the nature of the promises the insuring organization can make; the nature, size, and timing of the collection of the consideration it exacts from its promisees; the methods it can use in soliciting expressions of interest in the performance it offers; the qualifications of the individuals who solicit these expressions of interest; the methods the insuring organization can use in reacting to solicited or unsolicited expressions of interest it receives; the timing and manner of paying money or rendering specific performances upon occurrence of a specified contingency; the method of terminating contractual relationships with any promisee; the method and substance of record keeping and reporting to its several constituencies; and even the termination of its operations. Adaptation to such public control may consume a substantial portion of the insuring organization's resources. Furthermore, the insuring organization is normally subject to numerous and substantial taxes levied upon it by one or more governments.

Such, in skeletal terms, is the insuring process. Although the contemporary insuring process is embellished with an ingenious variety of useful appurtenances, it remains basically the same as sketched here. Any dependency of the process on a particular ethics

---

[7]For an interesting, highly quantitative account of the feedback control process at work in the repetitive procedure of ratemaking in fire insurance see Paul Swadener, "Fire Insurance Rate Level Revision Procedures," unpublished doctoral dissertation, Graduate School of Business, Indiana University, 1968.

or morality must be traceable to one or more of these steps. Remembering the steps in this process, let us now consider the institutional apparatus that these steps require.

THE INSTITUTIONAL APPARATUS

Even though the concept of the insuring process is fairly simple, the institutional apparatus necessary to support it is rather elaborate. While some of the elements of this apparatus are strictly neutral in terms of ethics and morality, other elements definitely are not neutral. They depend on an acceptance of certain ideas of right and wrong and on a behavior that is consistent with such ideas. Thus, as mentioned earlier, an understanding of the necessary institutional apparatus of insurance may be helpful to a discussion of the ethical foundation of insurance. We should bear in mind, however, that a distinction exists between the institutional apparatus and the ethical foundation. The former has to do with social organization; the latter with standards as to what man ought to do.

We should notice in passing that insurance is a remarkably adaptable phenomenon. Over time many changes occur in the objects, processes, and organizations subject to insurance. Moreover, the insuring process lends itself to improvements. Electronics and photography, for example, have enabled considerable streamlining of the insuring process.

Despite these changes, however, the basic steps in the insuring process remain the same and require a stable institutional apparatus. Given the nature of man, this apparatus is necessary for the long-run execution of the insuring process, whether the process is on a primitive or sophisticated level. The following description was developed from this point of view. The several parts of the apparatus are described without any implication as to the relative importance of sequential use.

A System of Exchange　　Since insurance is primarily redistributive, a means must exist to make the redistribution (that is, taking a little from many and giving substantial amounts to a few), while concurrently paying expenses, collecting yields, and accomplishing other sundry exchanges entailed in the insuring process. Conceivably, the redistributions could occur through bartering, but for practical purposes a system of money and credit is required.[8]

A System of Quantification   Because the insuring process makes heavy use of discrete and continuous magnitudes and relationships among these magnitudes, it calls for a system of quantification that is generally understood by those involved in the process. Measurement, classification, and manipulation must be used to set prices, evaluate results of contingencies, and arrive at other magnitudes and relationships.

A System of Communication   Every step in the insuring process requires communication, often exceedingly complex communication. With two or more persons necessarily involved—and a multitude normally involved—both a precise language and at least one communication medium are needed to communicate the information and other expressions that have to be exchanged. Hence, the institutional apparatus must include not only a language but also a communications network adequate to handle the volume and variety of expressions inherent in the insuring process with speed, accuracy, and subtlety.

Private Property   Without dominion by an individual (or some other entity smaller than the total population) over property, the phenomenon of insurance would have no place in the scheme of things. No resources would exist in the private sector to bring about the redistribution that is the essence of insurance. Redistribution of resources would only be accomplished in other ways, if at all.

---

[8]In connection with barter, some readers may recall the fabled practice attributed to the early Chinese merchant travelers who used the Yangtze River. As the story goes, the danger of losing their small boats loaded with cargo was great when the boats traversed the numerous rapids. Loss of one or more of the boats plus the cargo could be disastrous to one of these traveling merchants. The practice of putting some of each merchant's cargo in each boat in the convoy was adopted with the idea that the loss of a given boat and its diversely owned cargo would not produce consequences as damaging as those caused by loss of a boat that contained all or a substantial part of the stock of a single merchant. For a more detailed description of this practice see James L. Athearn, *Risk and Insurance* (New York: Appleton-Century-Crofts, Educational Division, Meredith Corporation, 1962), pp. 16-17, and John H. Magee and David L. Bickelhaupt, *General Insurance* (7th ed.; Homewood, Ill.: Richard D. Irwin, Inc., 1964), p. 40. Whether or not this practice actually constituted insurance could be debated at length. The proposition that a barter system of exchange could serve contemporary insurance hardly deserves discussion.

A Consumption Surplus   The institutional apparatus to support the insuring process must include not only private property but also a surplus of production over current consumption. The insuring organization must be able to accumulate sufficient resources to honor the promises it has made in the event one or more of the specified contingencies occur. This accumulation is impossible in an economy functioning at the subsistence level.

A Power System   The institutional apparatus of insurance requires a means of enforcing promises and settling disputes. Given the nature of man, promises might be made but not fulfilled in the insuring process in the absence of a system of enforcement. Given the nature of insurance, innumerable disagreements might be left unresolved in the absence of a system for settling disputes with finality. The insuring process, therefore, requires a system of law, an adjudicatory facility, and social coercion to force use of the legal system when at least one of the individuals involved feels so inclined. In the Western culture we normally think of the relevant law as that which includes contracts, torts, agency, and property, but no such classification is necessarily involved. Neither are courts of original and appellate jurisdiction required, nor police powers of a given type. The institutional apparatus of insurance simply must include some means of enforcing promises and settling disputes with finality. In practical terms this entails some sort of legal system.

Markets   Manpower and material resources are necessary for the execution of the insuring process. Consequently, an arrangement must exist for the marshalling of resources. The insuring organization must have accessibility to a market for the labor, equipment, and materials it requires. If the organization is to enjoy a yield on the resources it holds in its custody, it must also have access to an investment market. To be sure, the parties to the insurance transaction must have contact with each other in an insurance market.

A System of Management   Because the insuring process requires organization, motivation, and control of persons and things in order to accomplish given ends, the institutional apparatus must also include a system of management. In a world where disorder can easily occur, management is indispensable to the accomplishment of virtually any objective; certainly it is indispensable to the insuring process.

A System of Reporting   Insofar as it affects the well-being of participants with diverse interests, the insuring process requires some means by which to report the results of its execution to the individuals, organizations, and/or governments involved.

ETHICAL PILLARS OF INSURANCE

The institutional apparatus of insurance alone is not sufficient for the execution of the insuring process. In fact, every part of the apparatus could exist without the insuring process necessarily being enacted. Sustained and healthy execution of the insuring process depends on additional essentials, and these may be thought of as constituting the ethical foundation of insurance. In this discussion they will be referred to as "ethical pillars."[9] The order and length of discussion given to each pillar do not imply the relative importance of the pillars nor any sequence.

Achievement   Achievement is one of the ethical pillars upon which sustained use of insurance depends. For insurance to function, achievement must be generally valued by the insured society. Individuals using insurance must believe that achievement is both desirable and possible. With such a belief, such persons probably will possess strong incentives and will be motivated to work, husband their possessions, and risk their wealth in further achievement. Such conduct is likely to maximize insurance need and availability.

Insurance depends upon a concept of achievement that is close to but not identical with the Protestant ethic (also called the Puritan ethic), which is fundamental to much of the historical culture of the United States. The general idea of the Protestant ethic is that hard work, self-denial, and self-discipline along with steadfast and vigorous pursuit of one's calling provide serenity if not happiness in this life and ensure moral and spiritual progress toward the life that is to come.[10] Devotion to one's calling could even be taken as convinc-

---

[9]The ethical pillars will not necessarily coincide with the *desirata* of underwriters. Whereas underwriters may aim at the ideal qualities wanted in applicants in the short run, the ethical pillars, in contrast, have to do with the generally acceptable behavioral standards which are conducive to the long-range availability and use of insurance.

[10]For a detailed discussion of this aspect of ethics see Max Weber, *The Protestant Ethic and the Spirit of Capitalism*, translated by Talcott Parsons (New York: Charles Scribner's Sons, 1958).

ing evidence that one has methodically developed his own state of spiritual grace to a considerable degree.[11]

As it pertains to the ethical foundation of insurance, achievement is a similar concept but not necessarily as strong. For one thing, it need not have the ascetic flavor of the Protestant ethic, nor does it necessarily connote the idea that hard work and self-discipline are important preparations for the life after death. For the purposes of insurance, it is enough that achievement be pursued for the joys it can bring in this life both as a means and an end.

For achievement to be practiced in a society, freedom must be valued and must be provided for most, if not all, of the individuals. Insurance ethics calls for egalitarianism in the sense that individuals need to be equally free to achieve, but need not necessarily be equal in their achievements. In fact, given the differences among man's propensities and abilities to achieve, equality of achievement could come only by forcefully throttling some individuals and heavily aiding others. This sort of interference could quickly undermine insurance by removing both the incentive to achieve and the fear of the consequences of not achieving. If people generally come to believe that achievement is not good, the resulting indolence would breed carelessness, poor maintenance, lack of growth, lack of technological improvement, ignorance, and a general lack of concern. These qualities elicit loss-causing behavior, and losses above a certain frequency sound the death knell for insurance.

In short, insurance needs an achievement orientation both on the part of those making the insurance available and those using it. It needs the incentive, work, pride, husbandry, growth, and optimism that spring from a belief in achievement and from a society in which freedom to achieve is not only permitted but also encouraged.

Acquisitiveness   Insurance is also supported by the ethical pillar of acquisitiveness. In some uses this word has the ugly connotation of greed or of extreme and determined selfishness where gross accumulation is an end in itself. As it is used here, however, acquisitiveness means a desire to acquire and stops well short of avarice. Acquisition is a type of achievement. For insurance to prosper, acquisition, except through crime or tort, must be sanctioned by law

---

[11]The Methodists drew their name from the idea of methodical development of grace through work.

and must be considered right and good except perhaps at extreme magnitude.

As mentioned earlier in the chapter, insurance is essentially a redistribution of resources, except where the insurance facility is used as a savings medium. It follows, then, that in the insurance environment there must be some resources susceptible to redistribution. Other things being equal, the more resources, short of satiation of wants, the greater the usefulness of insurance. Without an acquisitiveness common to virtually all of the members of a given society, the society is not likely to have the income, real property, and other possessions that are the usual objects of insurance. Without this acquisitiveness on the part of virtually all the members of the society, no form of economic and social organization is likely to be productive. With acquisitiveness accepted and approved, any form of economic and social organization is likely to be productive, and insurable objects are likely to accumulate.[12]

The earlier discussion of the institutional apparatus of insurance emphasized that insurance depends on a system of private property, with considerable freedom to use the property as one chooses.[13] In addition, the sustained use of insurance demands that those using it view ownership not only as legal but also as a positive good. Insurance users must feel that an individual should be able to own at least a large fraction of the fruits of his labor and that ownership should transcend the grave through the right of an individual to bequeath a large fraction of his estate. Without such an attitude of ownership, life insurance would atrophy, and other insurances might normally be terminable at the death of an insured. Insurance depends on an ethics that blesses ownership and honors the institution of private property.

Perhaps insurance does not necessarily depend on individual ownership. Organizations could conceivably own the property with-

---

[12] The larger the group doing the acquiring and the accumulating, however, the less may be the need for insurance (assuming that insurance is defined as involving a payment from outside the group). As the group grows, it will become increasingly able to regularize its activities and budget the demands upon its resources. Ultimately, it will become self-sufficient, albeit perhaps at the minimum level of subsistence.

[13] While it is certainly far-fetched, the insurance system itself conceivably could become sufficiently powerful to limit individual freedom severely. For a preposterous science fiction account of a tyrannical insurance system which eventually acts as the government, see Edson McCann, *Preferred Risk* (New York: Dell Publishing Company, 1955).

out defeating the use of insurance. These organizations, however, would have to be small enough in comparison to the whole society to permit individuals in the organizations to see a clear relationship between their efforts and their rewards.

The history of insurance is linked closely with the history of private enterprise; where enterprise has flourished, insurance has also. At least part of the connection has to be attributed to the acquisitiveness that characterizes enterprise.

Preservation   A third ethical pillar of insurance is the desire to preserve. The word "preserve" means to keep safe from injury, harm, or destruction, to keep alive, keep intact, maintain, or protect from decay. This word is quite important to the successful operation of a system of insurance. Insurance requires that people generally have a distaste for loss of value, whatever the circumstances attending the loss, whether the loss is inadvertent or by design. This is not to say that destruction of value can never be countenanced in an insured society. The point is, rather, that waste must be generally disdained and profligacy eschewed, while thrift and frugality are preferred as virtues and practiced at least moderately.

It is not enough that the general populace be merely indifferent to destruction or other decrease in value. The decrease must be a source of displeasure; otherwise, too many persons in the society may become too tolerant of destruction of value. Over time, toleration of the destruction of value is the nemesis of insurance because much of the value destroyed is likely to be subject to insurance.

This basic concept of distaste is sometimes spoken of as an "aversion to loss."[14] The expression is colorful and effective but perhaps slightly inaccurate for our purposes. Aversion may be too strong a word and loss too weak. Aversion connotes a revulsion, a repugnance, but in the context of the present discussion, distaste does not necessarily have to go that far. On the other hand, loss has a personal quality about it, implying a personal deprivation. If one did

---

[14]"Aversion to loss" is a concept quite close to, but a bit stronger than "aversion to risk" as discussed by Milton Friedman and L. J. Savage in "The Utility Analysis of Choices Involving Risk," *Journal of Political Economy*, vol. 56 (August, 1948), pp. 279-304. The "aversion to risk" concept is developed definitively in Harry Markowitz, *Portfolio Selection* (New York: John Wiley & Sons, Inc., 1959) and is treated also in Harry C. Sauvain, *Investment Management* (3rd ed.; Englewood Cliffs, N.J.: Prentice-Hall, Inc., 1967), pp. 119-20 and in Mark R. Greene, *Risk and Insurance*, pp. 44-50.

not feel personally involved, he could observe a decrease in value without feeling a deprivation and thus a loss. In the meaning of this discussion the distaste must extend to a general decline in value whether or not the decline causes a personal deprivation. This ethical pillar of insurance requires that one have a distaste for value destruction whenever, wherever, and to whomever it occurs, regardless of whether he would have been in a position to enjoy the value in the absence of the decline.

A well-established point in insurance literature is that an insurable interest is a necessary prerequisite to insurance.[15] This prerequisite means that one must be in a position to be deprived of something he has and wants to keep in order to qualify as an insured. As one of the ethical pillars of insurance, the idea of preservation is stronger than that of insurable interest. For insurance to function, the people in a society must in general loathe to see anyone, anywhere, suffer a loss of value in his possessions, regardless of the narrow question of insurable interest and regardless of whether the loss stems from acts of God, vagaries of nature, violence of man, personal accident, disease, death, wear and tear, litigation, blight, or whatever.

As with the other ethical pillars discussed in this chapter, any given insured society can tolerate some exceptions. Insurance is still manageable even if a few persons, or occasionally slightly more than a few persons, are indifferent to or actually relish the destruction of value. A few deviations can be absorbed in the system. Quantification of the maximum tolerable deviation is probably im-

---

[15]In the following excerpt, William D. Winter applies the "insurable interest" concept to marine insurance: "No person may become a party to a marine insurance contract unless he has an insurable interest. That is . . . [he] must bear such a relation to the insured subject that, directly or indirectly, he may be benefited by its safe arrival or continued existence and be injured by its damage or loss. . . . A person may not legally take out insurance on certain property for his own benefit merely because such property is subject to marine hazards. The party seeking such insurance must bear some probable relation to the property itself in order to insure it for his own benefit, or a legal relation of agency must exist to enable one to take out insurance for the benefit of another who has a valid insurable interest." William D. Winter, *Marine Insurance—Its Principles and Practices* (3rd ed.; New York: McGraw-Hill Book Company, 1952), p. 126. Copyright © 1952 by McGraw-Hill Book Company. Used with permission of McGraw-Hill Book Company. The general theory of insurable interest is developed in William R. Vance, *Handbook on the Law of Insurance* (3rd ed. prepared by Buist M. Anderson; St. Paul: West Publishing Company, 1951), pp. 156-61.

possible except with the use of overly simplified assumptions. About all that can be said meaningfully is that a preponderance of the members of a society must exhibit this distaste consistently.

One troublesome aspect of the topic of distaste remains to be examined. Not all destruction of value must be regarded as wrong. Some destruction of value is necessary for progressive change. Our precept must allow us to realize that in certain circumstances intentional destruction of value is the only means of creating greater value. A popular term for the destruction of value in order to gain greater value is "renewal."

Renewal becomes increasingly important as a society matures and grows more crowded. Moreover, advances in technology make renewal increasingly attractive. The old must give way to the new for a society to progress or even to persist. A disinclination to see value destroyed does not necessarily connote abhorrence but rather a sort of prima facie presumption that can be overcome. Business practice and social engineering are replete with examples of destruction of a machine, a building, a facility, or even a community followed by the substitution of something more efficient. Economic costs and benefits are normally measurable within sufficient tolerances to permit business firms to make economic decisions fairly easily. At the social level, however, decisions of this type are much more difficult to make because both the costs and the benefits resist accurate measurement. Hence, there may easily be disagreements as to the relative worths of the new and the old. Renewal is compatible with a general disinclination toward destruction so long as the new is demonstrably better than the old—demonstrable at least to a majority of those persons affected by the change.

In short, the ethics essential to insurance requires the overwhelming majority of the people, whether or not they are insured, to cherish and want to preserve value. For the sake of progress, the preservation has to be tempered with a cautious readiness to improve well-being by intentional destruction of things that are still functional but that stand in the way either of improved efficiency in the existing order or of a new and better order.[16]

Apprehension   Apprehension that is mild but nevertheless real constitutes the fourth ethical pillar of insurance. A person who ex-

---

[16]This rationale, short of war, is not extended to decisions about human life.

periences no excitement or fear about the future but faces it in utter complacency probably has no interest in insurance. Neither does one who views the future with abject futility and despair. Only the individual who has a somewhat apprehensive, yet positive, concern about the future will be motivated to use insurance in an effort to preserve his options to the maximum. Only he will feel that the future is sufficiently threatening, yet sufficiently manipulable, to give insurance a place in his preparations. The ethics of insurance requires that a moderate degree of apprehension be regarded as a commendable trait among all members of society and as particularly befitting those to whom others look for financial support.

Contracts of insurance are characteristically long run. While some are ad hoc or of only a few months' duration, many contracts remain in force for at least a year. An increasing number run continuously until cancelled. Some, particularly in life insurance, span generations. Use of insurance over the long run, then, requires that the duration of an individual's concern be at least as long as the minimum duration of insurance.

The *maximum* length of time for which a prudent individual should make plans depends on both the particular situation and the planner. For some individuals in some situations a few seconds into the future may form a long enough time span. For other individuals in other situations the minimum planning span may be a hundred years. Widespread availability and use of insurance in a society occur only where most people make many of their plans in a climate of mild apprehension and plan ahead for a period of years instead of weeks or months.

Honesty   Honesty is the fifth ethical pillar of insurance. In the absence of honesty as the normative and expected mode of conduct, the insuring process would never begin or would soon falter. Unless most persons in the society are honest in most little matters and unless virtually everyone is scrupulously and compulsively honest in big matters, insurance will not function. The use of insurance is a testimony to the basic honesty of a society.

Not much ingenuity is required to think of ways to cheat in an insurance transaction. In the eyes of the law, insurance has long been a matter of good faith and in some respects, as in marine insurance, a matter of utmost good faith. *Uberrima fides* is an ancient and honored doctrine that still applies. Good faith is a necessary accompaniment of the insurance transaction because of the looseness and the ambiguity of so many of the promises, restrictions, and other provisions in the contracts. Indeed, these provisions invite abuse. Who is to say whether an insured who has been disabled for at least 60 months under a long-term disability is in fact unable "to engage in any gainful occupation for which he is reasonably fitted in consideration of his training, education, experience, or prior average earnings"?[17] What is really meant by the following provision pertaining to additional living expense insurance?

This policy covers the necessary increase in living expense resulting from loss by a peril insured against to the property covered hereunder incurred by the Named Insured to continue as nearly as practicable the normal standard of living of the Named Insured's household for the applicable period described . . . below.[18]

In settling a business interruption insurance claim, how is one really to know what the insured business would have produced in gross receipts had the interruption not occurred? Who can challenge an insured after a fire loss when he includes in his claim a request for payment for 20 bed sheets, four of which had never been used? These hypothetical cases, which have their counterparts in loss adjustment practice everyday, illustrate the extreme honesty on which the redistributive system of insurance, inexact as it is, depends. While insurers are very adept at detecting occasional attempts at fraud, the system would soon break down if dishonesty became the normative conduct.

High standards of honesty are not confined to those who are parties to the insurance contract. Medical advisers, attorneys, jurists, repairmen, hospital administrators, claims adjusters, and others who are related to the contract have ample opportunity, despite the most elaborate safeguards, to succumb to dishonesty. Insurance also requires honesty as the customary and dependable action of other persons in society who are not in any way involved in insurance transactions. To illustrate the point, numerous types of insurance contracts promise payment or replacement in kind in the event of certain types of loss by theft. If theft becomes so rampant that losses become excessively common, redistribution of the burden of theft losses will become impractical, and the burdens will have

---

[17]The actual wording from a long-term disability income policy.
[18]From Coverage D of Section I of Homeowners Policy, Form 2.

to remain where they fall. As mentioned previously, quantification of the limits of tolerability is impossible except through the use of overly simplified assumptions. In any given situation the exact location of the saturation point is open for debate, but the existence of such a limit is hardly debatable.

In short, insurance is sustained by honesty.[19] Major breaches of honesty at any level of society weaken the viability of the insuring process. At some undetermined frequency the breaches wreck the process.

Obedience A willingness to obey the law is the sixth ethical pillar of insurance. It is not difficult to see that insurance requires a certain orderliness in human affairs. While nature is erratic in many respects, it displays an underlying orderliness which renders some types of events fairly predictable. The same degree of orderliness is needed in human conduct, especially as it has to do with insured losses. We have seen that the insuring process normally requires the rate-makers to make an estimate of the cost of insured losses well in advance of the occurrence of the losses.[20] Thus, they

---

[19]The topic in discussion here does not extend to the concept of "adverse selection," which is simply the exercise of an option by a person in his own favor and against the interest of the insurer in a case where his and the insurer's interests are not the same. An example is the choice by a beneficiary of life insurance proceeds to allow the proceeds to remain with the insurer when the guaranteed interest rate is more favorable than that obtainable elsewhere, or contrariwise, to take the proceeds in cash (assuming he has such an option) instead of leaving them with the insurer when the effective rate is greater elsewhere. Another example is the tendency of less healthy individuals to exercise the right of converting group coverage to individual coverage. Adverse selection is not immoral but simply the choice of an individual to use a provision made available to him in the contract. The insurer is behooved to anticipate such selection and price the insurance accordingly.

[20]If a policy is "participating" so that any excess premium can be refunded to the policyholder, the ratemakers have a margin of safety on the "top side" of the price. They can deliberately add a contingency element in the rate with the explicit intent of refunding it should it not be needed. Even if a policy is not participating, any superfluity in a rate can be eliminated by adjustments for the next policy period. To the extent that the body of policyholders is consistent from one period to the next, this sort of adjustment is a reasonable approach to equity. The difficulty arises, however, in errors on the "bottom side" of the price. Except in the rare instances of assessable policies or "retrospective rating," the insurers have no recourse to the policyholder for more premium in respect to a given policy and policy period in the event that loss experience is worse than predicted. While they normally can increase the rate for new contracts (or sometimes for existing contracts) in subsequent periods, they cannot normally increase rates retroactively. Therefore, ratemakers must be particularly careful to set rates that will be adequate. If they err, the insurers must pay the unanticipated losses from previously accumulated resources. They can do only so much of this without facing insolvency.

have to be able to make predictions within reasonably narrow limits of tolerance. For such a prediction to be made, human affairs must be orderly, but order is not likely to come fortuitously.

The principal means of guaranteeing order in human behavior is through the creation and enforcement of law. Mark R. Greene has commented on law and regularity, observing that individuals in a society can suffer loss because other individuals do not conform to the usual and expected patterns of behavior. He classifies the deviations from expected behavior as "intentional" or "accidental." Crime is an example of intentional deviation. Although he does not say so, Greene might agree that the tort of negligence is an example of accidental deviation from expected behavior.[21] Greene's concept can be used to form the generalization that the law influences or at least reflects the patterns of human behavior expected in a society. The ethical foundation of insurance demands the establishment of laws that minimize long-run loss. In this sense, then, the law is an institution for regularizing human behavior through the maintenance of the status quo or through the encouragement of nonwasteful change. When law serves such a function, violations can normally be thought of as destructions of value or as socially repugnant appropriations of value by one person or organization from another. In numerous circumstances either one of these types of violation can produce an insured loss and evoke a redistribution of resources. Therefore, if the insuring process is not to be overwhelmed, the violations must be relatively few. There must be general enthusiasm for or at least tolerance of the law. The law generally must be respected and obeyed so that behavior will be predictable and losses will fall within tolerable limits.[22]

---

[21]Under "accidental deviation" Greene includes personal injuries or accidents stemming from no-fault, nonintentional mishaps in human conduct as well as from unexpected events in nature. In connection with "intentional deviation," he has treated the subject of crime in a paper entitled "A Sociological View of Insurance," presented at the 1965 Risk Theory Seminar of the American Risk and Insurance Association held in Chicago.

[22]Mehr and Cammack, in *Principles of Insurance*, pp. 40-41, comment on this as follows: "No insurance company can afford to insure a type of loss that is likely to happen to any great percentage of those exposed to it. . . . Insurance is an arrangement whereby the unfortunate few who lose are indemnified by the fortunate many who escape loss. If the many, however, suffer the loss, then the few will prove inadequate to indemnify them properly, except at an uneconomic premium" (used by permission). The authors state that unemployment insurance (on a voluntary basis) "runs aground of this requisite" of insurance.

An interesting paradox now demands attention. While insurance requires that obedience to the law be regarded as ethical and that obedience be the prevailing moral practice, some types of insurance, particularly dishonesty insurance, require instances of nonconformity to the law. Theft is a violation of the law. Yet theft insurance presupposes some theft. Thus, the ethical foundation of a few types of insurance rests upon human conduct that is not perfect but which, rather, includes occasional aberrations. If thefts did not occur frequently enough to justify concern, no one would want theft insurance. Similarly, if no one ever committed an intentional tort, insurance relating to liability for intentional torts would be useless.

For insurance of a given type to be used, the contingency must occur often enough to produce protective action. For example, only the most unusual person would seek insurance that pays a claim if and only if the insured is killed or injured by a newly formed geyser. The estimated probability is simply too low to provoke worry. An individual's intuitive estimate of the responsibility of some unwanted event has to be above some minimum worry limit before he is motivated to seek insurance. Doubtless, the minimum worry limit varies considerably from one person to another and perhaps for a given person from one time to another.[23]

Here, then, is a peculiar situation in which the existence of a few—but only a few—types of insurance actually depends on violations of the law. For these insurances to be successful there must be a few persons whose morality can accommodate an occasional infraction of the law. We must recognize, however, that even here the number of nonconformities must remain very small in relation to the number of conformities. The domain of insurability is narrow. As the probability of loss during a given period rises enough to induce concern, insurance becomes increasingly less appropriate as a loss-sharing device until the point is reached where it is altogether useless.[24]

We should also recognize clearly that most types of insurance do not depend in any way on disobedience of the law. For most insurances, such as direct damage, consequential, health, and life, na-

[23]The relationship of such a limit to one's age is a subject for a potentially fascinating study.

[24]Some might argue that when the probability of loss during a given period increases above the minimum worry limit, insurance becomes increasingly more useful, and that only when the probability of loss increases to a certain magnitude does the usefulness of insurance decline. This view is interesting but debatable.

ture provides all the losses that the system needs—and sometimes more than enough. Fires, storms, illnesses, injuries, accidents, and premature deaths unfortunately have a probability which leaves most of us wanting to insure.

Tradition   The seventh ethical pillar of insurance is tradition. Law is not in itself sufficient to introduce and maintain the full degree of order necessary for insurance to function. One reason is that it is not static but is subject to change. Normally, the changes are cautious, deliberate, and predictable. Occasionally, however, the implications for insurance of a judicial decision or a new statute can be profound and immediate.[25] A second reason is that many customs, practices, and other expressions of behavior are outside the law, not because they are violations, but rather because they are not covered by the law. Legally speaking, such forms of behavior are neutral but can influence the number and frequency of losses. Examples are the way people get to and from work, forms of recreation, preferences for and uses of lighting fixtures, the generally accepted ways of dancing, and even eating habits.

For insurance to be made available and used over a long period of time, the legal and extra-legal aspects of life must be orderly enough to permit predictions. Members of the society, therefore, must show at least moderate respect for tradition; they must generally feel that both the individual and the society ought to maintain some sort of tradition and that tradition in itself is good.

Tradition does not have to be sacrosanct. The requirement is only that loss-causing legal or extra-legal behavior change slowly enough to be predictable in time for incorporation into insurance prices. Tradition must be honored at least to the extent that this much stability in human conduct be maintained. As techniques for prediction become more accurate and of a longer range, and as techniques for data collection and processing are improved, insurance can adapt itself to a commensurately faster pace of change. In fact, the pace has quickened significantly in recent years. The only limitation is that the changes must be sufficiently predictable and

---

[25]An example might be an unusually high judgment in a liability case that becomes a pace-setter for other judgments in the same and neighboring courts. Another example could be a precedent-setting ruling to the effect that an accidental injury to an employee during an off-premises coffee break is an injury "arising out of and in the course of employment" for purposes of workmen's compensation. Another could be a new statute establishing a no-fault system of compensating automobile traffic victims.

their loss propensities sufficiently understood far enough in advance to permit rates to be made, approved as required, and put into use before the changes manifest themselves in insured losses.[26] In short, insurance can live with, and indeed thrive upon, ordinary change. It cannot live with revolution.

Personal Responsibility   The eighth ethical pillar of insurance is the simple but profoundly significant concept of personal responsibility. Sustained use of insurance requires widespread conviction, growing out of love, pride, and prudence, that each individual is *personally* responsible and accountable for himself and "his own." Without personal responsibility an individual might not feel sufficiently motivated to defer current consumption in order to pay insurance premiums. An individual who is personally responsible has a cogent rationale for discipline. Two aspects of this ethical pillar, duty and accountability, shall be considered here.

Personal responsibility is a perceived duty on the part of an individual (particularly an insured or prospective insured) to provide necessities for himself and his dependents. Such responsibility often reflects a wish if not a duty on his part to go beyond minimum provisions. His concern also transcends the present and even his own death. This attitude and its consequent implemental actions stand in sharp contrast to one who is willing to do without or to be supported through the largess of another, be it friend, family, church, or state. Individual responsibility is the wellspring of insurance. A welfare mentality, on the other hand, is its bane.

Personal responsibility is not construed here to include extreme self-reliance, or individualism. The individual who feels not only fully responsible but also fully confident that he can negotiate any eventuality by himself might spurn all forms of loss-sharing. Such superconfidence runs counter to an ethical component mentioned earlier, namely, an apprehension of the future. Extreme individualism can spring from another source too. Some individuals with the noblest of motives, for example the Amish, seem to regard the purchase of insurance, at least certain types of insurance, as sinful.[27] They regard insurance as evidence of a lack of faith in the pro-

---

[26]The discussion here presumes that the phenomenon in question does not generate a loss frequency that renders the phenomenon uninsurable.

[27]For an interesting and detailed treatment of this subject, see Myles A. Tracy, "Insurance and Theology: The Background and the Issues," *Journal of Risk and Insurance*, vol. 33 (March, 1966), pp. 85-93.

vidential concern of God. They apparently feel that with God's help, one's strength and resources will be adequate to the occasion, especially in view of the assistance one renders to and can expect to receive from one's brothers in the faith.[28] Extreme individualism, as illustrated by either of these examples, is probably a rare commodity in this country in this age.

Second, personal responsibility is a presumption of accountability for one's actions. While an individual can entertain any one of several ideas about accountability, he must, in the spirit of this concept, believe that he will ultimately be accountable to something or somebody. An individual may believe that he is accountable only to himself and that his conduct depends only on his own innate sense of right and wrong. On the other hand, he may believe that within and beyond the law he is accountable only to other men. He may believe that he is accountable to God both here and now and in the life hereafter. Such persons have often been described as "God fearing." They may believe that in the life hereafter there is a heaven and hell, or they may believe that the quality and form of their present life will determine the nature of another reincarnation on earth. Whatever the rationale, an individual's feeling of being personally accountable is likely to engender in him a restraint which is beneficial to insurance. Unless a majority of the individuals in a society manifest this restraint most of the time, insured losses stand to become too frequent and too large. The spirit of this accountability is pointed up in the biblical admonition, "whatever a man sows, that shall he also reap" (Galatians 6:7).

Charity   A final pillar of insurance is charity. In order for a society to use insurance for any length of time, the members of that society must generally exhibit charity. The word here is used in the sense of a general disposition to goodwill, kindliness, and sympathy.

As already observed, insurance necessarily involves redistribution. Consequently, some who pay insurance premiums (except for permanent life insurance) will, during a given policy period, collect nothing except perhaps a relatively small refund from the insurer and possibly not even that. In fact, the clear majority of insureds

---

[28]One might argue that this reciprocity is a form of insurance in itself or that it belies the genuine individualism to which this paragraph is addressed. If either really is the case, then this example was poorly chosen.

will be in this position. A few stand in just the opposite position and will receive compensatory payments, some of which will be inordinately large compared to amounts that have been paid to the insurer. Insurance necessarily involves an averaging. If insurance were priced so that each insured paid exactly for his own loss (plus his share of the cost of the insuring process), the purpose of insurance would be defeated. Only in an unusual circumstance does one recieve what he has paid.

This fundamental reality of insurance is no great mystery. Insureds through their own observations can easily perceive this characteristic fact. They also can understand that from the standpoint of any one individual, the prospect of receiving indemnifying payment in the event adversity strikes is worth the high probability of not recovering one's own premium payments. Each individual recognizes that he may be the one needing indemnification. He can also sympathize with others in a similar circumstance at least to the extent that he will pay a premium that probably will not be recovered.

This is the sense in which charity underlies insurance. Each insured has to be willing for his premiums to be used to pay both the losses of others and the expenses of the insuring process, in exchange for protection. In a limited sense this protection is a quid pro quo. Unless the insured has some charity in his blood, however, he is tempted to do without insurance—unless creditors give him no option. For the purposes of insurance, then, charity need not be strong as love; but, when viewed in the long run, it is something more than pure selfishness. It involves an indulging, perhaps even begrudging, participation in a formalized loss-sharing process which takes a little from many and gives much to a few.

PUBLIC MORAL HAZARD

In concluding this chapter, the discussion of the ethical foundation of insurance is related to the concept of "moral hazard" as customarily treated in the insurance literature. Insurance scholars seem generally to agree that a moral hazard can exist. An illustrative statement follows.

> The ethical insured also endeavors to prevent loss. The so-called "moral hazard" does not. Moral hazard is a term which embraces more that merely the criminally minded insured. The phrase also covers the insured who fakes or exaggerates claims, and the one who grows careless merely because he carries insurance. The behavior of the insured who conspires to cheat the insurance company on the cost of an automobile repair job may

prove as serious in its economic consequences as that of the arsonist. The burden in both instances falls on the entire community of insured persons.[29]

An old maxim is often heard among insurance underwriters to the effect that "the moral hazard is uninsurable at any price." This admonition is supported by Mowbray and Blanchard, who have written: "Hazard due to violation of the insured is known among insurance men as 'moral hazard.' This risk (sic) has not been found to be stable and both for this and more obvious reasons of public policy is uninsurable on any terms."[30] Textbook literature is not uniform in concurring with this maxim. Athearn, for example, implies some exceptions by saying:

> Moral hazard also affects the chance of loss. Dishonesty or lack of integrity of the individual can increase the chance of loss to 100 percent. A dishonest insured may burn his own home or rob his own store in order to collect the insurance. When such a person buys insurance, loss becomes a certainty. Because, as will be shown later, the operation of an insurance scheme involves the law of chance, moral hazard may make a risk uninsurable. [Italics added][31]

Similarly, Huebner, Black, and Cline state that some of the moral hazard is reflected in rates based on loss experience.[32]

Other authors, however, generally avoid stating either that the moral hazard is categorically and without exception uninsurable or that it is insurable under given circumstances and within given limitations. In general, they caution the underwriter to be ever vigilant and to refuse to accept any application which he feels is contaminated in any way by the moral hazard, but they stop short of saying that the transaction is not insurance if the underwriter errs in his judgment and accepts a tainted application.

Perhaps the maxim is slightly overstated. It is very likely that some dishonest claims are paid because the dishonesty is concealed from the adjusters. Other moral hazards probably also result in claims being paid for losses which never were suffered or which

---

[29]Pfeffer, *Insurance and Economic Theory*, p. 118, used by permission.

[30]Albert H. Mowbray and Ralph H. Blanchard, *Insurance—Its Theory and Practice in the United States* (5th ed.; New York: McGraw-Hill Book Company, Inc., 1961), p. 21. Copyright © 1961 by McGraw-Hill Book Company. Used with permission of McGraw-Hill Book Company. The 1969 edition of this text, coauthored by C. Arthur Williams, Jr., does not list "moral hazard" in the index and apparently does not include this passage.

[31]Athearn, *Risk and Insurance*, pp. 47-48, used by permission.

[32]S. S. Huebner, Kenneth Black, Jr., and Robert S. Cline, *Property and Liability Insurance* (New York: Appleton-Century-Crofts, 1968), pp. 211-12.

were provoked by the insured. These payments are made within the insuring process. It is awkward to insist that they do not embody insurance. Perhaps they do not. Still, the stronger position seems to be that the transactions are within the pale of insurance even though the institution can absorb only so many without facing disintegration.

This reasoning is consistent with views developed in discussing the ethical pillars. Some deviation is inevitable, but the insuring process can absorb it only as long as it occurs infrequently. The question of whether moral hazard is categorically uninsurable or partially insurable may be a matter of hairsplitting anyway. The really pertinent point is that insurance writers have almost unanimously emphasized the threat posed by moral hazard to insurance.[33]

Some authors distinguish between "moral hazard" and "morale hazard." The following quotation illustrates the distinction.

A moral hazard is a condition which increases the chance that some person will *intentionally* [italics added] cause a loss. Some unscrupulous persons can make, or believe that they can make, a profit by bringing about a loss. Others abuse the insurance protection by (1) making claims which are not warranted, thus spreading through the insurance system losses which they should bear themselves (e.g., claiming automobile liability when there is no negligence on the part of the defendant), (2) over-utilizing the services (e.g., staying in a hospital beyond the period required for treatment), (3) charging excessive fees for services rendered insureds, as is done by some doctors and garages, and (4) granting larger awards in liability cases merely because the defendant is insured. Some of these abuses are fraudulent; others indicate a different (and indefensible) code of ethics where insurance is involved. . . .

A morale hazard is a condition which causes persons to be less careful than they would otherwise be. Some persons do not consciously seek to bring about a loss, but the fact that they have insurance causes them to take more chances than they would if they had no insurance.[34]

Whatever the meaning attributable to moral hazard, the conclusion is that this hazard does not extend merely to the insured and his associates; it also extends to society at large. Unless vir-

---

[33]Two illustrative articles, both from the *Journal of Insurance*, are O. D. Dickerson, "The Problem of Overutilization in Health Insurance," vol. 26 (Spring, 1959), pp. 65-72; and Richard F. Schmidt, "Does a Deductible Curb Moral Hazard?" vol. 28 (September, 1961), pp. 89-92.

[34]Williams and Heins, *Risk Management and Insurance*, p. 51. Copyright © 1964 by McGraw-Hill Book Company. Used with permission of McGraw-Hill Book Company.

tually all the people all of the time exhibit a morality consistent with the several ethical pillars, insurance in the society cannot be provided and used over the long run.

Insurance presupposes a yearning for achievement, a drive of acquisitiveness, a desire to preserve what is valuable, a bit of apprehension about the future, a readiness to obey the law, a sense of honesty, a fondness for tradition, a willingness to accept personal responsibility and accountability, and a measure of charity toward others in society. This ethical foundation is a prerequisite for an enduring insurance system.

Some authors do not feel that this distinction is worth making. According to O. D. Dickerson when speaking in the context of health insurance:

> Moral hazard refers to the intangible loss-producing propensities of the individual assured. Its characteristics are . . . difficult to illustrate since such intangibles are difficult to define and identify. Any situation or circumstance that might indicate a desire on the part of the assured that the loss occur is evidence of moral hazard. Dishonesty, carelessness, lack of pertinancy, and ignorance on the part of the assured are elements of moral hazard. Some authors have distinguished between moral hazard, which refers to situations of potential dishonesty and the like, and *morale* hazard, which refers to potential carelessness. However, such a distinction is not particularly useful in practice, and it is frequently impossible to distinguish one from the other.[35]

The ethical foundation of insurance, as discussed in this chapter, clearly encompasses more than the *intentional* abuse of the insurer by the insured or vice versa. Hence, the distinction between moral and morale hazards seems a bit superficial and of little use. In the context of our discussion, morality refers to the totality of an indi-

---

[35]O. D. Dickerson, *Health Insurance* (rev. ed.; Homewood, Ill.: Richard D. Irwin, Inc., 1963), p. 463, used by permission. Denenberg and others agree that the distinction is impractical, but refer both to moral hazard and morale hazard (see Denenberg and others, *Risk and Insurance*, pp. 8, 151). For those who apparently do not make the distinction, see Winter, *Marine Insurance—Its Principles and Practices*; Dan M. McGill, *Life Insurance* (rev. ed.; Homewood, Ill.: Richard D. Irwin, Inc., 1967), p. 393; and Edwin J. Faulkner, *Health Insurance* (rev. ed.; New York: McGraw-Hill Book Company, Inc., 1960), pp. 326-64. Pfeffer considers the distinction superficial, but he recognizes it as possible (see *Insurance and Economic Theory*, pp. 62, 118). Among the works already cited, the following draw the distinction and use it: Athearn, *Risk and Insurance*, p. 48; Greene, *Risk and Insurance*, p. 10; Huebner, Black, and Cline, *Property and Liability Insurance*, pp. 211-12; Magee and Bickelhaupt, *General Insurance*, pp. 6-7; Mehr and Cammack, *Principles of Insurance*, pp. 22-23; Mowbray and Blanchard, *Insurance—Its Theory and Practice in the United States*, pp. 21-22.

vidual's conduct as measured against his ethics or standard of what he feels he ought to do. Slothfulness or indifference can be just as wrong as lying. Consequently, the distinction between intent and inexcusable inadvertence is not pertinent to our purpose and need not be made.

Most of the textbook writers who have discussed moral hazard confine the meaning of the term to the insured himself.[36] Some writers impute a slightly broader scope to the term and include not only the insured but also others who are involved in the insurance process as beneficiaries, loss adjusters, or persons who can influence the size of the claim once the loss has occurred.[37]

G. F. Michelbacher has taken the broadest possible view of the application of the moral hazard, which, he says, "is the bogeyman who will catch the unwary insurance man." He uses the term to include "every adverse manifestation of human nature that may be encountered in the insurance transaction." He says further:

From this . . . viewpoint moral hazard is every deviation from correct human behavior that may pose a problem for an insurer. . . . Moral hazard may be found, therefore, wherever people are touched by or can influence some phase of the insurance transaction. There are three such possibilities, involving (1) the insured personally, (2) those intimately related to or associated with the insured, and (3) others who may cause or influence the misfortune insured against or who may suffer as the result of that misfortune.[38]

Michelbacher gives as examples of the second possibility the careless youthful driver, the ruthless foreman who ignores safety rules and drives his men, the business associate who invents a burglary to cover his own defalcations, the careless employee

---

[36] Examples include Athearn; Denenberg and others; Dickerson; Greene; Huebner, Black, and Cline; Magee and Bickelhaupt; McGill; Mehr and Cammack; Mowbray and Blanchard; Pfeffer; and Winter in the writings already cited. Additional authors who do the same thing are Edwin W. Patterson, *Essentials of Insurance Law* (New York: McGraw-Hill Book Company, Inc., 1935), p. 280; and William H. Rodda, *Property and Liability Insurance* (Englewood Cliffs, N.J.: Prentice-Hall, Inc., 1966), p. 4.

[37] Williams and Heins regard the moral hazard as possibly involving several classes of persons other than insureds. Faulkner, in *Health Insurance*, p. 328, says that the moral hazard involves the attitude of the applicant "and others affected" but does not say specifically who the others might be.

[38] G. F. Michelbacher, *Multiple-line Insurance* (New York: McGraw-Hill Book Company, Inc., 1957), pp. 214-31. Copyright © 1957 by McGraw-Hill Book Company. Used with permission of McGraw-Hill Book Company.

who unwittingly sets the plant on fire, and the cashier who consorts with criminals. Examples of the third possibility include all other individuals who become involved at some stage of the insurance transaction. These may be jurors, criminals, victims of the insured's acts, or certain others.[39] Michelbacher does not distinguish between moral and morale hazards.

The Michelbacher concept of moral hazard is more closely aligned with the concept of the ethical foundation of insurance than are the other concepts of moral hazard referred to in this discussion. In some respects, however, even the Michelbacher concept is too narrow. Our discussion of the ethical components of insurance suggests that, except for relatively few instances, everybody in the society must embrace all the ethical pillars of insurance. Even individuals who might not fall within Michelbacher's third classification may influence persons who, in their turn, influence those in that class. To be consistent with the concepts developed in this chapter, Michelbacher's third group must include virtually everyone in the society who is not in the first two groups. Perhaps this is the meaning Michelbacher intended to convey.

[39]Michelbacher, *Multiple-line Insurance,* pp. 221-22.

3

POPULATION
PROSPECTS

If not restrained, population growth in time would provoke major changes in ethics and morality, which would interfere with the availability and use of insurance. Unrestrained population growth doubtless would also change the frequency and severity of occurrences against which insurance is sought to such an extent that the insuring process would be seriously threatened. Of all the possible sources of disturbance to the institution of insurance, population growth may be the most formidable. For the purposes of this study, we need to appraise the danger of population overgrowth as clearly as possible in order to deal realistically with its implications for insurance. If the problem is easily manageable, we need to recognize what should be done; if the problem is likely to resist control, we need to be forewarned.

Since realism requires attention to considerable detail, this chapter is devoted to a discussion of population history and outlook. Historical and projective estimates of population are presented for both the world and the United States. No special attention is paid in this chapter to insurance. Consideration of the insurance implications of the ethical and moral consequences of the population growth projected in this chapter is reserved for Chapter 4.

Many population experts write of the imminent calamity that awaits us as the result of continued population growth. Others minimize the problems or assure us that advancing technology will permit commensurate growth in food production and in the production of other necessities. The latter group mentions the need for adaptation and the likelihood of some inconveniences but downgrades the probability of disaster. The extreme of viewpoints on this subject can be illustrated by two brief excerpts from recent publications. William and Paul Paddock, one an agronomist with considerable experience in the tropics and the other a retired foreign service officer of the U.S. State Department, use the following frightening metaphor to describe the impending population-food crisis:

A locomotive is roaring full throttle down the track. Just around the bend an impenetrable mudslide has oozed across the track. There it lies, inert, static, deadly. Nothing can stop the locomotive in time. Collision is inevitable. Catastrophe is foredoomed. Miles back up the track the locomotive could have been warned and stopped. Years ago the mud-soaked hill could have been shored up to forestall the landslide. Now it is too late.

The locomotive roaring straight at us is the population explosion. The unmovable landslide across the tracks is the stagnant production of food in the undeveloped nations, the nations where the population increases are greatest.

The collision is inevitable. The famines are inevitable.[1]

In sharp contrast is a statement reflecting the typical Marxian attitude toward population and food production. On March 23, 1965, the Soviet representative on the Population Commission of the United Nations Economic and Social Council delivered a speech. He is reported to have said that while certain countries might experience food shortages in particular years, in the long run it is possible, according to many experts, to feed not only the present world population but a population *one hundred times greater.*[2]

Laymen can easily be left in a quandary because of the irreconcilable nature of two such divergent statements. Laymen may be further confused upon observing that optimism about food production in the face of expanding population is not restricted to spokes-

[1]William and Paul Paddock, *Famine 1975! America's Decision: Who Will Survive?* (Boston: Little, Brown and Company, 1967), pp. 8-9, used by permission.

[2]P. G. Podyachikh as reported in *U.N. Summary Record of the One Hundred and Eightieth Meeting* and as discussed by Robert C. Cook in his article, "Soviet Population Theory from Marx to Kosygin," *Population Bulletin,* vol. 23 (October, 1967), p. 97.

men from Marxist countries. In 1953 Sir John Boyd-Orr, the former director-general of the United Nation's Food and Agriculture Organization, wrote: ". . . with a modern agricultural engineering and chemical science, the only practical limit to food production is the amount of capital, labour, and research we are willing to devote to it."[3]

The more defensible—albeit much less comfortable—position is that held by the Paddock brothers. Some indication exists that even the Russians are edging away from their traditional insistence that food shortages are nothing but the handiwork of capitalism.[4] The viewpoint espoused in this chapter is that a worldwide and deeply serious population threat is looming.

POPULATION GROWTH TO DATE

Realistic speculation about future population growth and the resultant changes in moral behavior require a perspective about the growth that has already occurred. Ideally we should ascertain the vital statistics of the human race since the beginning. Unfortunately, population counts are a fairly recent phenomenon. The first census for the United States was authorized as of 1790. Apparently most countries (except a few in Western Europe) did not maintain reliable population data before that time. Even now, vital statistics for many parts of the world are based on fairly crude estimates. John D. Durand, a demographer-sociologist at the University of Pennsylvania, reminds us that population studies for various parts of the world are based on historical estimates which are not much better than projections.[5] Nevertheless, the estimates are adequate to

---

[3]John Boyd-Orr, *The White Man's Dilemma: Food and the Future* (London: George Allen and Unwin Ltd., 1953), p. 80, used by permission. Interestingly enough, Lord Orr's successor in the Food and Agriculture Organization, Binay R. Sen, took a much less sanguine view of the world food outlook and issued repeated warnings of possible impending disaster. One such warning was in these terms: "The next 35 years . . . will be a most critical period in man's history. Either we take the fullest measures to raise productivity and to stabilize population growth, or we will face disaster of an unprecedented magnitude. We must be warned . . . of unlimited disaster." Quoted by Lloyd V. Berkner, "Man versus Technology," *Population Bulletin*, vol. 22 (November, 1966), p. 93.

[4]Cook, "Soviet Population Theory from Marx to Kosygin," pp. 85-86, 99-105.

[5]John D. Durand, "World Population Estimates," *Proceedings of the World Population Conference—Belgrade, August 30-September 10, 1965*, vol. 2 (sales no. 66XIII.6; New York: United Nations, 1967), pp. 17-22.

FIGURE 1

Estimated World Population Growth and Doubling Times at Various Rates

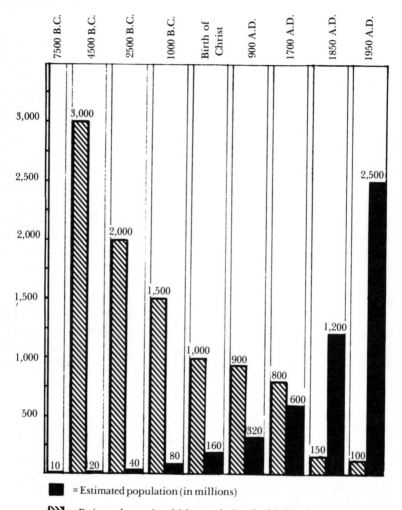

■ = Estimated population (in millions)

▨ = Estimated years in which population doubled in size.

Source: Adapted from Fritz Baade, *The Race to the Year 2000* (Garden City, N.Y.: Doubleday & Company, Inc., 1962), p. 4.

TABLE 3

Estimated World Population Growth and Doubling Times at Various Rates

Year	Estimated Population (in millions)	Estimated Time in which Population Doubled in Size
7500 B.C.	10	
4500 B.C.	20	3,000 years
2500 B.C.	40	2,000
1000 B.C.	80	1,500
Birth of Christ	160	1,000
900 A.D.	320	900
1700 A.D.	600	800
1850 A.D.	1,200	150
1950 A.D.	2,500	100

Source: Adapted from Fritz Baade, *The Race to the Year 2000* (Garden City, N.Y.: Doubleday & Company, Inc., 1962), p. 4.

convey the principal demographic outlines. Let us look first at the world data and then at some figures for the United States.

Growth of World Population

World population data are at best learned estimates. Nevertheless, they are accurate enough to show an alarming trend. Fritz Baade, a German economist, presents some estimates based on data of L. Dudley Stamp and Walter F. Wilcox.[6] Baade estimates that 10 million human beings existed as of about 7000 B.C. He depicts the doubling time as slowly falling over the centuries until in 1950 it was only one-twenty-fifth as long as in about 4500 B.C. (see Table 3). Figure 1, based on the same figures, emphasizes the recent dramatic upshoot. Another estimate, telling much the same story, was prepared by J. L. Cloudsley-Thompson, professor of zoology at the University of Khartoum and Keeper of the Sudan Natural History Museum (see Figure 2).

Having seen and heard so many references to the population explosion, perhaps we have ceased to be impressed by the phrase or

[6]Fritz Baade, *The Race to the Year 2000* (Garden City, N.Y.: Doubleday & Company, Inc., 1962). Baade bases his estimates on data from the following books: L. Dudley Stamp, *Our Undeveloped World* (London: Farbes and Farbes, 1953) and Walter F. Wilcox, *Studies in American Demography* (Ithaca, N.Y.: Cornell University Press, 1940).

FIGURE 2

Growth of World Population

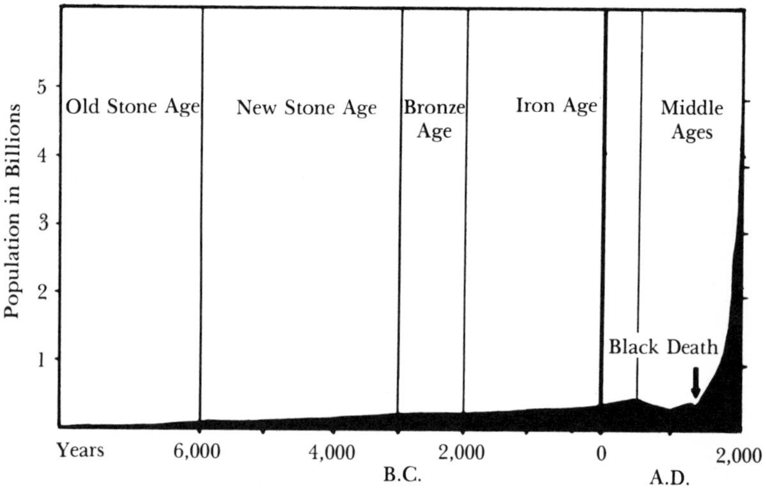

Note: Not all of the Old Stone Age is represented here; if it were, the base line would extend 15 feet to the left.

Source: J. L. Cloudsley-Thompson, *Animal Conflict and Adaptation* (Chester Springs, Pa.: Dufour Editions, Inc., 1965), p. 148, used by permission. Cloudsley-Thompson indicates that he relied on the estimates of A. Desmond in S. Mudd, ed., *The Population Crisis and the Use of World Resources* (The Hague: Junk, W. A. A. A. 2, 1964).

have grown weary of its heavy use. Yet, the preceding diagrams leave no room for doubt that the phrase is timely. Growth built upon growth, in compound interest fashion, truly reaches explosive force in due time. Exponential growth has always been at work on the human race but historically has been restrained by tenaciously high death rates. With improvements in personal and community hygiene, pesticides, and health care, the exponential is showing its awesome power. The doubling of the number of human beings that is believed to have occurred between about 7500 B.C. and about 4000 B.C. required about 2,500 years (longer than since the days of Socrates) but produced only about 10 million additional people. In contrast, the estimated doubling between about 1850 and 1950 produced a net addition of perhaps 1.3 billion people in about 100 years. The *annual* net increase is estimated now at close to 75 million. As Sir Julian Huxley has said, "Clearly this business of doubling

TABLE 4

World Population Estimates of the Population Reference Bureau, Inc., Mid-1970

	Population (billions)	Current Growth Rate (percent)	Doubling Time (years)	Birth Rate Per 1,000 Population	Death Rate Per 1,000 Population
World	3.632	2.0%	35	34	14
Northern America	0.228	1.1	63	18	9
Latin America	0.283	2.9	24	38	9
Europe	0.462	0.8	88	18	10
USSR	0.243	1.0	70	18	8
Oceania	0.019	2.0	35	25	10
Africa	0.344	2.6	27	47	20
Asia	2.056	2.3	31	38	15

Note: All rates are annual. Current growth rate is found by dividing the year's population growth by the population at the beginning of the year.

Source: 1970 World Population Data Sheet (Washington, D.C.: Population Reference Bureau, Inc.). The source indicates that the figures were derived from data maintained by the Population Reference Bureau, Inc. and obtained from governments, from the United Nations, and from other international agencies. The data sheet presents population information for 142 countries.

cannot go on indefinitely, or indeed for more than a few decades, without leading to disaster."[7]

Table 4, based on data published by the Population Reference Bureau, Inc., summarizes population estimates as of mid-1970 for the several continents or other major demographic units of the world. Perhaps the most striking aspect of Table 4, aside from the sheer magnitude of the population figures, is the disparity in the current growth rates among the several countries of the world. The PRB, Inc. publication from which the table is derived shows the current growth rate for individual countries as well as for major demographic units. Using these growth rates, let us arbitrarily assume that 2.0 percent or more represents an alarmingly high annual population growth rate. Table 5 gives all of the countries that fall into this category.[8]

[7]Julian Huxley, *The Human Crisis* (Seattle: University of Washington Press, 1963), p. 52. Copyright © The University of Washington Press, 1963; used by permission.
[8]The 2.0 percent demarcation, while convenient as a lower limit for the category, is actually much too high if a long-range view is taken of population growth. In the long run even a 1.0 percent average annual growth rate is alarmingly high and quite uncharacteristic of the development of the human race.

TABLE 5

Countries with an Estimated 1970 Population Growth Rate of 2.0 Percent or More Per Year

Rate	Nation	Rate	Nation
8.3	Kuwait	2.7	Turkey
3.8	Costa Rica	2.6	Dahomey
3.4	Colombia		India
	Dominican Republic		Nigeria
	Ecuador		Tanzania
	El Salvador		Togo
	Honduras		Uganda
	Iraq	2.5	Afghanistan
	Mexico		Haiti
	Paraguay		Hong Kong
	Philippines		Korea, South
	Southern Rhodesia		Laos
	Venezuela		Malawi
3.3	Jordan		Mauritius
	Morocco	2.4	Bolivia
	Pakistan		Ceylon
	Panama		Chad
	Syria		Guadeloupe
	Thailand		Israel
3.2	Algeria		Ivory Coast
	Sudan		Mali
3.1	Kenya		Senegal
	Libya		Singapore
	Mongolia		Somalia
	Peru		South Africa
	Reunion	2.3	Burma
3.0	Cambodia		Burundi
	Iran		Chile
	Lebanon		China (Taiwan)
	Nicaragua		Guinea
	Swaziland		Sierra Leone
	Tunisia	2.2	Bhutan
	Zambia		Botswana
2.9	Ghana		Cameroon, West
	Guatemala		Central African Republic
	Guyana		Congo (Brazzaville)
	Indonesia		Congo (Democratic Republic)
	Niger		Mauritania
	Rwanda		Nepal
2.8	Brazil	2.1	Angola
	Korea, North		Ethiopia
	Malaysia, East and West		Jamaica
	Saudi Arabia		Mozambique
	Southern Yemen		North Vietnam
	UAR		South Vietnam
	Yemen		Upper Volta
2.7	Albania	2.0	Martinique
	Madagascar		Southwest Africa (Namibia)

Source: 1970 World Population Data Sheet (Washington, D.C.: Population Reference Bureau, Inc.)

The array permits several useful observations:

1.   Generally, the relatively high population growth rates are in the relatively undeveloped areas of the world. One is tempted to generalize that the rate of population growth shows a high inverse correlation with economic development. Perhaps it does. One does not need to go that far, however. It is enough simply to notice that the relatively high population growth rates occur, with few exceptions, in countries generally classified as less developed. This is not to say that all the less-developed countries have experienced high recent population growth rates.[9] Nevertheless, conspicuously absent from the array are the industrialized countries such as the United States, Canada, Japan, Australia, the USSR, and European countries other than Albania.[10] Thus, population growth truly is proceeding most rapidly in those parts of the world where economic development already is distinctly in arrears.

2.   Latin America appears to be the major area of highest current growth rates; numerous Latin countries have growth rates well in excess of 3 percent.

3.   With few exceptions African countries fall in the 2.0 to 3.0 range.

[9]The data sheet, for example, shows Equatorial Guinea with a 1970 estimated growth rate of 1.3 percent and Gabon with 0.9 percent.

[10]Another conspicuous absence from the array is mainland China, whose population and growth rate have not been recently reported and can only be crudely estimated in the Western world. Irene B. Taeuber, Office of Population Research, Princeton University, wrote of the difficulty of making estimates for mainland China: "The area of mainland China includes one-fifth to one-fourth of the world's total population. In 1953 and 1954 the Government of China (mainland) conducted a census and investigation of the population. The population as of mid-1953 was reported as 583 million for the mainland. This single figure is accepted as the base for retrospective and projective estimates by all analysts. The Government also published an age pyramid for the population as of 1953, and vital rates for the years from 1952 through 1957. These data are rough approximations only. Hence the future population of 20 to 25 percent of the world's population involves a hypothetical age structure and hypothetical vital rates to move from 1953 to 1965 and then from 1965 to the end of the century. The range of the demographically possible is enormous. Assuming the fertility of rural Taiwan in the late 1930s along with declining mortality, the population would be 2,000 million by the end of the century. Assuming the swift realization of the Government's goal of late marriage, postponed births, and a two-child family, the population would be only 1,000 million by the end of the century," Taeuber, "Future Population Trends and Prospects: Statement by the Moderator," *Proceedings of the World Population Conference—Belgrade, August 30-September 10, 1965*, vol. 1 (sales no. 66XIII.6; New York: United Nations, 1966), pp. 195-96. In their projections the U.N. demographers chose to use 900 million for the low variant to the year 2000 and 1,500 million for the high variant.

4.   The population of the countries in the category of alarmingly high population growth rates represents close to 55 percent of the total world population. If mainland China, whose growth rate is questionable, were included in the group, the figure would be close to 75 percent. In either case considerably more than half of the 75 million or so additional human beings added to the world's population in 1970 will reside in the countries in the "alarmingly high" growth rate category.

5.   Although color has no necessary causal connection whatever, the fact remains that the population of the predominantly nonwhite areas of the world is growing as a whole at a rate much faster than that for the predominantly white areas.[11]

6.   Considering the power of the exponential, these growth rates portend great evil for the future. An average annual growth rate of 5 percent means a doubling about every 14 years; a rate of 4 percent means a doubling about every 18 years; 3 percent, every 23 years; and 2 percent, every 35 years. Such growth rates are clearly intolerable. Even a 1 percent average annual growth rate leads to a doubling in about 70 years. The world population cannot double many more times. With 3.5 billion as the starting point, only 10 doublings produce a figure of 3,584 billion, a horrible number even to use as an illustration of human population.

Growth of U.S. Population

The population of the United States has grown tremendously fast. The first federal census of the population, conducted as of August 4, 1790, yielded a figure of 3,929,214. A recent release by the Bureau of the Census estimated total population residing

---

[11]Formal discussion of such a phenomenon long has been taboo, however, in international demographic circles because of the possible racial implications and the readiness of communist propaganda agencies to seize on the discussion as evidence of white capitalists' fear of Asian, African, or South American Indian economic and social development. Particularly taboo has been the recommendation from any Western source that fertility control be adopted in Asia, Africa, or Latin America. With the dangers of population growth becoming increasingly recognized, the propaganda value of recommendations for fertility control fortunately is being lost. For a discussion of this matter see Frank Lorimer, "Issues of Population Policy," in The American Assembly, *The Population Dilemma* (Englewood Cliffs, N.J.: Prentice-Hall, Inc., 1963), pp. 143-78.

in the United States (excluding Armed Forces abroad) at about 204,509,000.[12] Given recent growth rates, a reasonable estimate of the 1970 end-of-year population is about 206 million. Discounting spurious accuracy, the growth from 1790 to 1970 approximates over 200 million for this span of about 180 years. The increase in population in the United States during the 1960s was larger than the total population of the United States recorded in the 1850 census. The average annual compound rate of growth, for whatever that figure is worth, has been about 2.2 percent.

Population growth in the United States has been tremendously influenced by immigration to and from the United States. Any analysis of our population history should reflect net immigration figures. Unfortunately, no official immigration statistics were collected and maintained until about 1820 after the passage of a law in 1819 requiring that the master of each incoming ship carrying passengers report certain information to the collector of customs. The earliest emigration figures, other than for aliens being deported, appeared in 1908.

Even these published figures for movement into and out of the United States are awkward to use in estimating net immigration. The definition of "immigrant" has been changed several times to fit the changing immigration patterns.[13] Moreover, the definition of "emigrant" does not necessarily include all citizens and immigrants who leave the United States for permanent residence abroad. Consequently, net immigration estimates should be used only within a wide range of tolerance.

In view of the crudity of the data, only rough estimates of net immigration can be made here. We can begin our estimates as of

---

[12]U.S. Department of Commerce, Bureau of the Census, *Population Estimates, Current Population Reports*, series P-25, no. 443 (February 1, 1970), p. 1.

[13]The early figures for immigration included only persons arriving by ship at Atlantic and Gulf coast seaports of the United States. Arrivals on the Pacific coast were counted during and after 1850. After 1892 aliens arriving by ship in Canada but destined for the United States were also included in the immigration tallies. Aliens arriving over land borders, aside from those arriving by ship in Canada and included under the 1892 ruling, were first reported in 1904. About that time the basis of reporting was also changed to exclude those arrivals who were not permitted to enter the United States. For more details see U.S. Department of Commerce, Bureau of the Census, *Historical Statistics of the United States—Colonial Times to 1957* (Washington, D.C.: U.S. Govt. Printing Office, 1960), pp. 48-49.

1820,[14] provided that we can estimate the annual volume of emigration through 1907. Specialists who have worked on the problem have assumed that emigration was about 10 to 15 percent as large as immigration in the 1820-1870 period; about 25 percent as large from 1871-1880; about 33 percent from 1881-1900; and about 45 percent from 1901-1910.[15] These percentages have been used in the preparation of Table 6, which provides an estimate of net immigration since 1820. The table reveals that net immigration may well have been greater than 30 million since 1820.

If, for working purposes, we can accept the net immigration estimates given in Table 6, we are ready to look at the decennial census of population figures and estimate the amount of growth that stemmed from natural increase as well as net immigration. Table 7 and Figure 3 show in approximate terms the two components of the population growth. Despite likely inaccuracies in most of the figures,[16] the enormous growth is undeniable.

[14]No official immigration data are available for the years before 1820. Taeuber and Taeuber make the following statement about earlier immigration: "Most people who have studied the history of the period and whatever local records were available believe that something less than a quarter of a million white immigrants entered the country in the 30 years from 1790 to 1819." Conrad and Irene B. Taeuber, *The Changing Population of the United States*, Census Monograph Series (New York: John Wiley & Sons, Inc., 1958), p. 51, used by permission. Most of those who entered before 1790 presumably were included in the first census. The authors also report a Bureau of the Census estimate that about 400,000 Africans were brought to this country as slaves in the early nineteenth century. Presumably, slaves were included in the first census but Indians were excluded. The Bureau of the Census document *Heads of Families at the First Census of the United States in the Year 1790* (Washington, D.C.: U.S. Govt. Printing Office, 1907), p. 4, indicates that the form used provided for enumeration of slaves.

[15]Taeuber and Taeuber, *The Changing Population of the United States*, pp. 54-55. The authors cite an estimate made by Simon Kuznets and Ernest Rubin in *Immigration and the Foreign Born*, Occasional Paper 46 (New York: National Bureau of Economic Research, 1964) as the source for the estimates of the rates of emigration before 1911.

[16]The immigration figures are not the only ones that are suspect. The census data themselves are not above suspicion. Taeuber and Taeuber say that the first census covered only about half the land claimed at that time by the government. Much of the rest was occupied at least partly by hostile Indians who were not included in the census. Neither were white settlers, if any, in such territories. As new territories were included within the national boundaries, the proportion of land area covered by the enumerators in the successive censuses varied and became 100 percent only with the census of 1890. See Taeuber and Taeuber, *The Changing Population of the United States*, p. 9. The census data, and consequently the growth rates, are also affected by the population of the new territories included within national boundaries. Alaska and Hawaii are recent examples.

TABLE 6

Estimated Net Immigration in the United States, 1820-1970

Census Year	Estimates for 10-Year Period Ending with Census Year*		
	Immigration	Emigration	Net Immigration
1820-1830	152	23	129
1830-1840	599	89	510
1840-1850	1,713	257	1,456
1850-1860	2,598	390	2,208
1860-1870	2,315	247	2,068
1870-1880	2,812	703	2,109
1880-1890	5,247	1,731	3,516
1890-1900	3,688	1,217	2,471
1900-1910	8,795	3,958	4,837
1910-1920	5,736	2,180	3,556
1920-1930	4,107	1,027	3,080
1930-1940	528	451	77
1940-1950	1,035	114	921
1950-1960	2,515	302	2,213
1970	3,300	300	3,000
Total	45,140	12,989	32,151

*All figures are given in thousands.
Sources: Immigration data for 1820-1966 were taken from U.S. Department of Commerce, Bureau of the Census, Statistical Abstract of the United States, 1969 (90th ed.; Washington, D.C.: U.S. Govt. Printing Office, 1969), p. 88; data for 1967 and 1968 were taken from the 1967 and 1968 editions of U.S. Department of Justice, Immigration and Naturalization Service, Annual Report of the Immigration and Naturalization Service (U.S. Govt. Printing Office), p. 31. Immigration data for the years 1969-70 were estimated. Emigration data for 1820-1910 were computed from estimates in Conrad and Irene B. Taeuber, The Changing Population of the United States (New York: John Wiley & Sons, Inc., 1958), pp. 54-55; for 1911-57 they were computed from data in U.S. Department of Commerce, Bureau of the Census, Historical Statistics of the United States—Colonial Times to 1957 (Washington, D. C.: U.S. Govt. Printing Office, 1960), Table C-156, p. 64. Emigration data given for the years 1958-70 were estimated.

The upturn in the rate of natural increase during the 1940s and 1950s is quite noticeable. Table 7 and Figure 3 also show the declining absolute and relative importance, after 1910, of net immigration as an element in population growth. Net immigration was largest in the decade ending in 1910, when it amounted to almost 5 million and accounted for about 30 percent of the population increase for that decade. By contrast, it only accounted for roughly 10 percent in the 1960s. The population growth occurring since 1940 reveals the power of exponential growth even in the face of declining average growth rates. The growth by about 75 million since 1940 fully justifies our anxiety about the future.

The population growth of the United States has been characterized by several major long-term trends that may continue indefi-

TABLE 7

U.S. Population—Net Immigration and Natural Increase, 1790-1970

| | | Estimated Increase* (in millions) | | | Estimated Average Annual Compound Rate of Increase+ | |
| | | | | | Natural Increase Only | Total Including Net Immigration |
Year	Population (in millions)	Net Immigration	Natural Increase	Total Increase‡		
1790	3.9	—	—	—	—	—
1800	5.3	—	—	1.4	—	3.1%
1810	7.2	—	—	1.9	—	3.1
1820	9.6	—	—	2.4	—	2.9
1830	12.8	0.1	3.1	3.2	2.8%	2.8
1840	17.1	0.5	3.7	4.2	2.6	3.0
1850	23.2	1.4	4.7	6.1	2.5	3.1
1860	31.4	2.2	6.0	8.2	2.3	3.1
1870	39.8	2.1	6.3	8.4	1.9	2.4
1880	50.1	2.1	8.2	10.3	1.9	2.5
1890	62.9	3.5	9.3	12.8	1.7	2.3
1900	76.0	2.5	10.5	13.0	1.6	1.9
1910	92.0	4.8	11.2	16.0	1.4	1.9
1920	105.7	3.5	10.2	13.7	1.1	1.4
1930	122.8	3.1	14.0	17.1	1.2	1.5
1940	131.7	0.0 (1)	8.9	8.9	0.7	0.7
1950	151.3	0.9	18.7	19.6	1.3	1.5
1960	179.3	2.2	25.8	28.0	1.6	1.7
1970§	206.0	3.0	23.7	26.7	1.2	1.4

*For decade ending with the census year shown in leftmost column.
+For each year of the decade ending with the census year shown in leftmost column.
‡Because of rounding errors previous figures in the "population" column plus figures in the "total increase" column do not always equal the new population figure.
§All the figures for 1970 are estimated.
Sources: Table 6 and U.S. Department of Commerce, Bureau of the Census, Statistical Abstract of the United States, 1968 (89th ed.; Washington, D.C.: U.S. Govt. Printing Office, 1968), p. 5.

nitely. Consequently, they deserve brief expostulation at this point in the discussion.

1.   The population growth rate has shown a general but irregular decline since about 1860. Even so, because of the enlarged base, the absolute natural increase in population during the 1950s was about 20 million more than that during the 1850s. The absolute growth during the 1960s was only slightly less than that of the 1950s.

FIGURE 3

U.S. Population—Net Immigration and Natural Increase, 1790-1970

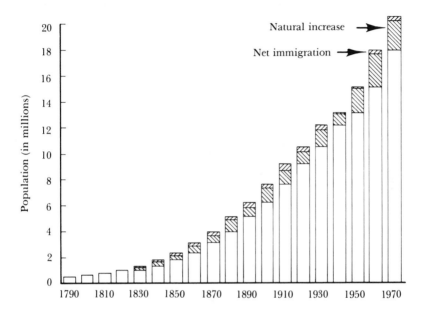

Source: Table 7.

2.   Negro population as a percentage of total population declined from about 11.6 percent in 1900 to about 10.0 percent in
1950. Since then, it has risen back up to about the 1900 level and
this relatively faster Negro growth trend is expected to continue.
Table 8 summarizes white and nonwhite birth and death rates.[17] The
nonwhite death rate is now about as low as the white death rate.
The nonwhite birth rate, however, has not declined nearly as rapidly
as the white birth rate and as of 1970 is expected to be 150 percent

[17]Bureau of the Census data are categorized into white and nonwhite. Negro and
nonwhite growth patterns are probably quite similar.

TABLE 8
U.S. Birth and Death Rates per 1,000 Population,
1800-1970

	Live Births			Deaths (excluding fetal deaths)		
Year	White	Nonwhite	Total	White	Nonwhite	Total
1800	55.0	—	—	—	—	—
1810	54.3	—	55.2	—	—	—
1820	52.8	—	—	—	—	—
1830	51.4	—	—	—	—	—
1840	48.3	—	51.8	—	—	—
1850	43.3	—	—	—	—	—
1860	41.4	—	44.3	—	—	—
1870	38.3	—	—	—	—	—
1880	35.2	—	39.8	—	—	—
1890	31.5	—	—	—	—	—
1900	30.1	—	32.3	17.0	25.0	17.2
1910	29.2	—	30.1	14.5	22.4	14.7
1920	26.9	35.0	27.7	12.6	17.7	13.0
1930	20.6	27.5	21.3	10.8	16.3	11.3
1940	18.6	26.7	19.4	10.4	13.8	10.8
1950	23.0	33.3	24.1	9.5	11.2	9.6
1960	22.7	32.1	23.7	9.5	10.1	9.5
1970*	16.8	25.0	17.8	9.4	9.5	9.4

*Figures for 1970 are estimates.
Sources: U.S. Department of Commerce, Bureau of the Census, *Historical Statistics of the United States—Colonial Times to 1957* (Washington, D.C.: U.S. Govt. Printing Office, 1960), pp. 23,27, and *Statistical Abstract of the United States, 1969* (90th ed.; Washington, D.C.: U.S. Govt. Printing Office, 1969), pp. 47, 48, 55.

of the white birth rate. Interestingly, with the exception of the jump reflected in the figures for 1950, Table 8 shows steadily declining birth rates for both white and nonwhite populations. The postwar upturn in the birth rates for whites peaked in 1957 at 24.1 and for nonwhites in 1956 at 35.4.

3.   Urban population for many years has been increasing faster than nonurban population. The Bureau of the Census designates certain heavily urbanized areas in the United States as "Standard Metropolitan Statistical Areas" (SMSAs). An SMSA is designated as a city, or two contiguous cities, with population of at least 50,000, according to the most recent census of population, and with certain other urban characteristics. In 1900 the proportion of population inside the SMSAs was about 42 percent. The estimate for

1970 is in excess of 65 percent. Kingsley Davis has estimated that in 1960 about 53 percent of the population lived in areas comprising only about 0.71 percent of the total land area of the United States.[18] As of 1970, the concentration probably is even more pronounced.

4. A pronounced decrease in the proportion of the population engaged in agriculture has been allied to the urbanization process. For example, according to the Bureau of the Census, the farm population declined from almost 16 million in early 1960 to slightly more than 12 million by the end of 1964.[19] As of 1970, farm population probably constitutes little more than 5 percent of the total population of the United States. This figure appears exceptionally small when compared with the 70 to 80 percent reported for such countries as Turkey, India, Pakistan, and Egypt.[20]

5. The concentration of the Negro population in the SMSAs has also been allied to the urbanization process. While only about 27 percent of the total Negro population resided in SMSAs in 1900, about 65 percent of the considerably larger Negro population was in the SMSAs in 1960.[21] The 1970 figure is probably about 70 percent.

[18]Kingsley Davis, "Urbanization—Changing Patterns of Living" in Hoke S. Simpson, ed., *The Changing American Population* (New York: Institute of Life Insurance, 1962), pp. 59-68. Davis has also wryly observed that most of the nation's automobiles are often crammed into this small space too. Another treatment of the subject by the same author appears in "The Urbanization of the Human Population," *Scientific American*, vol. 213 (September, 1965), pp. 40-54. A different treatment of urbanization by Philip M. Hauser is found in "Urbanization—Problems of High Density Living," in Richard N. Farmer and others, eds., *World Population—The View Ahead* (Bloomington, Ind.: Bureau of Business Research, Graduate School of Business, Indiana University, 1968), pp. 187-217.

[19]U.S. Department of Commerce, Bureau of the Census, *America at Mid-Decade* (Washington, D.C.: U.S. Govt. Printing Office, 1966), p. 13.

[20]For detailed estimates of the proportions of several national populations engaged in agriculture see Baade, *The Race to the Year 2000*, pp. 93-95. Incidentally, Baade makes the point that agriculture in these countries is grossly inefficient because too many people are farming too many plots that are too small. Economies of scale cannot be enjoyed. The United States, however, may be approaching the limit of economies of scale so that the relative proportion of the population engaged in agriculture cannot decrease substantially.

[21]Detailed figures can be found in U.S. Department of Commerce, Bureau of the Census, *Population Trends in the United States 1900 to 1960*, by Irene B. Taeuber, Bureau of the Census Technical Paper no. 10 (Washington, D.C.: U.S. Govt. Printing Office, 1964), Table 2, pp. 99-139.

6.   After World War II the average number of children per family in the United States increased somewhat. A comparison of estimates for 1950 with those for 1965 shows the following:[22]

	1950	1965
No children under 18	42%	35%
One child under 18	23	20
Two children under 18	19	19
Three or more children under 18	16	26
Total	100	100

As we shall observe later, the behavior of the average number of children per family variable is crucial to population control over the long-range future. The postwar upturn in this variable after its decline during the Great Depression led to substantial population growth. Recent behavior of the birth rate suggests that the average may be declining again.

THE LONG-RANGE OUTLOOK

Having observed the increasing momentum of population growth, we cannot help but shudder and wonder about what will happen in the future. Among the questions to ponder are the following: Is there any practical limit to the number of human beings for whom life can be sustained on this planet? Does man have any automatic biological controls by which his numbers will be limited short of this ceiling? Will future growth rates be jaggedly uneven from continent to continent and from race to race? By what now appear to be reasonable expectations, how many people are likely to inhabit the globe by the turn of the century; and of that number, how many are likely to reside in the United States? These are difficult questions, and we can do no more than grope for the answers.

Maximum Potential Growth

A popular game is to try to estimate the number of human beings who could be squeezed on to the surface of the earth. R. A.

---

[22]U.S. Department of Commerce, Bureau of the Census, *America at Mid-Decade*, p. 24. The data are for U.S. families with family head under 65 years of age.

Piddington reports in a 1956 publication that Sir Charles Galton Darwin (not Charles R.) performed some interesting calculations to show that, at the then current rate of increase, the living space of every human would shrink to "standing room only" by 3954 A.D. [23]

Such a calculation would be factitious if taken as a prediction that such a condition would ever come to pass. Doubtless, starvation and plague would set in, and reproduction would slow down in ample time to prevent such a development. However, the calculation is hardly factitious when one inquires what the ultimate limit of the population increase is. Surely, there is such a limit; otherwise potential population growth would be infinite! Any continuing positive rate of growth eventually leads to astronomically large numbers.

Those who have wrestled with this subject seem to regard the question of an ultimate limit in the number of human beings as meaningless. Probably they are correct; at least they are practical. Energy, food, water, health care, individual space requirements, social requirements, and utilization of space off the surface of the earth (such as in high-rise structures or in craft not resting on the dry surface of the earth) are dependent on technology. Perhaps little is to be gained by wondering whether future technological advancement faces some absolute limit and, if so, where that limit is located. Perhaps the technological limit, if it does exist, is so far removed as to be totally irrelevant to us now. The concept of an ultimate limit on technology, and thus on the size of the human race, is nevertheless interesting to consider in our less practical moments.

Sir Julian Huxley cautioned us against worrying now about the ultimate maximum number of human beings. He said that we

---

[23]R. A. Piddington, *The Limits of Mankind: A Philosophy of Population* (Bristol: John Wright and Sons, Ltd., 1956), p. 2. The eerie term, "standing room only," was used by Karl Sax, professor of botany at Harvard University, as the title of his highly readable book dealing with the inadequacy of the earth's resources to accommodate a long continuation of the rapidly expanding human population. See Karl Sax, *Standing Room Only* (Boston: Beacon Press, 1960). Darwin's calculations doubtless were made with tongue in cheek. His serious statement on the subject is found in his book, *The Next Million Years* (Garden City, N.Y.: Doubleday & Company, Inc., 1953).

should worry, rather, about our current population growth, which is surely outrunning our current technology. At the same time, however, he tacitly recognized such a limit by urging people to quit thinking of the population-technology relationship as a race; he deplored references to a race between production and reproduction or between food and people. Huxley elaborated by saying:

> This, I am sure, is a wrong approach. The essence of a race is that it can be won; but this is something that neither side can ever win. The present rate of human increase cannot continue for more than a century or so at the outside without leading to a completely absurd but completely disastrous result. And this is for a period that is insignificant in relation to the evolutionary time before us—time to be measured not in hundreds, not in thousands, but in millions and even hundreds of millions of years. No, we must give up thinking in terms of a race; we must think in terms of a balance. We must aim at achieving some sort of balanced relation between the rate of reproduction and the rate of production of food and other resources.[24]

Whether or not some absolute limit exists, we necessarily are much more interested in the limit relative to current technology. Even here much disagreement exists. Moreover, estimates can quickly become dated as the stream of events proves them to be erroneous. An interesting example is found in *The Biology of Population Growth,* a book published in 1925 by Raymond Pearl, an eminent biologist at the Johns Hopkins University. To appreciate the example we need to know that Pearl subscribed to the now widely accepted idea that population growth of the human race follows an S-shaped sigmoid growth curve. In a sigmoid-type curve the rate of growth after an increase eventually slows, and the curve approaches

---

[24]Huxley, *The Human Crisis,* p. 57, used by permission. Huxley uses two illustrations to emphasize that without control of reproduction the population grows quickly to use newly available resources. The Lloyd Barrage on the Indus River in Pakistan was at one time the largest irrigation scheme in the world. It made a large area productive. Within a few decades, however, it became as densely settled as adjacent areas. The High Dam at Aswan, Egypt, will permit greater food production, but it will amount only to a quite temporary and minor victory, again because of human increase. The only really troublesome point in Huxley's statement is the presumption about the hundreds of millions of years of human history yet to unfold. Not even Sir Julian could know whether life on earth will continue that long. We must recognize the possibility (without calculable probability) that the Creator of the universe can call an end to time and mortality at his own option.

an upper asymptote.[25] In 1925 Pearl was already widely known for his extensive studies of the growth of insect and other populations. Because of the "logistic" he was using, he placed the upper asymptote on the human population sigmoid curve at the level of 2,026 million and suggested that the curve would be very close to this upper limit by 1975.[26] In the same context Pearl took a rather negative view of an estimate made by another scholar by observing: "Penck estimates the 'potential' world population as 8,000 millions . . . but I am unable to convince myself that his estimate is justified by the evidence."[27] To Pearl's credit we must remember that he was writing in 1925. Indeed, many passages in the present book may be even more erroneous by the year 2015.

Another much more recent example of what probably will be an underestimation was made by Sir John Boyd-Orr, whose optimism

[25]The general shape is similar to a large S.

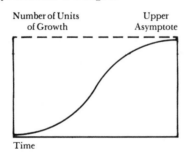

Lamont C. Cole, writing in 1948, recognized the general applicability of the sigmoid curve: "This type of growth is very general, and curves of this shape have been found to fit such diverse material as the growth in weight of vegetables, the number of victims of a communicable disease ('growth of an epidemic'), the growth of amount of lumber in woodlands, and the growth of populations of an extremely wide variety of organisms from bacteria to man. The sigmoid shape of the growth curve is usual no matter in what units the population is measured. For example, in fish populations a sigmoid growth curve is obtained whether the population is measured in number of individuals or pounds of fish per acre of water surface." See Lamont C. Cole, "Population Phenomena and Common Knowledge," *The Scientific Monthly*, vol. 67 (November, 1948), p. 343.

[26]Raymond Pearl, *The Biology of Population Growth* (New York: Alfred A. Knopf, 1925), p. 172.

[27]Pearl's reference is to A. Penck, *Das Hauptproblem der Physischen Anthropogeographie*. Sitzungsber. d. Preuss. Akad. d. Wiss. Bd. 32, 1924, pp. 242-57.

has already been noted. Perhaps that optimism was fed somewhat by his estimate of population growth. In 1953, he wrote:

There seems no reason to doubt the estimate made by agricultural experts, that if modern improved methods were applied to all the land at present cultivated or grazed the world supply of food would be doubled, and that if known measures were taken to increase the area of the earth under cultivation by irrigation, bush clearance, and other measures, the earth could support a population of 6,000 million. It is doubtful whether the world population will ever reach that level.[28]

More recently, and perhaps with better results, various resource specialists have attempted to gauge the world's resources and estimate the maximum supportable human population, given certain assumptions about productivity. In 1957 Harrison Brown, James Bonner, and John Weir of the California Institute of Technology published some carefully circumscribed speculations. They surmised that the earth perhaps could feed almost 8 billion people if (1) all potentially arable land were put into use, (2) the Japanese level of land productivity were attained in Asia, (3) the European land productivity level were attained elsewhere, and (4) the present Asiatic diet were followed in Asia and a European diet were followed elsewhere, each with 2,500 calories per day.[29] They opined that the maximum potential population might rise to about 11 billion if the whole world could attain the Japanese level of land productivity (a large "if") and content itself with an Asian diet of no more than 2,500 calories per day.

Another estimate was made along somewhat similar lines in 1959 by an Australian biologist-physician, Sir F. MacFarlane Burnet, who wrote of the approaching depletion of easily accessible, high grade sources of tin, lead, and zinc and of the tremendous demands for iron and copper. Burnet observed that the United States consumes about one-third of the world's production of fossil fuels and most other irreplaceable mineral resources. In Burnet's judgment, for the entire world to attain by the year 2000 as high a living standard as that of the United States in 1959, the annual production of oil, steel and certain other resources would have to increase about 13 times. According to Burnet, many scientists believe that if

---

[28]Boyd-Orr, *The White Man's Dilemma*, p. 79, used by permission.
[29]Harrison Brown and others, *The Next Hundred Years* (New York: The Viking Press, 1963), pp. 67, 164.

nuclear energy, exploitation of low grade ores, reuse of scrap metal, an increased use of aluminum and magnesium, and an increased use of synthetics can be realized, a world population of about 10 billion might be supported at a tolerable level of comfort. He then added the sobering observation:

But no form of sophistry can imagine that the irreplaceable resources of a small planet can continue to supply a population increasing in geometric progression, 6,500 million in 2000, 52,000 million in 2100 and 420,000 million in 2200.[30]

These several estimates and others that could be included are inconsistent in numerous respects. Yet, on one point they are clear. The particular limit of population growth depends heavily on the quality specified for the lives that are to be maintained. Considering present standards of living, we may have already passed the optimum level of population and may be plunging along toward the limit of the merely tolerable. Except for occasional spurts of accomplishment, mankind has been unable in recent years to increase its food production by more than 2 percent annually. People in many South American, African, and Asian countries have a lower average caloric intake today than in the late 1930s, and even then their diets were inadequate. Our only practical hope lies in stabilizing the size of the population. This sort of thinking probably motivated R. A. Piddington to comment that:

Not a single reason, material or spiritual, can be advanced for wishing to increase the world's population beyond its present total. On the contrary, there are at least a dozen grounds, ranging from the economic to the ethical, for hoping that it will soon be considerably reduced.[31]

What was true in 1956, when Piddington made his comment, is true today. What was urgent then, namely to bring about a drastic slowdown in the rate of population growth, is of greater urgency today. In this sort of setting it is almost unthinkable that the leader of any industrialized nation would speak out for a higher birth rate. That was precisely what happened recently, however, when Charles

---

[30]F. MacFarlane Burnet, *2000 A.D.—A Biologist's Thoughts on the Next Forty Years* (Melbourne: Adult Education Board of Tasmania in association with Melbourne University Press, 1959), p. 10, used by permission.

[31]Piddington, *The Limits of Mankind*, p. 149, used by permission.

De Gaulle implored the French for a higher birth rate to yield more Frenchmen.[32] Let us hope that the French and all others will find Piddington's reasoning more persuasive.[33]

Population Control

Whether man can and will control his numbers to avoid reaching the limit of his environment has been debated at least since the time of Machiavelli. The question is identified particularly with Thomas Robert Malthus, whose famous essay on population appeared in 1798.[34] Malthus's principle of population provided scholars with a

---

[32]"Higher Birth Rate Sought by De Gaulle," *Indianapolis Star* (December 15, 1968), p. 4.

[33]The De Gaulle point of view was not uncommon a few years ago. An example of such thinking can be found in a heavily documented publication of the International Labour Office, released in 1938. The author, Imre Ferenczi, argued that population was too low and said: "The decline in the birth rate constitutes, at least for some time to come, so great a danger in certain civilized countries, that . . . nations are now seeking and will make increasingly great efforts in the future to maintain or increase the present birth-rate, with the object of *preserving at least the present size* of the nation." See Imre Ferenczi, *The Synthetic Optimum of Population: An Outline of an International Demographic Policy* (Paris: International Institute of Intellectual Co-operation, League of Nations, 1938), p. 87. At that time governmental subsidies were used in many countries, and still are in some parts of the world, to encourage large families. In fact, the system of welfare payments currently used in the United States encourages large families by providing additional support as the number of children increases. To some extent federal income tax deductions for dependents do the same thing.

[34]The title of the first edition, published anonymously, is *An Essay on the Principle of Population, as it Affects the Future Improvement of Society, With remarks on the speculations of Mr. Godwin, M. Condorcet, and other writers.* Title and contents were revised during six subsequent editions. The principle differences arose as between the first and second editions, with the second being much expanded over the first. Robert Malthus (who prefered to drop the "Thomas") prepared the essay as a rejoinder to a paper by William Godwin that appeared in 1793. Godwin, a utopian, had said, in effect, that population could increase without practical limit for centuries to come without the earth being found insufficient to support its inhabitants; he then described an idyllic society that could and might come to fruition. In the preface to the second edition Malthus mentioned by name several persons, including David Hume, Robert Wallace, Adam Smith, and Benjamin Franklin, from whose writings he said he had deduced the principle of population. He was interested in using the principle to test the speculations that Godwin and others had made "on the perfectibility of man and society." In 1820 William Godwin published a lengthy rebuttal to Malthus. The full title of this work, which received relatively little publicity, is: *Of Population: An Enquiry Concerning the Power of Increase in the Numbers of Mankind, Being An Answer to Mr. Malthus' Essay on That Subject* (London: Longman, Hurst, Rees, Orme, and Brown, Paternoster Row, 1820).

virtually unlimited intellectual field for agreement or dissent; and they have been busy cultivating it ever since by producing books, tracts, and other literature. Malthus, nominally a minister but actually a professor of history and political economy at the East-India College at Hertfordshire, probably has been quoted or misquoted more often than any other social scientist except perhaps Adam Smith and Karl Marx. Malthus's publisher reportedly complained that "no work has been so much talked of by persons who do not seem to have read it, as Mr. Malthus' Essay on Population."[35]

Malthus's prognosis is exceedingly controversial; but if his reasoning is sound, it is exceedingly relevant to the future size of world population. Consequently, we have an incentive to appraise as best we can the position he really took. Perhaps the appraisal will indicate whether we have grounds for hoping that population growth soon can be curbed. The early pages of his essay convey his objectives, reasons for concern, and fundamental analysis.[36] Malthus said his purpose was to investigate the causes that had previously "impeded the progress of mankind towards happiness" and to examine "the probability of the total or partial removal of these causes" in the future (pp. 1-2). He considered the main impending cause to be "the constant tendency in all animated life to increase beyond the nourishment prepared for it" (pp. 2-3). He pointed to the result of this constant tendency by observing:

But as, by that law of our nature which makes food necessary to the life of man, population can never actually increase beyond the lowest nourishment capable of supporting it, a strong check on population, from the difficulty of acquiring food, must be constantly in operation. This difficulty must fall somewhere, and must necessarily be severely felt in some or other of the various forms of misery, or the fear of misery, by a large portion of mankind (p. 5).

On the basis of the evidence at his disposal he then surmised that, if unchecked, human population had the capacity under ideal

---

[35]This statement along with biographical and interpretive material about Malthus appears in Judy K. Morris, "Professor Malthus and His Essay," in "Malthus in Retrospect," *Population Bulletin,* vol. 22 (February, 1966), pp. 7-27. Another useful commentary about Malthus is found in the introduction to Gertrude Himmelfarb, ed., *On Population—Thomas Robert Malthus* (New York: The Modern Library, 1960).

[36]The quoted portions that follow come from volume 1 of Malthus' fifth edition (published in London in 1817 by John Murray). Page numbers for each quotation or paraphrase appear in parentheses.

conditions to double itself at least every 25 years.[37] He then noticed that, while the rate of increase in food production is not as easy to determine, it certainly is of a different nature than the rate of increase in population. He said that 1,000 million could be just as easily doubled every 25 years by the power of population as 1,000 but that the food to support the increase could by no means be "obtained with the same facility" because of gradually diminishing potential (p. 9). By contrast, "population, could it be supplied with food, would go on with unexhausted vigor . . . and this without any limit" (p 10).

He developed a supposition, concerning England and Scotland, constructed to show the potential for food production in as favorable a light as experience could possibly warrant. Using the supposition, he concluded that means of subsistence over the long run "could not possibly be made to increase faster than in an arithmetic ratio" (p. 14). Generalizing to the world as a whole on the basis of the supposition and considering human population at the time to be about 1 billion, he said that human population, if unchecked, would increase over two centuries in the numbers 1, 2, 4, 8, 16, 32, 64, 128, 256 (assuming a doubling every 25 years). Subsistence, on the other hand, could increase only in the numbers 1, 2, 3, 4, 5, 6, 7, 8, 9. By this supposition population in two centuries would be to subsistence as 256 is to 9 or in three centuries as 4,096 is to 13 (p. 15).

He was led to state that:

The ultimate check to population appears then to be a want of food, arising necessarily from the different ratios according to which population and food increase. But this ultimate check is never the immediate check, except in cases of actual famine.

The immediate check may be stated to consist in all those customs, and all those diseases, which seem to be generated by a scarcity of the means of subsistence; and all those causes, independent of this scarcity, whether of a moral or physical nature, which tend prematurely to weaken and destroy the human frame (p 17).

---

[37]Current growth in many parts of the world, as summarized earlier, indicates that 25 years is too long a minimum doubling period. Also, an interesting study by Joseph W. Eaton and Albert J. Mayer, *Man's Capacity to Reproduce*, showed that the Hutterites of North America (an anabaptist sect living in small colonies in the United States and Canada) were growing in the early 1950s at a rate of about 4.1 percent per year, which gives a doubling time of about 16 years (Glencoe, Ill.: The Free Press, 1954), reprinted from *Human Biology*, vol. 25, no. 3, (1954).

He classified the immediate checks as "preventive" and "positive." For man, the preventive checks are those actions or inactions that lead to a reduction in the rate of propagation (p. 18). The positive checks include "every cause . . . which in any degree contributes to shorten the natural duration of human life." They include "all unwholesome occupations, severe labour and exposure to the seasons, extreme poverty, bad nursing of children, great towns, excesses of all kinds, the whole train of common diseases and epidemics, wars, plague, and famine" (pp. 21-22).

Malthus concluded that the preventive and positive checks "are all resolvable into moral restraint, vice, and misery." He held that "the restraint from marriage which is not followed by irregular gratifications may properly be termed moral restraint" (p. 22). Delayed marriage, even if accompanied by promiscuity, he considered still a preventive check but one that is a form of vice.[38] He classified positive checks arising solely from the laws of nature (such as a death-dealing storm) as producing misery. He felt that there are other positive checks, such as wars, that are brought about by vice but produce misery. He concluded that the sum of these checks form the immediate hindrance to population growth and that the preventive and positive checks vary inversely with each other; that is, as preventive checks become less effective the positive checks become more so—and presumably vice versa (p. 24). Of all the checks, only moral restraint, in his judgment, does not produce or grow out of misery or vice.[39]

Any short summary of Malthus is necessarily an unsatisfactory one. The foregoing, however, does demonstrate the necessity for some sort of check on population growth. The disagreements arise in whether the checks must be the harsh "positive" ones directly associated with food shortages and space limitations.

After Malthus's essay appeared, the use of the steam engine made transportation to and from the new world much more efficient

---

[38]Apparently he considered contraceptives also as a preventive check but an "improper art" that he did not condone and one clearly falling "under the head of vice."

[39]Moral restraint is given more attention in subsequent editions of the essay than in the first edition. Apparently Malthus became a bit more optimistic in his later years about the hope of moral restraint. His optimism, however, was always bridled. See his *Principles of Political Economy* (2nd ed.; New York: Augustus M. Kelly, Inc., 1951), p. 226. The book was published in 1820, with the second edition appearing in 1836.

than it had been with sailing ships. The industrial revolution led to productivity gains. Subsequent general abandonment of draft animals in many parts of the world freed substantial food potential for human use. As a result, more persons in many parts of the world found "a place at nature's festive table" to eat a better diet than men generally had eaten previously. It became fashionable to say that time and events had thoroughly repudiated Malthusianism by demonstrating that food production could be expanded to keep pace with expanding population. Harold A. Boner wrote that by about 1860 the "guiding minds of most of the powerful parties or groups in England . . . far outstripped the upholders of Malthus both in numbers and prestige."[40]

With the sustained and increasingly rapid population growth, many persons who tended initially to scoff at the Malthusian principle experienced second thoughts. The increases in world population in the successive 50-year periods from 1800 have in fact almost formed a geometric progression.[41] Clearly, however, food production has grown in the interim faster than in an arithmetic progression. Even so, a view is becoming popular that in terms of centuries Malthus's thinking about both ratios will be proved correct. The view is that he merely failed to anticipate a welcome but temporary increase in the rate of growth of food production.

Whether he was fundamentally wrong in his emphasis on the importance of the positive checks or merely in error in his timing remains to be seen. The critical areas of Malthusian debate continue to be the relative importance of preventive versus positive checks and the potential of the food supply. The possibility of family planning (a technique that Malthus did not think would receive widespread practice) adds a new potential importance to preventive checks.

Perhaps we can learn something useful by examining how population seems to be controlled in nonhuman species. Such control has

[40]Harold A. Boner, *Hungry Generations* (New York: King's Crown Press, Columbia University, 1955), pp. 128-29, used by permission.

[41]Lord Simon of Wythenshawe, a British scientist, has argued that this resulting geometric increase has proved Malthus an uncanny prophet of population growth. See Lord Simon of Wythenshawe, *Some Aspects of World Population and Food Resources*, Occasional Papers on Eugenics, no. 9 (London: Cassell and Company Ltd. and the Eugenics Society, 1955), p. 6. This argument goes too far. Malthus only said that population, if unchecked, had the capacity to double itself every 25 years.

been the object of intensive study for many years. Although there is no necessary carryover to man, the studies suggest that the positive checks may not be as important as preventive checks in limiting populations of nonhuman species. The nature of the preventive checks, however, remains mysterious and defies understanding. Strangely, aside from unusual weather or relatively rare accidents, mass starvation and other obvious positive checks do not appear to be the primary limitations on population growth. Rather, many species of animals, birds, fish, insects, and reptiles somehow limit their numbers so as normally to fit the food supply and other constraints of their environment instead of reproducing to the point where the positive checks come into play.

Let us briefly examine several of the studies that have been reported:

1.   Raymond Pearl and his associates in 1922 set up an experiment to study the reproductive pattern of the fruit fly *(Drosophila)* in varying population densities. Numerous half-pint bottles were arranged, each with identical culture media coated with a standard amount of yeast (for food). The initial imago (adult insect) density in the bottles varied, ranging from one pair per bottle to 50 pairs per bottle. Record was kept of the offspring. As population density increased, fecundity (rate of actual reproduction) dropped sharply to establish what appeared to be a distinct inverse relation between crowding and reproduction, all within but apparently up to the limit, of the food supply.[42]

2.   Allee in 1932 discussed the study of laboratory populations of the flour beetle *(Tribolium)* that thrives in wheat flour. Numerous other studies have been conducted on the flour beetle since then. The objective of one was to see at what density, if any, the population would level off. Numerous containers, each with the same quantity of standardized flour, were used. One pair of imago beetles was "seeded" into each four grams of whole wheat flour at 27 degrees centigrade. The beetles and their larvae were periodically screened out of the flour and placed in a similar environment of fresh flour so as to keep the habitat uncontaminated by waste products of the beetle population. In

[42]Reported in Warder C. Allee and others, *Principles of Animal Ecology* (Philadelphia: W. B. Saunders Company, 1949), p. 349.

each case the population became practically constant at about 44 individuals per gram of flour after 100 days and remained at that level for the next 50 days at which time the experiment was terminated. Different types of flour were used in other containers under the same circumstances. The level at which the beetle population stabilized varied apparently in accordance with the food content of the flour. Some evidence of cannibalism was observed, but no evidence was seen of death by malnutrition or starvation.[43] Interesting questions are left unanswered: How are the beetles able to control their growth rate short of starvation? What determined who ate whom (or whose eggs) when?

3.   MacLagan and Dunn (1936) experimented with the grain weevil (*Sitophilus*) to show that within limits egg production per female decreased as weevil density increased. A peculiar phenomenon was observed. The females would not oviposit at their maximum rate unless the number of grains available for oviposition (egg deposit) was at least 11 times the number actually utilized. Any reduction in this number of grains was accompanied by a reduction in the number of eggs laid. It is strange that the insects would be aware of numbers in this fashion.[44]

4.   One of the strangest examples of population control is found in the behavior of lemmings, small rodents that live in the arctic tundra. Adult lemmings are about six inches long, including a tail about three inches long. The central Canadian arctic varieties gestate in 19-21 days. The litters vary from three to nine, giving lemmings a tremendous reproductive power.[45] Lemming population runs in about a 3- to 3½-year cycle. The cycle is fairly consistent over Lapland, Greenland, North America, and Siberia. At the height of the cycle some but not all the lemmings migrate to the sea, marching chiefly at night, generally in parallel lines with the lines about three feet apart. They normally travel in straight lines, eating through impediments, falling over cliffs, swimming streams. They may cover 100 miles before reaching the sea. They plunge into the sea and swim about until they drown. Their numbers

[43]Warder C. Allee, *Animal Life and Social Growth* (Baltimore: The Williams & Wilkins Company, 1932), pp. 85-88.

[44]Allee and others, *Principles of Animal Ecology*, p. 350.

[45]Charles J. Krebs, *The Lemming Cycle at Baker Lake, Northwest Territories, During 1959-62* (Montreal: The Arctic Institute of North America, 1964).

are so large as to form huge drifts.[46] Researchers do not know how the lemmings determine who migrates and who stays, how they know departure time has come, why they go, how they can find their way to the sea, and why they sacrifice themselves.

5.   Robert L. Stecker has reported two studies of population growth of house mice.[47] The general outcome of the first study was that the mice tended to remain very close to home territory but that they migrated when the colony began to press upon the food supply. Those that did not migrate were a fairly good cross section of the total population before migration. In the second study all egress from the colony was blocked, and the total food supply was held constant. Population growth stopped at such a level that the colony remained well fed and apparently quite healthy. Autopsies at the conclusion of the experiment revealed heavy deposits of fat on members of the population. Unfortunately, the experiment could not be continued beyond 11 months to ascertain the pace at which reproduction would be resumed as adult mice died.

6.   V. C. Wynne-Edwards (Regius Professor of Natural History at Marischal College at the University of Aberdeen in Scotland) has presented many cases of how animals and birds seem to regulate their populations.[48] Among other accounts is the description of how gannet birds on the Cape of St. Mary in Newfoundland isolate a part of the flock, prevent it from breeding, but hold it in reserve for contingencies. The size of the isolated part of the flock seems to depend on the outlook for food through the next breeding season. Various other birds and animals give evidence of having strict territorial systems coordinated, not with the existing food supply, but with the outlook for food at least during the period required to rear the young. The better the food outlook, the smaller seems to be the territory per individual. Pecking orders and other hierarchical structures seem to determine which individual in a species is allowed a territory or other

[46]Allee, *Animal Life and Social Growth*, pp. 89-94.
[47]A popular account is found in Robert L. Strecker, "Populations of House Mice," *Scientific American*, vol. 193 (December, 1955), pp. 92-94, 96, 98, 100.
[48]These studies are reported in his book, *Animal Dispersion in Relation to Social Behaviour* (New York: Hafner Publishing Company, 1962), especially Chapter 22. See also his article "Population Control in Animals," *Scientific American*, vol. 211 (August, 1964), pp. 68-74.

access to the food supply and, thus, which is allowed to breed. Much of the competitive selection, as in the case of starlings, red grouse, penguins, ducks, bats, frogs, cicadas, and certain fish and monkeys, apparently takes place at dawn or dusk with the rest of the time devoted to peaceful pursuits.

These and other studies led Wynne-Edwards to advance the hypothesis that in some if not all the nonhuman species automatic, "homeostatic" devices operate to limit population growth before it depletes the immediate food supply.[49] He observes that, while certain populations are cyclical, others seem to be fairly stable over the long run. Even the cyclical populations seem to fluctuate around some observable norm. Neither disease nor starvation appear to control population growth. Although predators certainly help to control the populations of the species on which they prey, not all species normally serve as prey. Even in the absence of widespread starvation and disease, however, population densities do seem to be directly related to, if not dependent on, the food supply.

The possibility of homeostasis in the population of subhuman species raises two interesting questions: (1) Is homeostasis a type of Malthusian check? (2) Do human beings possess any homeostatic qualities in respect to human population? The first question is difficult. One might argue that homeostasis is contrary to the constant tendency Malthus saw in all animated beings to increase *beyond* the available nourishment. The evidence seems to be that ordinarily no such increase occurs in the nonhuman species—not as much starvation relative to their numbers as in the case of man. Reduced fecundity occurs ordinarily in time to avert starvation. If the "constant tendency" concept does not hold, then Malthus's other generalizations lose relevance.

On the other hand, one might take the position that the homeostatic quality is in the nature of a Malthusian check. When it leads to cannibalism or self-destruction, it is a positive check. When it leads to the restraint of the constant tendency, it is a pre-

---

[49]"Homeostasis" is a tendency to maintain by use of internal control a relatively stable condition. Wynne-Edwards says that the creatures maintain the stability more by the use of "epideitic" behavior than by sheer force. "Epideitic" means that the behavior is designed primarily for demonstration or show. See Wynne-Edwards, "Population Control in Animals," pp. 68-74.

ventive check. Wynne-Edwards emphasized that the quality, if it exists at all, is automatic and instinctive (and, by implication, involuntary). Malthus said that numerous involuntary preventive checks applied in animal and plant populations.

With each of these opposing views possessing some plausibility, the first question must be left in abeyance for want of sufficient facts. The second question is not as difficult to answer. If homeostasis is involuntary, automatic, and instinctive, the answer almost certainly is in the negative. If, however, it embraces a conscious, intellectual weighing of consequences, then the answer is open. Little, really, is known about what motivates human couples to want more or fewer children, especially in a modern society where adults do not expect to be completely dependent for support in old age on their children.[50] In any case we have little reason to expect, even when humanity pushes harder on the food supply, that human fecundity automatically will drop.[51] The hope, such as it is, can be justified only to the extent that modern family planning will be quickly adopted in all parts of the world. Family planning may represent the last great hope for population stability in the human race.[52]

[50]For a digest of some nebulous theories that possibly apply to the United States see M. F. Elliott-Jones, "Population Growth and Fertility Behavior," *Conference Board Record*, vol. 5 (September, 1968), pp. 34-43. See also Irene B. Taeuber, "The Changing Population," *Urban Land*, vol. 26 (July-August, 1967), pp. 15-22. One example of the difficulty of theorizing on fertility behavior is abstracted in the *Population Index*, vol. 33 (July-August, 1967), p. 326. This study, "Income and Reproductive Motivation" by Judith Ann Blake, indicates that survey data from national samples do not confirm the expectation that a rise in family size preference would accompany a rise in income.

[51]A point of view has been advanced by Josue De Castro in his *The Geography of Hunger* (Boston: Little, Brown and Company, 1952) that hunger and certain types of malnutrition tend, within limits, actually to increase sexual impulse and human fertility. De Castro points to the "true law of population" as articulated by Thomas Doubleday in 1853 along the same line. He also refers to studies made in the 1920s by Slonaker. The De Castro view has not gained wide support and has been challenged by studies which do not show that any increase in fecundity accompanies malnutrition or hunger.

[52]A good cross section of literature pertaining to family planning is found in a book of readings, Louise B. Young, ed., *Population in Perspective* (New York: Oxford University Press, 1968). Several of the treatises deal directly with techniques; others with economical, political, religious, and social aspects of family planning. The readings bring out the lack of wisdom and perhaps the gross immorality of reducing death rates around the world without commensurately reducing the birth rates.

Even this hope is dimmed by the powerful opposition from the Roman Catholic Church and international communism.[53] As mentioned earlier, some signs are visable that the communist opposition on population control may be abating somewhat. On the other hand, the 1968 papal encyclical, "Humanae Vitae," offers little encouragement that official Catholic endorsement of full-range national family planning programs will be forthcoming.[54]

Unless man can learn from the demographic examples of the lesser creatures or from other teachers, he faces perilous prospects of population overgrowth. On balance, the evidence simply does not give us grounds for expecting that the human population growth rate will soon approach zero or even turn down significantly. Consequently, the dire projections, summarized in the next section, give no indication of being exaggerations.

Projections to the Turn of the Century

A statistical projection, as observed in Chapter 1, is simply the extension of some series based on one or more assumptions about size and direction of future change. We must remember that they are only projections and not foreordinations of what is to come; yet given the recent history of population growth, we cannot positively refute them.

Demographers affiliated with the Population Division of the Economic and Social Affairs Department of the United Nations reassessed world population prospects in 1963.[55] Four variants were developed and projected to the year 2000 (see Table 9). The constant fertility variant links an assumed fertility at average rates prevailing in various parts of the world in the 1950s with an assumed declining

---

[53]Robert C. Cook, President Emeritus of Population Reference Bureau, Inc., labeled this dual opposition a paradoxical axis that effectively blocked any direct participation by the United Nations in population policy for 20 years. See "Soviet Population Theory from Marx to Kosygin," p. 89.

[54]A lucid explanation of the historical Catholic and communist opposition to birth control appears in Philip Appleman, *The Silent Explosion* (Boston: Beacon Press, 1965), pp. 44-106.

[55]*World Population Prospects as Assessed in 1963*, Population Studies No. 41 (New York: United Nations, 1966).

mortality. The high, medium, and low variants embody successively lower fertility assumptions and slightly varying mortality assumptions. Two additional recent projections have received much attention, probably because they are lower than the U.N. projections. The projection by A. Y. Boyarsky, a Russian professor, was presented to the World Population Conference in Belgrade in 1965.[56] The other projection was made in 1966 by Donald J. Bogue, a professor at the University of Chicago (see Table 9).[57] Both have generated considerable skepticism as being too low. Even the U.N. projections have been considered possibly too low by J. D. Durand, who has commented that "the previous versions of world population projections issued by the U.N. have consistently undershot the short-range if not the long-range marks, and the test of time might well prove this latest version again to be too conservative an assessment of the growth that is in store."[58]

In March, 1968, the Bureau of the Census published revised projections for the United States.[59] These projections include four variants: series A through series D. Each variant uses the same assumptions about mortality and migration but each is based on a different assumption about the parity, or average number of children per woman. In series A the assumed parity is 3.350; in B it is 3.100; in C it is 2.775; and in D, 2.450. The four variants, when projected to the year 2015, result in the figures indicated in Table 10.

Bureau of the Census officials say forthrightly that no way exists to assign an accurate probability to any one of the series. Thus, the projected population for 2000 falls between 280 and 360 million, producing a range of about 80 million. Furthermore, neither the highest nor the lowest projection is sacred; actual population could be outside the range in either direction.

---

[56]Boyarsky's paper, "A Contribution to the Problem of World Population in the Year 2000," appears in volume 3 of the *Proceedings of the World Population Conference—Belgrade, August 30-September 10, 1965.*

[57]"The Prospects for World Population Control," mimeographed, University of Chicago, 1966.

[58]J. D. Durand, "Comments on Macura," in Farmer and others, eds., *World Population—The View Ahead* (Bloomington, Ind.: Bureau of Business Research, Graduate School of Business, Indiana University, 1968), p. 45.

[59]"Summary of Demographic Projections," in U.S. Department of Commerce, Bureau of the Census, *Current Population Reports,* series P-25, no. 388 (March 14, 1968).

TABLE 9

World Population Estimates, 1980 and 2000

Author and Variant	Population (in billions)		Variability Index (U.N. medium=100)	
	1980	2000	1980	2000
United Nations (1963)				
High	4.551	6.994	105	114
Medium	4.330	6.130	100	100
Low	4.147	5.449	95	89
Constant Fertility	4.519	7.522	104	125
A. Y. Boyarsky (1965)				
Maximum	—	5.036	—	82
Main Estimate	—	4.626	—	75
Minimum	—	4.216	—	69
D. J. Bogue (1966)	4.061	4.527	—	74

Source: Milos Macura, "Long-Range Outlook—Summary of Current Estimates," in Farmer and others, eds., *World Population—The View Ahead* (Bloomington, Ind.: Bureau of Business Research, Graduate School of Business, Indiana University, 1968), p. 20.

As we have observed, the U.S. birth rates have fluctuated considerably. Because of the rising proportion of women of child-bearing age (15-44) in the population, each of the series contemplates some increase in the birth rate and a subsequent decline. Series A projects a birth rate (live births per 1,000 population) that goes up to about 25.5 by 1977 and then recedes to 25 by 1990. Series D projects a much lower rate that gets up to about 20 by 1983 and falls back to about 18 by 1990.

These projections for the world and the United States may prove to be wildly erroneous. Nevertheless, one must be impressed by them. They represent the most professional demographic thinking available. Clearly, the most disturbing aspect of the projections is that even the lowest—which, as far as we know, is no more probable than the highest—represents a frightening increase in human population. A world population by 2000 of even 4.2 billion (the Boyarsky minimum projection) and a U.S. population of 280 million (series D) are highly unpleasant to contemplate.[60] A world population of 7.5

---

[60]World and U.S. minimum projections do not both have to prove accurate for one to be accurate; the same relationship holds for the maximum projections.

TABLE 10
Projected U.S. Population to 2015, Including Armed Forces

Year	Series A*	Series B*	Series C*	Series D*
Estimates:				
1960	—	180.7	—	—
1965	—	194.5	—	—
Projections:				
1970	208.6	207.3	206.3	204.9
1975	227.9	223.8	219.3	215.4
1980	250.5	243.3	235.2	227.7
1985	274.7	264.6	252.9	241.7
1990	300.1	286.5	270.8	256.0
1995	328.5	309.8	288.8	269.5
2000	361.4	336.0	307.8	282.6
2005	398.4	365.2	328.7	296.4
2010	437.8	396.0	349.4	309.7
2015	482.1	430.2	373.5	324.5

*All figures are in millions and are calculated for July 1 of each year given. Source: "Summary of Demographic Projections," in U.S. Department of Commerce, Bureau of the Census, Current Population Reports, series P-25, no. 388 (March 14, 1968), p. 2.

billion (the United Nation's constant fertility variant) and a U.S. population of 360 million (series A) by 2000 or at any time could be genuinely tragic.

Even if only the lowest world and U.S. projections are fulfilled by the year 2000, little comfort can be taken. Unless mankind learns how to stabilize his growth below the Malthusian levels of misery and vice, the projections that are too high for 2000 are likely to be too low for 2050—and so on through the years until all agree that Malthus has been vindicated.

4

POPULATION PRESSURES

If the outlook sketched in the preceding chapter is accurate, then certainly one of the most telling adjectives to describe the near future is "crowded." Crowds, waiting, congestion, traffic jams, noise, large-scale facilities and activities, long minimum lead times, and close quarters will occur to a much greater extent than they do today. Whatever else comes—whether it be abundance or scarcity, peace or war, progress or decay—increased crowding seems to be the most reasonable expectation for life during the remainder of this century.

Population growth doubtless will have a dramatic effect on insurance. Premium volume is almost sure to soar, at least in the short run. The number of people associated with private and public insuring organizations probably will rise substantially. New coverages are likely to be introduced and old ones abandoned. New uses of insurance are likely to replace old ones. New concepts, calling for new terminology and new techniques, may be created in response to the demands engendered by population growth.

Little is known as to how increasing density and the changes that follow in its wake may affect human behavior, especially in relation to ethics and morality. There is little accumulated knowledge that seems relevant; and there are no historical or projective estimates, comparable to those dealing with population growth, that can be used to indicate possible future changes in morality and ethics. Population growth does appear to have produced some changes in moral behavior already. Magnification of these changes and manifestation of certain other changes would seem to be the logical consequences of further population growth. One can never be sure, however, that he is not allowing his own biases and preconceptions to influence his thinking. By the very nature of the undertaking, we are forced to suffer these inadequacies and to resort to conjecture in order to pursue the topic at all. The topic remains important despite the lack of research materials to use for documentation.

This chapter reflects an effort to find among recent trends a few hints of the way population growth in the future may directly influence ethics and morality, and thereby indirectly influence insurance. The substance of the discussion is speculative and is intended only for speculative use. The speculations are supported—to use De Jouvenel's expression—with "intellectual scaffolding" when the scaffolding seems capable of lending support. Nevertheless, they remain speculations.

RISING CRIME LOSSES

If population continues to grow, increasing numbers of people (1) may lose interest, or never acquire any interest, in preserving property from loss; (2) may forego honesty as a normal standard of conduct; and (3) may disdain respect for authority and obedience of the law. Thus, three ethical pillars of insurance could fail over the years to give the necessary support to the institution of insurance. Surely, the pillars will not fall; yet, we cannot be so confident that they will not lean. The leaning may come about through a relatively large number of people in the long-range future either becoming criminals or growing inured to and tolerant of crime in the belief that it is an inextricable part of modern society. Perhaps the second danger is greater than the first. Crime could swell to such an extent that insurance would no longer be useful in redistributing numerous types of crime losses that so far have been treatable by insurance.

There is no question but that a large spurt of crime has already occurred in the United States.[1] While we certainly have no grounds for attributing the growth of crime solely to the growth of population, we have some justification, as discussed later, for suspecting some sort of causal relationship. If the recent dual upsurge in population and crime is anything but concomitant, this country faces a mammoth crime problem that could have awesome repercussions for insurance.

Before contemplating the insurance implications of growing crime in a growing population, let us review a few figures. Crime data for the United States are compiled and published by the Federal Bureau of Investigation of the U.S. Department of Justice. The FBI publishes, in addition to monthly documents and other releases, annual editions of *Uniform Crime Reports,* a convenient source of aggregate data on crime frequency and law enforcement in the United States.[2] The uniform crime reporting program provides data on two major classes of crime: (1) crimes of violence: murder; forcible rape (carnal knowledge of a female forcibly and against her will); robbery (unlawful taking of property from another by violence or threat of violence); and aggravated assault (unlawful attack by one person upon another for the purpose of inflicting severe bodily injury); and (2) crimes against property: burglary (unlawful taking of property from another through forcible, felonious entry); larceny

---

[1]Although crime does not appear to be increasing in every country, the United States is not alone in experiencing rising crime. The number of offenses known to the police in England and Wales, for example, for 1966 was about 60 percent larger than that for 1960. *Annual Abstract of Statistics, 1967* (London: Central Statistical Office), p. 66. In Sweden the number of offenses against the penal code in 1966 was about 47 percent larger than in 1961. *Statistical Abstract of Sweden* (Stockholm: Central Bureau of Statistics, 1967), p. 295. In New Zealand the number of total criminal charges in the magistrate courts was about 80 percent larger in 1966 than in 1960. *New Zealand Official Yearbook, 1968* (73rd ed.; Wellington: Department of Statistics), p. 249. In Tanganyika, to take a country with a different degree of development, the number of criminal convictions increased almost 50 percent from 1959 to 1962. *Statistical Abstract, 1963* (Dar Es Salaam: Republic of Tanganyika, Central Statistical Bureau, Directorate of Development Planning, 1964), p. 174.

[2]The 1968 edition is entitled *Crime in the United States—Uniform Crime Reports— 1968.* The data are gathered from law enforcement agencies throughout the country. The system of preparing the uniform crime reports has been gradually improved over the years, and a major change occurred in 1958. Thus, figures in the *Uniform Crime Reports* for years prior to 1958 are not strictly comparable with those appearing after that date.

FIGURE 4

Crimes of Violence, 1960-1968, Percent Change over 1960

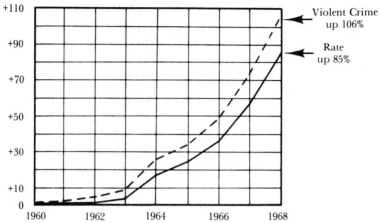

Limited to murder, forcible rape, robbery, and aggravated assault.

Source: U.S. Department of Justice, Federal Bureau of Investigation, *Crime in the United States—Uniform Crime Reports—1968* (Washington, D.C.: U.S. Govt. Printing Office, 1968), p. 3.

(unlawful taking of property equal in value to or in excess of $50 from another without use of force, violence, or fraud—examples are shoplifting, purse-snatching, or bicycle theft); and automobile theft (unlawful taking of an automobile of another). A crime index, based on the number of reported crimes, and a crime rate, based on the number of crimes per 100,000 of the population, are computed and published. Figures 4 and 5 give the crime index for 1960-68 as compared with, respectively, the rate for crimes of violence and that for crimes against property.[3]

Crimes against property are much more numerous than crimes of violence. In 1968 the former constituted 87 percent of the total

[3]Since each curve represents changes in a *rate* and shows a value greater than zero for the end of 1960, the percentage changes must have been computed against some base earlier than the rate for 1960, presumably 1959.

FIGURE 5

Crimes Against Property, 1960-1968, Percent Change over 1960

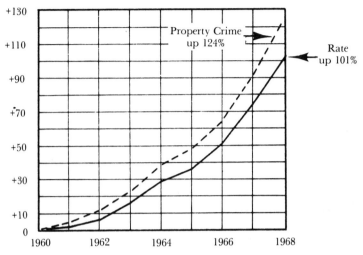

Limited to burglary, larceny $50 and over, and auto theft.

Source: U.S. Department of Justice, Federal Bureau of Investigation, *Crime in the United States—Uniform Crime Reports—1968* (Washington, D.C.: U.S. Govt. Printing Office, 1968), p. 3.

crimes reported in the two major classes. Figure 6 shows the crime index and the crime rate for the two major classes of crime for 1960-68, as related to the population change.[4] Table 11 breaks down the crime rate figures for 1968 into the specific crimes and indicates percentage changes for each crime over the same rate for 1960 and 1967.

As the three figures indicate, the increase in crime has been astounding! The number of serious crimes reported to the police in 1968 was 17 percent larger than that for 1967, and the 1967 figure

[4]The problem discussed in footnote 3 is pertinent to two of the three curves in this figure. The population curve does probably show the percentage change in population compared to the estimated magnitude as of the beginning of 1960. The other two curves, pertaining as they do to estimated changes in rates, reflect percentage changes against the respective rates before the beginning of 1960; presumably the percentages were computed against the 1959 rate levels.

TABLE 11

Crime Rates in the United States by Type of Crime, 1968

	1968 Rate Per 100,000 Population	Percent Increase Over: 1960 Rate	1967 Rate
Murder	6.8	36.0%	11.5%
Forcible Rape	15.5	64.9	13.1
Robbery	131.0	118.7	28.3
Aggravated Assault	141.3	66.8	10.4
Burglary	915.1	82.8	12.8
Larceny (at least $50)	636.0	125.3	20.2
Automobile Theft	389.1	114.3	17.6

Source: U.S. Department of Justice, Federal Bureau of Investigation, Crime in the United States— Uniform Crime Reports—1968 (Washington, D.C.: U.S. Govt. Printing Office, 1968), p. 5.

was 16 percent larger than that for 1966. While some of the increases during the 1960s might be explained by an improvement in reporting and the possibility of relatively more of the total committed crimes being reported, no reasonable allowance can explain away the steep uptrend in the figures. The FBI studies indicate certain distinct trends in the rate of crime growth. First, a high proportion of criminals commit more than one offense. Second, an increasing proportion of total arrests in recent years has involved young people. For example, total arrests of juveniles for serious crimes in 1968 were about 78 percent higher than in 1960. During the same time the number of persons in the 10-to-17 age group increased by about 25 percent. Third, narcotic offenses have increased rapidly. For example, arrests for violations of the Narcotic Drug Law were four times as many in 1968 as in 1960, with arrests in 1968 being up about 64 percent over 1967, primarily for offenses involving marijuana.

The first trend, pertaining to repeated criminal offenses, warrants further description. The 1968 edition of Uniform Crime Reports (pp. 35-42) includes a description of the "Careers in Crime" data program being maintained by the FBI in cooperation with state and local law enforcement agencies. The program is facilitated by the exchange of fingerprint records, which permits the FBI to obtain each offender's criminal history. The aim of the program is to ascertain the extent to which repeated offenses by the same criminals add to total crime.

FIGURE 6

Crime and Population, 1960-1968, Percent Change over 1960

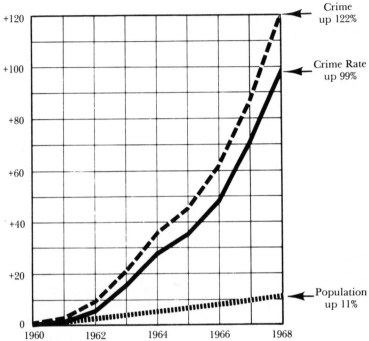

Crime = Crime index offenses
Crime rate = Number of offenses per 100,000 population

Source: U.S. Department of Justice, Federal Bureau of Investigation, *Crime in the United States—Uniform Crime Reports—1968* (Washington, D.C.: U.S. Govt. Printing Office, 1968), p. 2.

The degree of repetition is astonishing. The program shows for a group of 94,467 offenders processed because of an arrest for a serious crime in 1967 or 1968 that 39 percent had previously been arrested for one or more such violations. About 80 percent had prior arrests of some sort; 70 percent had at least one prior conviction; and almost half had been imprisoned on a prior sentence for at least

90 days. The data also show that the rearrest rate is higher the younger the age group and that it is higher for blacks than for whites.

Another part of the "Careers in Crime" data program involves observing the records of 18,333 offenders released from the federal criminal justice system in 1963. By the end of 1968 about 63 percent had been rearrested at least once. Of these, 21 percent had been rearrested only once; 13 percent twice; 9 percent three times; and 20 percent four or more times. Although one or more biases may have been at work in producing the results, the figures are still discouraging. Of those who were acquitted or had their cases dismissed in 1963, 91 percent were rearrested for new offenses before the end of 1968. Of those given probation in 1963, about 55 percent were rearrested before the end of 1968. The comparable figure for those receiving a sentence of a fine and probation was 36 percent; for parolees it was 61 percent; for those subject to mandatory release after serving prison time, 74 percent.

The figures on rearrest by type of offender also reveal a very high rate of rearrests. For example, 80 percent of the persons who had been arrested for auto theft and released in 1963 were rearrested on some charge before the end of 1968. For those arrested for burglary and released in 1963, the percentage rearrested on some charge before the end of 1968 was 77. The comparable figure for assault offenders was 74 percent; for forgery offenders 68 percent; for narcotics offenders 69 percent. Even granting that these released offenders may have been watched especially closely, the figures appear high.

Beckwith's speculations about the next 500 years were mentioned in Chapter 1. Another passage from his book is interesting in the context of crime. He comments:

> The average personal risk of losing property or income through any misfortune—unemployment, sickness, accident, flood, earthquake, crime—will be steadily reduced throughout the next 500 years in all countries. In other words, all personal property and income will become more and more secure. This trend is already centuries old in advanced countries. It has been due to the growth of peace and order, the rise of private and public insurance, improvement in medical care, the spread of monopoly, and the growth of free distribution.[5]

---

[5]B. P. Beckwith, *The Next 500 Years* (New York: Exposition Press, 1967), p. 31, used by permission.

The FBI crime data indicate that the risk of becoming a victim of a serious crime increased about 16 percent in 1968 over 1967 with an average of over two victims in each group of 100 inhabitants. These figures do not fit comfortably with the Beckwith comment unless one regards the recent criminal behavior atypical of that to be expected in the long run. Probably none of us would dispute Beckwith's implication that property and person are much more secure from criminal abuse than was the case, say, in 1600 in Europe or in 1850 on the western frontier of the United States. Several might argue that adverse changes have occurred in many parts of the world since about 1950. Perhaps this period is much too short in terms of assessing trends for centuries or longer. Still, this period is quite relevant to what may happen between now and the turn of the present century, our principal concern in this study. In respect to crime at least, the Beckwith assurance should be accepted only if room is left for wide short-run fluctuations.

We would be naive to assert that the cause of the terrible increase in crime was the increase in population or population density in given areas. Crimes have increased much faster than the population and at rates quite dissimilar among the several types of crime indicated. We might be equally naive, however, to assume that the widening spread between the rate of population growth and the rate of crime growth (as depicted in Figure 6) will continue. Hopefully, crime will be sufficiently deterred to permit the spread to narrow.

Despite not knowing the causes of the growth of crime, we would be remiss in completely disassociating crime from population growth. A statement pertinent to this point appears in the 1968 edition of the *Uniform Crime Reports:* "The number of crimes per unit of population is . . . highest in the large metropolitan centers and in those areas where populations are growing the fastest."[6] Table 12, a summary of crime rates for urban, suburban, and rural areas, shows the inordinately high crime rates in metropolitan centers.

Something about high density living seems to encourage crime and other sordid kinds of behavior to increase more rapidly than density itself. Perhaps some multiplier effect is at work. Several studies on the physiology and behavior of animals subjected to severe crowding have indicated that the stresses produced by crowd-

---

[6]*Uniform Crime Reports*, p. 5.

TABLE 12

Crime Rates in the United States by Type of Crime and by Area, 1968

Crimes Per 100,000 Population

	Total U.S.	Cities Over 250,000	Suburban	Rural
Murder	6.8	14.2	3.3	6.3
Forcible Rape	15.5	31.8	12.0	8.8
Robbery	131.0	432.6	45.1	12.2
Aggravated Assault	141.3	294.6	85.1	81.1
Burglary	915.1	1,665.8	761.0	387.2
Larceny (at least $50)	636.0	1,080.9	564.8	217.4
Automobile Theft	389.1	933.6	237.3	66.7
Total	*2,234.8*	*4,453.5*	*1,708.6*	*779.7*

Source: U.S. Department of Justice, Federal Bureau of Investigation, *Crime in the United States—Uniform Crime Reports—1968* (Washington, D.C.: U.S. Govt. Printing Office, 1968), p. 5.

ing are severe. A study, for example, of Minnesota jack rabbits revealed that at the peak of their population cycle many of these rabbits suffered fatty degeneration and atrophy of the liver. Others suffered brain, adrenal, thyroid, or kidney hemorrhage.[7] No reasons, other than the stresses produced by crowding, seem to account for these difficulties. Many of the rabbits experienced convulsions before death. At this period in the population cycle the rabbits died at an average younger age than at other periods in the cycle.

Studies of other animals show hypertension and overactivity of the adrenal and pituitary glands. Wynne-Edwards, whose work was referred to in Chapter 3, has described experiments showing "that social stress can have depressing and injurious effects on the animal body just as severe as those produced by the stresses of disease, hunger, fatigue or exposure to physical hardship."[8]

---

[7]As reported by Hudson Hoagland, "Cybernetics of Population Control," *Bulletin of the Atomic Scientists*, vol. 20 (February, 1964), pp. 2-3.

[8]V. C. Wynne-Edwards, *Animal Dispersion in Relation to Social Behaviour* (New York: Hafner Publishing Company, 1962), p. 550, used by permission. In Chapter 22, pp. 530-56, he cites numerous manifestations of social stress in animals, birds, and reptiles produced by crowding. These manifestations include eating or destroying eggs, infanticide, fratricide, and other pathological behavior.

J. B. Calhoun has reported the results of a laboratory study of a domesticated albino strain of the Norway rat. His report reveals that rats, when placed in high density confinement, soon sink to a very ugly level of behavior despite an abundance of food and water.[9] Sexual aggression, parental neglect, fratricide, infanticide, and harrassment became commonplace although not all of the animals descended to what Calhoun called the "behavioral sink." He concluded that the behavior produced by the experiment was so abnormally acute that it could have led to the extinction of the population.

The relevance of these studies to human behavior under the stress of crowding is not known. Some professional opinion does suggest, however, that crowding takes its toll even in human relations. If so, crime could well be one of the manifestations. Philip M. Hauser, in discussing the social changes produced by high density living, observed:

> It follows . . . that greater size and density of population, especially if accompanied by heterogeneity, diminishes the power of informal social controls. Informal social control, effected largely through the play of folkways and the mores, gives way to increased formal control, the control of law, police, courts, jails, regulations, and orders. The breakdown in informal social controls is in large measure responsible for greater personal disorganization as manifest in juvenile delinquency, crime, prostitution, alcoholism, drug addiction, suicide, mental disease, social unrest, and political instability. Formal controls have by no means proved as efficacious as the informal in regulating human behavior.[10]

If density does aggravate crime and other social ills, our nation (and the world) faces the prospect of increased aggravation. Perhaps Malthus had such developments in mind in his emphasis on vice as a population check. The possiblity of a relationship between crime and density is not a cheerful one to contemplate because urbanization is likely to continue. Efforts to decentralize through the establishment of new cities have not been on a large enough scale

[9]J. B. Calhoun, "Population Density and Social Pathology," *Scientific American*, vol. 206 (February, 1962), pp. 139-46, 148.
[10]Philip M. Hauser, "Urbanization—Problems of High Density Living," in Richard N. Farmer and others, eds., *World Population—The View Ahead* (Bloomington, Ind.: Bureau of Business Research, Graduate School of Business, Indiana University, 1968), pp. 105-6.

to relieve the increasing densities.[11] If density really is a causal element in the climbing trend of crime, the outlook for control of crime is not pleasant. Probably no amount of police protection against criminals would be enough to reverse the trend.[12]

IMPLICATIONS FOR INSURANCE
OF RISING CRIME RATES

If the uptrend in the crime rate should develop into a sustained phenomenon or if the rate should stabilize at a relatively higher level than it is now, serious insurance problems could result. In fact, some already exist. For one thing, theft might become a peril no longer susceptible to insurance treatment because of the intolerably high frequency and severity of losses. Before this type of insurance would be withdrawn from the market, we might see the deductibles

---

[11]The huge sums spent already on new model cities give some clue as to the magnitude of the problem of dispersal. Making the present cities livable is also an expensive proposition. Back in 1963 the National Planning Association published a study by Peter Wagner entitled *The Scope and Financing of Urban Renewal and Development*, NPA Planning Pamphlet 119 (Washington, D.C.: National Planning Association, n.d.). Wagner estimated that in 1960 about $48 billion of private and public funds were spent for purposes related to urban renewal and development. He visualized that even without any formal urban renewal program, perhaps an average of about $80 billion would be spent annually over the next 20 years in an attempt to keep the cities livable. He saw the urgent need for a comprehensive, coordinated development program that would commit an additional $30 billion of private and public funds annually for renewal and development in the cities, excluding that put into new industrial plants and the cost of undeveloped land (pp. *xii-xiii*).

[12]No implication of recommended laxity should be read into this statement. The statement simply has to do with what could happen despite our best efforts at crime prevention and control. At the August, 1968, annual meeting of the American Bar Association a defeatist theme was sounded time and again in respect to the crime problem. Attorney General Clark, Chief Justice Warren, and others related crime to poverty, corruption in local politics, slum conditions, racial ill will, and despair. The general conclusion seemed to be that the United States will have mounting crime as long as the social ills remain and that jurisprudence could do little to deter the criminal acts. Little attention was given, except by international visitors, to the idea that law enforcement and strict punishment for crimes should be primary concerns of the American Bar Association. A report of the meeting can be found in "Lawyers Look to Social Reform, Not Law to Cure Crime Problem," *National Observer* (August 12, 1968), p. 4. In view of the prospects for rapid population growth, continued urbanization, persisting slums, and continuing poverty (which has never been eradicated in the history of man), the outlook for control of crime through the avenue of remedying the underlying social ills is not bright, to say the least. See *Annual Report of the American Bar Association Proceedings of the Ninety-second Annual Meeting* (Chicago: American Bar Association, 1969).

FIGURE 7

Ratio of Automobiles Reported Stolen to Automobiles Registered,
United States, 1955-1968

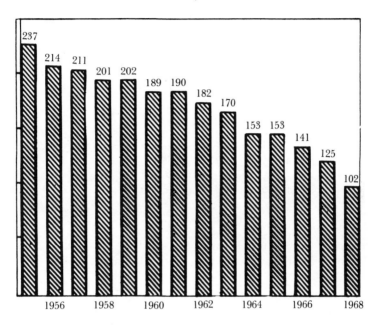

Source: Information provided by William J. Davis, secretary and manager of the Western Division of the National Automobile Theft Bureau, in a letter to the author, July 22, 1968.

consistently enlarged, urbanized territories increasingly excluded, and the list of uninsurable properties considerably broadened.

A serious problem already exists in respect to automobile thefts and wanton damage to or destruction of automobiles. Automobile thefts, according to *Uniform Crime Reports,* have increased sharply since 1960. In 1967 they occurred in the United States on the average of one every 48 seconds. Information about reported automobile thefts compiled by the National Automobile Theft Bureau shows an adverse movement in the ratio of reported car thefts to total car registrations (see Figure 7). The data reveal that in 1955, 1 passenger car out of every 237 registered passenger cars was reported

TABLE 13

Insured Automobile Theft, Vandalism, and Malicious Mischief Losses as Percentage of Total Automobile Comprehensive Losses, 1964-1968

| Statistical Years Ending | *Percent of Total Automobile Comprehensive Coverage Losses (Class 01 Plus Class 06) Accounted for by:* | | | | | |
| | *Theft Losses* | | *V & MM Losses* | | *Total Losses* | |
	No. Losses	*$ Losses*	*No. Losses*	*$ Losses*	*No. Losses*	*$ Losses*
1964	19%	19%	14%	14%	33%	33%
1965	18	25	18	11	36	36
1966	19	28	20	13	39	41
1967	20	31	20	12	40	43
1968	21	36	20	12	41	48

Source: Countrywide recapitulation of motor vehicle experience of Insurance Rating Board (and predecessor organizations).

stolen; in 1958, 1 in 201 was stolen; in 1961, 1 in 190; in 1964 1 in 153; in 1967, 1 in 125; in 1968, 1 in 108; and in 1969, 1 in 102 (estimated).[13]

The increasing number of thefts along with the increasing instance of vandalism of course are reflected in the data on insured losses paid. Table 13 summarizes for one rating bureau the growing relative importance of theft, vandalism, and malicious mischief as causes of loss among the total losses associated with nationwide automobile comprehensive insurance. While the period for which data are presented does not coincide with the period for which reported car thefts are shown, the trend, nevertheless, is distinctly discernible and distinctly disturbing. Unless halted, the trend may lead to the withdrawal from the market of insurance to cover automobile theft and probably vandalism and malicious mischief as well.

Another example of the underwriting problems being experienced by theft insurance in the face of growing crime rates is found in the enlarged proportion of claims attributable to the theft coverage in homeowners insurance. Table 14 shows the deteriorating situation on a nationwide basis as reflected in the loss data of the Multi-Line Insurance Rating Bureau. The figures reveal that during

[13]Information provided by William J. Davis, secretary and manager of the Western Division of the National Automobile Theft Bureau, in letters to the author.

TABLE 14

Homeowners Theft Losses as Percentage of Total
Homeowners Losses, 1963-1968

Statistical Years Ending	Percent of Total Homeowners Losses Due to Theft	
	No. Losses	$ Losses
1963	12%	11%
1964	12	13
1965	14	14
1966	17	15
1967	17	16
1968	20	18

Source: Recapitulation sheets included in correspondence with Frank J. Caso, director of research, Multi-Line Insurance Rating Bureau.

the middle 1960s the theft component of homeowners losses rose disturbingly, both as a percentage of the number and as a percentage of the dollar amount of losses paid under the terms of the homeowners policy.

The unpleasant homeowners policy situation can also be illustrated on a more detailed basis by examining recent loss data for one company. We should remind ourselves that the figures are not highly credible even though the insurer is fairly large and services what appears to be a fairly representative cross section of residential property owners in the United States and Canada. There could be a slight bias toward relatively more urban than suburban or small-town policyholders. Even so, the figures are interesting in revealing a drift toward increasing importance of losses related closely to dishonesty. Theft, vandalism, malicious mischief, and mysterious disappearance losses accounted on a nationwide basis for the following percentages of the dollar amount of all Section I and Section II losses paid under homeowners policies by this particular insurer for the years indicated: 1961, 17 percent; 1962, 21; 1963, 21; 1964, 19; 1965, 15; 1966, 26; 1967, 23; and 1968, 24. The increase from 17 percent in 1961 to 24 percent in 1968 (about 40 percent of the 1961 position) is sufficiently large to indicate that all is not well. A further fact, not revealed by the figures here, is that the theft and related losses for certain years amounted to more than nine times as much as the total Section II (liability, medical payments, and physical damage to property of others) claims paid by the company. Over the period, they amounted to about 60 percent of the total fire and lightning claims and to about 115 percent of the windstorm claims.

If we recall the prevailing thinking during the development of the homeowners policies and remember that theft, vandalism, and mysterious disappearances were thought of as ancillary coverages to fire, wind, and liability, we can appreciate all the more the unexpected and unwelcome growth of the theft and vandalism losses.[14] In the experience of the particular insurer just referred to, the theft, vandalism, malicious mischief, and mysterious disappearance components of the losses paid exceed the total losses paid for the fire and lightning component for several states for several years. In a few instances the theft and related losses exceeded all the other Section I losses. When this sort of loss experience is suffered even by one large insurer, the situation is alarming. Unless the trends are halted, sooner or later the theft, vandalism, and mysterious disappearance perils will have to be deleted from the homeowners policies. Assuming extrapolation of present trends, there is little prospect that these types of losses could be insured any more readily in one or more separate contracts divorced from the homeowners policies.

The point is simply that loss frequency and loss severity may become too high. For theft and related coverages to be provided at all, they might have to be subsidized by premiums ostensibly paid for other coverages. Moreover, with theft so prevalent in urban areas, long-run provision of theft and related insurances might require that urban policyholders be subsidized by other policyholders. Whether or not this sort of subsidy will be undertaken and maintained is a matter for speculation later in the chapter. If no subsidy is provided, the theft and related insurances may ultimately be withdrawn.

Still another indication of the progressive difficulty in providing insurance for theft losses is found in the extreme increases in the loss ratios of the "burglary and theft" category of insurances provided by both stock and mutual insurance companies. Looking at the aggregate industry figures published by Alfred M. Best Company,

---

[14]To be objective, we should keep in mind that not all the mysterious disappearance losses paid by insurers are caused by theft. Common sense (not always an infallible guide) suggests that a large percentage stems from dishonesty on the part of insureds who claim reimbursement for improper losses.

Inc., we can see elephantine increases since 1950 in the reported ratios of loss plus loss adjustment expenses incurred to premiums earned. For stock companies this ratio moved from 40.7 percent in 1950 to 65.2 percent in 1967; for mutuals the ratio went from 38.4 percent in 1950 to 82.4 percent in 1967.[15] In the case of each group of companies the trend was sharply upward despite minor oscillations in the figures from year to year, and this trend developed despite frequent rate increases made to hold the ratio stable.

Some explanation of the increasing loss ratio might be found in the increased adverse selection resulting from development of multiple line policies that also include theft coverages. Perhaps a worse class of business has remained in the separate "burglary and theft" category. Another explanation might be found in the increased efficiency of the insuring process and the decreased profit margin, both of which would have the effect of leaving a larger proportion of the premium dollar for the payment of losses and loss adjustment expenses. Neither one of these decreases, however, is large enough to account for the violent changes in the loss ratios. Changes in the liability with which claims are paid or changes in the ratio of insurance carried to value exposed also could affect the loss ratios. With respect to liberality of claims settlement, the policy provisions are reasonably clear and lend themselves to reasonably accurate loss adjustment. We have no reason to suspect any increasing generosity in claims practices. Changes probably have occurred also in the average ratios of insurance to value in the direction of insuring a larger proportion of a policyholder's exposed properties. Since most theft losses are small relative to the property exposed, the effect of this change, other things being the same, would be to lower, not to increase, the loss ratio.

Thus, we are left with the conclusion that the climbing loss ratios reflect alarming increases in the criminal acts of burglary, robbery, and other types of theft. This conclusion is quite consistent with the behavior we have observed in the crime statistics. Another variable affecting the loss ratio could be a change in the tendency of policyholders to report insured losses, although we would be hard pressed to find evidence of any major change in respect to these types of

[15]Figures for both stocks and mutuals can be found in *Best's Aggregates and Averages* (30th ed.; Morristown, N.J.: Alfred M. Best Company, Inc., 1969) and earlier editions.

losses, which under the policies being discussed have characteristically been regularly reported. The trend of the rising loss ratios for these lines of insurance cannot long continue unabated. Even substantial rate increases have not prevailed against the trend. Either the trend halts or these coverages, too, ultimately will disappear from the market.

Another aspect of the discussion of theft insurance, but one needing separate treatment, has to do with the insuring of employers against loss from the dishonesty of employees. Over the long-range future fidelity insurance, to use the generic term for this type of coverage, could pose difficult problems, aggravated by population growth. The fact of the matter is that insured fidelity losses, in real terms, have risen since 1950 in the United States at a considerably faster rate than has gross national product. In a growing economy an increase in insured fidelity losses relative to GNP seems much more significant than simply an increase in the absolute losses. With the economy growing, the latter is to be expected, but not the former.

Table 15 shows the changing relationship between insured fidelity losses and loss adjustment expenses, on the one hand, and GNP, on the other. The figures in Table 15 were calculated in a roundabout fashion that should be explained. For each year, 1950 through 1968, earned fidelity premiums for stock companies and mutuals were multiplied by the respective incurred loss (and loss adjustment expense) ratios as reported in *Best's Aggregates and Averages*. The annual dollar fidelity insured losses for the industry (stocks plus mutuals) were then estimated for each year by adding the two products (that is, stock incurred losses plus mutual incurred losses). Finally, for each year the resulting insured fidelity losses were expressed as a percentage of GNP. Despite the crudity, the method has enough consistency to make the figures useful.

The table suggests that the ratio of insured fidelity losses to GNP was about 30 percent larger in 1968 than in 1950. Taken by itself, this growth is not necessarily meaningful; it could simply reflect an increasing tendency for employers to use fidelity insurance. Furthermore, the change in the ratio could be completely independent of any population pressures toward more crime. However, the change might also constitute another piece of evidence of future difficulty in insuring criminal losses. Although the fidelity losses relative to GNP are minuscule, the change in the ratio is distinctly adverse and

TABLE 15

Insured Fidelity Losses and Gross National Product for the United States, 1950-1968

Year	Insured Fidelity Losses* as a Percentage of GNP
1950	.000073%
1951	.000085
1952	.000084
1953	.000086
1954	.000092
1955	.000078
1956	.000086
1957	.000096
1958	.000102
1959	.000089
1960	.000105
1961	.000113
1962	.000082
1963	.000116
1964	.000096
1965	.000094
1966	.000097
1967	.000098
1968	.000094

*Including loss adjustment expenses.
Sources: Best's Aggregates and Averages (21st ed.; Morristown, N.J.: Alfred M. Best Company, Inc., 1969) and earlier editions. U.S. Department of Commerce, Business Statistics, 1967—A Supplement to the Survey of Current Business (16th Biennial ed.; Washington, D.C.: U.S. Govt. Printing Office, 1967), pp. 1, 38. Survey of Current Business, vol. 49 (January, 1969), pp. S-1, S-7.

could bode ill for the future. The limit of insurability of employee fidelity, expressed as a percentage of GNP, may, itself, be very low. Unless the trend in the ratio is halted or reversed, employee fidelity to employers could ultimately become uninsurable.

Another harbinger of difficulties for insurance that may be caused by the rising crime frequency is found in the recent change in arson statistics. The National Fire Protection Association compiles and publishes data on suspected arson losses and on fires whose origin is unknown. The latter probably has a high, although undeterminable, arson content. Table 16 gives some clue to the increasing importance of arson as a cause of damage to or destruction of buildings.

TABLE 16

Estimated Incendiary, Suspicious Fires and Fires
Whose Origins are Unknown or Undetermined, 1950-1968

	Incendiary, Suspicious*		Unknown or Undetermined*		Total*	
Year	No. Losses	$ Losses	No. Losses	$ Losses	No. Losses	$ Losses
1950	0.9%	2.2%	8.1%	30.7%	9.0%	32.9%
1951	0.9	2.2	8.1	30.3	9.0	32.5
1952	0.9	2.3	9.2	31.5	10.1	33.8
1953	1.0	2.4	9.9	31.3	10.9	33.7
1954	1.2	2.9	9.4	30.7	10.6	33.6
1955	1.2	2.9	9.2	31.6	10.4	34.5
1956	1.4	2.5	8.2	31.5	9.6	34.0
1957	1.8	2.5	8.0	28.7	9.8	31.2
1958	2.4	3.0	7.4	27.0	9.8	30.0
1959	2.3	2.6	6.4	28.8	8.7	31.4
1960	2.7	2.7	5.8	30.1	8.5	32.8
1961	2.7	3.1	5.8	29.6	8.5	32.7
1962	2.7	3.1	5.9	31.7	8.6	34.8
1963	3.4	3.9	6.0	33.7	9.4	37.6
1964	3.4	5.0	7.2	36.4	10.6	41.4
1965	3.7	5.1	7.7	35.8	11.4	40.9
1966	3.9	6.2	9.3	35.1	13.2	41.3
1967	4.6	8.7	12.9	38.9	17.5	47.6
1968	5.1	7.3	14.4	40.8	19.5	48.1

*Given as a percent of total building fires.
Source: Data provided to the author by Daniel Pingree, statistician, National Fire Protection Association. In June, 1970, Pingree mentioned in a phone conversation that preliminary 1969 figures indicated a continuation of the increases in all the percentages.

An important characteristic of Table 16 is that it indicates a fourfold increase in arson-suspected fires as a percentage of total building fires since 1950. Relative money losses have also quadrupled. These figures suggest that arson, which is quite separate from the incendiarism associated in recent years with civil disorders, has been growing with alarming speed. Traditionally, arson has connotated stealth as opposed to blatant and open igniting of fires. The sweep of the figures in Table 16 suggests that arson in the traditional sense is a serious and growing problem.

Experts responsible for investigation of fires in which arson is suspected classify arson under several headings. One is "fraud arson" in which the fire may be set by the owner, perhaps in the hope of extracting an insurance settlement larger than the value to him of the property burned. Valued policy laws, requiring payment of the total amount of insurance instead of the actual cash value of a total loss, probably contribute to arson of this type.[16] Defense against this type of arson, however, is possible to a limited extent through underwriting selection and through the possibility of denying claims where fraud arson can be proved. A related type of arson, subject also to some underwriting selection, is "mobster arson," resulting from action of single gangsters or syndicates using arson as a weapon for extortion.[17] Another and increasingly irritating type of arson is "fun arson" or "juvenile arson"; this type of destruction is usually directed at public buildings, especially public schools.[18] An arson investigation official has commented:

> A review of the 1965 fire reports received by the NFPA (National Fire Protection Association) showed that 60% of the school fires so reported were of incendiary origin—set by intruders. . . . An estimated 4,200 "incendiary, suspicious" school fires occurred in the United States during 1965 causing approximately $18 million damage.[19]

The insurance consequences of this type of arson are made especially troublesome by the fact that such losses, even if arson is proved, have to be paid anyway; but very little can be anticipated by underwriters to guide them in the selection of school buildings to insure.

In discussing the arson trends, we should remember that arson is elusive and difficult to prove, that the figures are only estimates, and that the trends are open to interpretation. Several arguments could be made to explain the trends. It could be argued, for example, that

[16]An old saw has it that many total losses in valued policy states are caused by friction, the friction of a mortgage rubbing against a valued policy statute.

[17]Defensive underwriting against mobster arson is becoming increasingly difficult, however, with the increasing restrictions being imposed upon insurers in their ability to decline applications or cancel or refuse to renew existing contracts in areas suspected to be subject to gangster influence. Moreover, the losses have to be paid even when arson is proved.

[18]In terms of frequency and perhaps in terms of dollars, vandalism is even more of a problem.

[19]Statement by R. C. Steinmetz of the International Association of Arson Investigators in a speech entitled "Arson Developments," at the Mutual Insurance Technical Conference, Hotel Roosevelt, New York City, November 16, 1966. The speech was subsequently published as "Arson Developments," *Best's Insurance News* (Fire and Casualty edition), vol. 67 (February, 1967), pp. 20-24.

the standards for the "incendiary, suspicious" category may have been lowered over the years, with the result that more fires are placed in this category. No evidence exists to support such a development, however. In fact, the stronger argument would seem to be that the technology of ascertaining fire losses has improved over the years so that what might have appeared erroneously in earlier reports as a suspicion of arson can now be identified as something else. If this argument holds (and it may not), a fairly stable percentage of the building fires of "unknown or undetermined" origin might have a higher arson proportion than was previously the case. Neither argument is really strong. We should merely recognize that the figures, being estimates, are subject to errors in either direction.

Arson is ugly. It represents a value system that is the antithesis of the values upon which insurance is based. The extent of arson from traditional causes is not yet unmanageable. Again, however, the trend is adverse and the slope of the trend is steep enough to create major problems even within a decade. Unless the trend is halted, it is inevitable that sooner or later insurance will no longer lend itself to treatment of arson losses. One defensive measure insurers may be forced to take is to decline certain types of property, such as public schools. One needs little imagination to anticipate the public reaction to such an underwriting practice. Another defensive measure might be to reword the fire policy to exclude payment for arson losses. This measure is equally unpalatable, however, and points again to the urgency for deterring crime.

Surely, the most menacing implication for insurance in the rising crime frequency is the emergence of civil disobedience as a technique for pursuing social or political ends. The idea of disobedience itself undermines the ethical foundation of insurance. The violence and destruction that often accompany the disobedience are completely antithetical to the ethical foundation of insurance. In the past, crimes have been associated predominantly with motives of avarice, greed, revenge, lust, or anger directed toward some individual or small group. The committing of crimes of murder, mayhem, arson, pillage, vandalism, and the like on a mass scale as demonstration of gross dissatisfaction with the social order adds an enormous new dimension to insuring against crime losses. The initial estimates of physical loss usually exceed by a substantial margin the physical losses actually covered by insurance. The discrepancies occur not only because the loss estimates are often high but also because numerous damaged or destroyed properties are uninsured or underinsured.[20] Still, the concept of mass protest and selective disobedience of civil law unquestionably poses a grave threat to the insuring process, be it private or public. When any sizable proportion of the population within an organized community becomes intent on destruction instead of preservation of lives or property, whatever the motives, insurance is vitally threatened. This problem, which strikes at the very essence of insurance, is treated at greater length in the next section and in Chapter 8.

INSURANCE AS AN INSTRUMENT OF SOCIAL POLICY

Let us turn now to the possibility of quite a different kind of change in ethics and morality and to its implications for insurance. Over the long-range future a large number of people may decide to use insurance to achieve a considerably wider redistribution of wealth than that traditionally achieved by insurance. Their behavior may come to reflect a belief that insurance—private as well as public— ought to be used to fight social ills and that underwriting should be subordinated to the more important considerations of public well-being. The people may decide that it is right and proper for insurance to be used to favor the property owner in a blighted area, the aged automobile owner, the slum dweller, the racially disadvantaged, the destitute, and others in difficult circumstances not primarily of their own making. Disadvantaged individuals may not be able or may not want to buy insurance at rates that reflect their loss potential. If the sentiment to use insurance to favor certain groups of people becomes widespread in a democratic society, the force of government will become available to encourage or even coerce the change.

This is not to say that the inclination to use insurance as an instrument of social policy has arisen or will arise because of population growth. No causal relationship can be proved. Yet, it seems reasonable to think that rapid population growth aggravates urban blight,

---

[20]For the first ten months of 1968, for example, the amount paid by insurance companies for the physical damage of civil disorders, according to one source, came to about 45 percent of the initial estimate of the damage.

poverty, slums, racial disturbances, civil disorder, automobile congestion, rising costs of health care, and comparable social ailments. These are some of the ailments for which alleviation is already being sought through use of insurance. Further rapid population growth may be expected to aggravate these and other social ills, creating even more pressure for expansion of the institution of insurance. Hence, the relationship between rapid population growth and use of insurance as an instrument of social policy seems close enough to justify a discussion of it at this point.

As noted in Chapter 2, insurance necessarily involves a spreading of losses. The incidence of insured losses is rearranged. Losses do not remain where they initially fall. This rearrangement, as we saw, is essential to insurance; otherwise each individual would have to retain the burden of his own losses or shift it by some other means such as charity. A troublesome question in insurance theory and practice, however, has been and continues to be whether the averaging of losses should be widespread or narrow. At one extreme every insured would pay a rate based on his own unique exposure to loss.[21] At the other extreme the rate would be the same for every insured in the program, regardless of differences among insureds as to loss potential.

As the insuring process has developed over the years, continuing efforts have been exerted to relate the cost of the insurance to the loss-causing propensities of the insured. Successively refined groupings have produced relatively small classes of insureds, with the members within each group believed to comprise fairly homogeneous units of exposure to risk. The sets have been defined, depending on the types of insurance, in terms of age, medical history, size, occupation, use, territory, construction, weight, history of insured losses, loss prevention practice, sex, and numerous other criteria.

In a competitive insurance market, be it private or public, a tendency exists to fragment rating classes by creating new and smaller classes of insureds. Each new class may be defined more narrowly than the predecessor class and may be subjected to a different rate.

---

[21]Imperfections in the actuarial system have so far prevented any danger of an insured being assigned his own loss cost in advance. The science of prediction simply is not that good, and whether it ever will be involves a prediction that probably should not be attempted.

James M. Cahill, having had the opportunity as an actuary and manager of a large rating bureau to observe this process, has written:

The variations within one line of insurance call for the establishment of rate groupings which will reflect the often sizable differences inherent in one group as contrasted to another. Ratemaking would be much simpler if it were practicable to have only a few very broad groupings of risks for rating purposes. But consistent pressure for the fragmentation of a line of insurance into more and smaller rate groups is created by the competition in rates among insurance companies. In any rate group the worse-than-average risks are in fact paying less than their loss-potential would indicate, and the better-than-average risks are paying more. The alert competitor can offer the better-than-average risks a lower rate by setting them apart in a new grouping based on criteria designed to effect such differentiation.[22]

Mr. Cahill comments further that at some point the cost of establishing still another class coupled with the decreased credibility of the loss data for that class will bring the process of fragmentation to a halt.

Recognition of differences in loss-causing propensities among insureds does not necessarily stop, however, with the stabilization of rate classes. The recognition of differences may be carried further by "individual risk modification" or some similarly named technique. The practice is commonplace and the idea simple. An individual insured within a given class may display characteristics (usually manifested by loss experience) substantially different from the average for the class of which he is a member. If so, he may find his rate modified from that charged for the class, subject to upper and lower limits of modification. For example, suppose that a particular insured had better loss experience (that is, fewer dollars of insured losses) for the period under observation than the average contemplated for the class of insureds in which he was placed. His rate for the next (or the current) rating period would be adjusted downward as long as it did not fall below some minimum. If, however, his loss experience was worse than the average contemplated for the class, his rate would be raised commensurately, subject to some maxi-

[22]James M. Cahill, "Ratemaking in Liability Insurance and Related Lines," in John D. Long and Davis W. Gregg, ed., *Property and Liability Insurance Handbook* (Homewood, Ill.: Richard D. Irwin, Inc., 1965), p. 691, used by permission.

mum.[23] The same concept of rate modification is also commonly applied in group life insurance; automobile physical damage and medical payments insurance written on a fleet basis; and large contracts of marine, fidelity, and several other lines of insurance where a single insured's loss experiences are frequent enough and large enough to possess some credibility.

Thus, the tendency clearly has been toward progressive refinement of insurance rates to match the anticipated losses of a particular insured for a particular period.[24] This refinement has been viewed as progress, as improvement, as an approach to equity, and as commendable. However, over the long-range future this trend may be reversed. The public may decide, at least for certain types of insurance, that the losses should be spread over relatively large groups without the usual attention to actuarial finesse. The concept of what constitutes equity in ratemaking may undergo a change that, in turn, stems from the moral conviction that insurance is an instrument which should be used to combat besetting social ills.

This sort of feeling could be produced by a growing and widespread doubt that ordinary individuals in the future will be able to exercise significant control over their lives. Many people probably think that the classic assertion "I am the master of my fate; I am the captain of my soul"[25] has always been a self-delusion. In the future, however, they and others may be persuaded that the bold declaration, aside from its religious oversights, rings an even more

[23]A highly detailed and excellent treatment of "Individual-Insured Rating Plans" is found in C. A. Kulp and John W. Hall, *Casualty Insurance* (4th ed.; New York: The Ronald Press Company, 1968), pp. 874-957.

[24]Reinsurance is somewhat different in that, except for truly catastrophic losses, reinsurers aim toward helping a primary insurer average its own annual losses over a longer period of time. The amount a particular primary insurer has to pay for its reinsurance is closely related, with allowance for an appropriate time lag, to what the reinsurer pays in reinsurance claims to that particular primary insurer.

[25]The concluding two lines of William Ernest Henley's "Invictus." An interesting observation was made on this general point by newspaper writer Hal Boyle in an Associated Press account of the crippling snowstorm that engulfed New York in February, 1969. Boyle in a February 10 release commented that such an event, with all its inconveniences, did have an exhilarating effect by causing New Yorkers to feel that people are more important than machines. Many of the machines failed. The further implication was that the victory would be short-lived because New Yorkers would soon revert to the patterns of life dictated by the machines on which, in the long run, all life in crowded greater New York (and elsewhere) depends.

hollow note than it did formerly. The possibility does exist that individuals may lose any meaningful control over their job security, the security of their savings, the quality and extent of education of their children, and other equally important facets of their lives.

This loss of control, as already intimated, might be abetted and hastened by the increased crowding and the growing complexity of technology. As individuals become more dependent on and involved in the web of large-scale economic activity, and as they become progressively removed from nature in their urbanized groupings, they may feel less able to control their destiny. They may also, quite understandably, feel less personal responsibility for the situations in which they find themselves.

In such a frame of mind a sufficiently large block of the voting and insuring public may readily embrace the "social action" use of insurance to implement the change. Some of those involved probably will be acting out of desperation; others will act without any clear understanding of the issues and the implications but in the fuzzy expectation of gaining more than they lose. In this kind of setting the trend toward rate refinement may thus eventually yield to a trend toward rate uniformity, all in the name of social justice. In the early stages of the change, assuming it does develop, the wider averaging may be confined to a few lines of insurance to meet problems of special urgency. Over a matter of decades, however, the wider spreading of losses may extend to additional lines of insurance and, indeed, may contribute to an obliteration of the distinctions among the lines.[26]

There is no reason inherent in insurance theory why insured losses cannot be shared widely. Conceivably, a given insurance program could cover everybody in the world against a given type of loss with each insured paying an identical premium. For that matter, the program theoretically could be expanded to an "all risk" coverage, and the premium could be assessed against each household (or other unit) in some inverse relationship to income without the program ceasing to be insurance. As long as the benefits payable are

---

[26]If this obliteration occurs, then the withdrawal from the market of theft and related insurances, as discussed earlier in this chapter, could be postponed indefinitely. The postponement may be accomplished by the consolidation of present lines of insurance, which would result in the subsidizing alluded to in the earlier discussion.

confined to those required as indemnity (or those deemed to be the valued policy equivalent) for losses arising out of "pure risk,"[27] the arrangement described could remain within the domain of insurance.

The potentially troublesome issue involved if larger groupings are to be used is not that the arrangement would at some point cease to be insurance. Rather, the really pertinent issue is whether the reversal of the trend toward rate refinement would in the long run increase or decrease the usefulness of insurance to individuals and to society as a whole. Whatever the answer on the matter of usefulness, the change would probably mean that a larger redistribution would be produced by insurance than would result from a more narrow averaging of the losses.

In some cases, averaging losses has increased the usefulness of insurance, as for example, in packaging or reinsurance.[28] Each of these techniques builds on a wider averaging of losses. Each, however, still involves grouping relatively homogeneous units of exposure into separate rate classes, even though the exposure may be extremely broad. Futhermore, reinsurance is largely a spreading of a primary insurer's losses over time rather than a spreading of a single period's losses among many primary insurers. Each of these

---

[27]"Pure risk" is used here in the customary sense of uncertainty as to loss but certainty of no gain. When we describe insurance in such extremely broad terms, we cannot help but be curious as to how insurance differs conceptually from collectivism. The answer appears to lie in the fact that, by definition and by practice, insurance is restricted to changing the incidence of loss arising from pure risk, whereas collectivism is not restricted to treatment of pure risk. To phrase this distinction in another way, insurance involves redistribution of wealth only to indemnify, while collectivism involves common ownership (or control) of wealth without regard to indemnity. Pure collectivism would seem to obviate the need for the insuring process to operate within the collective organization because individuals, not owning property, could not suffer indemnifiable loss in the first place. The collective organization as a whole, however, may need indemnification for loss suffered and may therefore need insurance provided by resources external to the collective organization. Thus, we may observe the phenomenon of a collectivist government buying insurance from a foreign insurance organization.

[28]Another example is found in the type of averaging that occurs in the treatment by insurance of unique or unusual but not unique losses. Insurers do not possess sufficient information about any one of the loss probabilities to permit setting a meaningful rate. Only by averaging *all* of the unique and unusual losses in a single rate calculation can an insurer or a group of insurers develop a meaningful rate that would make the coverage available at all. The "special risk" departments of many insurance companies operate precisely in this fashion. As loss data become available for particular coverages, the base for averaging losses may tend to narrow.

techniques is essentially different from abolishing, say, the territorial distinctions for a given type of insurance and the differences in their individual exposures. The territorial abolition is a type of broadening which, conceivably, could be produced by the new approach to averaging.

Whether individuals would lose the incentive to avoid loss as ratemaking becomes further removed from individual loss experience is a great unknown. Whether the insuring process would become progressively less efficient as individuals begin to use it as an agency for social reform also is unanswerable at this time. Whether the use of insurance as an instrument of social policy really would alleviate social ills is likewise unanswerable pending more experimentation.

The discussion of the scale over which insured losses are to be averaged has been abstruse. An example may serve to indicate the kind of changes in loss sharing that may take place. Fire and allied insurances to cover residential and commercial properties in the nation's "inner cities" have been increasingly difficult to provide. The hardships faced by insureds and the underwriting difficulties encountered by insurers have been the subject of wide attention. In several states commissioners of insurance even have prohibited insurers from canceling or have forced them to renew policies in numerous lines, especially automobile and homeowners coverage. With loss frequencies and loss severities frightfully high and with ceilings being maintained on the prices of insurance issued to cover urban core properties, insurers naturally have been less than enthusiastic about selling the insurance.

In an effort to keep the insurance market for these properties open, state insurance officials during the early and middle 1960s approved several "urban plans." The principal characteristic of most of these urban plans was that insurers were freed, within limits, from the ceilings on insurance rates and were allowed to charge higher rates under certain conditions, depending on the nature and location of the property being insured. Even with more price freedom on the part of insurers, however, insurance did not become readily available for all inner city properties. Despite the possibility of a surcharge, many of the properties remained unattractive to underwriters. Some probably were uninsurable at any price; others were poorly maintained or were located in blighted areas with a dangerous conflagration potential; and still others were subject to undue crowding or uses inconsistent with loss prevention.

The difficulties of providing an insurance market were then compounded by the succession of destructive riots that occurred in the cities during the second half of the 1960s. The riot damage often was concentrated among the very properties most difficult to insure before the rioting occurred. The insurance aspects of the civil disturbances became so grave that the President's National Advisory Panel on Insurance in Riot-Affected Areas was created to review the problems and recommend a course of action. The report of this distinguished panel and its highly capable staff is well known, and several of its recommendations have already been implemented.[29] The omnibus Urban Property and Reinsurance Act of 1968 contained the initial implementive legislation.[30]

Two aspects of the panel's recommendations that were enacted into law are especially pertinent to this discussion. First, the law places considerable pressure on the insurance industry to issue not only "fire and extended coverage" insurance on the inner city properties but also to provide insurance against "vandalism and malicious mischief" as well as theft.[31] The industry, in cooperation with the several states, is encouraged by the law to establish plans to provide urban core property owners with "fair access to insurance requirements" (FAIR plans). The central idea is that the insurers should provide insurance on every property which, after inspection and with continuing maintenance, can be brought to minimum underwriting acceptability, assuming no negative underwriting consideration whatever is given to the location of the property. The "environmental hazard" is not to be considered in the underwriting decision to accept or reject the property or in the establishment of the rate for the property. While surcharges are allowed, as under the previous urban plans, they are to relate to hazards other than

---

[29]The report, published in January, 1968, is entitled *Meeting the Insurance Crisis of Our Cities;* a companion volume, *Hearings Before the President's National Advisory Panel on Insurance in Riot-Affected Areas* (November 7-8, 1967), was also published.

[30]*Urban Property Protection and Reinsurance Act of 1968, United States Code Annotated* (1969), Title 12, Subchapter IX-C, Section 1749 bbb, pp. 593-611.

[31]No inference is made that the insurance industry did not exercise its voice in the drafting of the legislation. Three of the seven panel members, in fact, were insurance company presidents. Additionally, the panel and later Congress received substantial testimony from individuals affiliated with the insurance industry. The testimony suggests general industry endorsement of the recommendations made by the panel.

those produced by the environment. The intent of the law is that owners of these properties as a class are not to be required to pay the full losses their properties are expected to generate. A statement in the panel's report makes this intent quite clear:

> We recognize the need for flexible and adequate rates. A risk must bear an appropriate rate; if a property is significantly more hazardous than average, it must yield a commensurately higher premium. Nevertheless, we hope that the states will consider placing a maximum limit on surcharges. Excessive or discriminatory rates must not be permitted to undermine the goals of the FAIR Plan.[32]

Here, then, is a striking example of pressure to spread insurance losses over a much wider area than that dictated or even allowed by customary underwriting and actuarial practices. Furthermore, the new law suggests that state pools be used as necessary to supplement FAIR plans and that, if necessary, each state assess insurance companies inside or outside its pool, or use general or special tax revenues to subsidize through the pool those insureds buying coverage under the FAIR plans.

The second especially pertinent aspect of the panel's recommendations, as enacted into law, is the creation of the National Insurance Development Corporation.[33] The purposes of this organization include the provision of federal "reinsurance against the risk of extraordinary loss from civil disorders" so as to remove "the burden from a single group of persons or segment of the insurance industry. . . ."[34]

The clincher in the arrangement is that federal "riot" reinsurance is available only to an insurance company that (1) pays a reinsurance premium to the fund and (2) participates fully in the FAIR plans and in the state pools in each state where the company operates and where the state, itself, agrees to retain "a layer" of the riot losses.

FAIR plans were established in 34 states, Puerto Rico, and the District of Columbia before the expiration of the initial 90-day dead-

---

[32]*Meeting the Insurance Crisis of Our Cities*, p. 11.
[33]Called the "National Insurance Development Fund" in Section 1749 bbb-13 of Title 12 in *United States Code Annotated*.
[34]*Meeting the Insurance Crisis of Our Cities*, p. 13. Sections 1749 bbb-7 through 1749 bbb-15 (pp. 600-609) relate to reinsurance.

line for eligibility for reinsurance specified in the federal act.[35] Consequently, the new approach appears to be generally acceptable, at least until it shows major flaws, and losses stemming from urban blight and civil disorders will be spread more widely than if the legislation had not been enacted. The prospect of wider loss sharing is further strengthened by the fact that even before the passage of the new federal law, several rating bureaus and independent filers had succeeded in adding in most states a specific riot loading to the rates for the insurance contracts that provide riot coverage.[36]

Much could be said about the advisory panel's role in developing enlightened solutions to extremely difficult problems. Our interest, however, centers on the possibility that the work presages a major philosophical change in the way insurance should be priced and used in times of acute social stress. If the recommendations of the panel along with the riot loadings made by the bureaus and independent filers do set a precedent, they may also call for a fundamental reexamination of several conceptual issues.

One of the concepts needing reexamination pertains to unfair discrimination in setting rates. For example, the new "social action" approach to insurance may conflict with the insurance statutes of several states insofar as they pertain to ratemaking. These statutes, perhaps without exception, require the duly constituted state official to see that the rates are adequate, not excessive, and not unfairly discriminatory.[37] The prohibition against unfair discrimination is

---

[35]According to a count in Alexander Picone's article "1968: The Year of Truth," *Journal of Insurance Information*, vol. 30 (January-February, 1969), p. 22, and "FAIR Plan Status at a Glance," a chart developed by the American Mutual Insurance Alliance as of December 10, 1968, and updated by "General Bulletin 69-10," January 29, 1969.

[36]In most states the loading took the form of a percentage addition to the rate. In most states the addition was 4 percent of the unloaded rate for counties and cities with a population of 250,000 or more and 2 percent for all other areas. For a brief description of the rating bureau proposals see "Changes Developed by Three Bureaus for Civil Disorders," *National Underwriter*, vol. 72 (March 29, 1968), pp. 1, 5.

[37]The relevant Indiana statute, for example, reads in part: "The purpose of this act . . . is to promote the public welfare by empowering the commissioner of insurance to regulate insurance rates to the end that they shall not be excessive, inadequate, or unfairly discriminatory, and to encourage reasonable competition among insurance companies . . . and to permit and regulate, but not require, cooperative action among insurers, as to rates, rating systems, rating plans and practices, and other matters within the scope of this act." *Burns Annotated Indiana Statutes*, 1968 Cumulative Pocket Supplement to 1965 Replacement Volume, vol. 8, part 1, section 39-5239, p. 38 (Indianapolis: The Bobbs-Merrill Company, Inc.).

the provision that could prove troublesome in light of the wider sharing of insured losses. The insurance commissioner of Arkansas, for instance, is on record as having disapproved a bureau request to include riot loading in certain policies issued in Arkansas.[38] His refusal apparently was based on the belief that Arkansas policyholders should not have to help pay for losses caused by riots in other states.

This point of view does raise interesting questions as to what constitutes unfair discrimination within the context of state statutes. Is a South Dakota farmer who is forced to pay riot loading in order to buy a farmowners policy being unfairly discriminated against? Should New York City policyholders in turn be assessed to help pay for South Dakota crop hail losses? Should the insurance premiums paid by a California vineyard owner include loading for vandalism losses in Miami? Should a rural Ohio resident have to pay more state taxes to support state reinsurance payments under an Ohio FAIR plan? Should he have to pay more federal taxes to support a federal reinsurance plan to help cover riot losses in Cleveland or Washington, D.C.? Is it equitable for the premium in a FAIR plan to include no environmental charge whatever when the environment contains the most probable ingredients of insured loss?

The advisory panel in the passage quoted earlier stated that discriminatory rates must not be permitted to undermine the goals of the FAIR plans. Could it be that the goals of the FAIR plans can be achieved only if the rates discriminate in favor of inner city property owners and against all other property owners? Even if the FAIR plans are admitted to be unfairly discriminatory, does such an admission carry any implication that FAIR plans should be abandoned?

These are thorny questions. Fortunately, the answers can be whatever the public wants them to be. Laws can be reinterpreted; statutes can be reworded. If the public, because of a change in its ethical thinking (or any other reason), wants to share insurance losses on a wider basis in the hope of solving social problems, changes may be made fairly easily in the way insured losses are averaged. Elderly operators of automobiles can be subsidized in respect to their insurance costs; hospital insurance rates can be juggled to favor the poor; low premium life insurance can be sold to

[38]"Ark. Denies Riot Charge," *Business Insurance*, vol. 72 (May 20, 1968), p. 1.

inner city residents; transportation insurance for buses, trains, ships, or planes can be subsidized out of general tax revenues; fire insurance on schools can be kept lower than objective analysis of loss data would indicate; and so on.[39]

As mentioned earlier, the loss sharing over the long range could eventually spill over lines of insurance so as to blur the distinction from line to line. This process is different from merely packaging multiple coverages within a single contract. Coverages can be packaged with each coverage being separately rated through the use of loss data compiled and maintained in respect to that coverage. This practice can prevail even though the package is marketed as being indivisibly rated. On the other hand, the tendency toward wide loss averaging could become so pronounced as to render redundant certain traditional distinctions among lines. The ultimate limit of such a tendency would be one tremendously broad form of insurance that could, as far as this nation is concerned, represent a countrywide pooling of losses arising from virtually any kind of peril subject to treatment by insurance. Of course, such a development is not likely within our current social and democratic system.

Somewhat more likely as time goes on is a reduction of the number of separately rated lines of insurance in this country and the merging of individual bodies of loss data into larger and more generalized data banks. The result could be that policyholders suffering certain predominant types of losses could be subsidized by other holders of the same type of policy who do not suffer that same predominant type of loss. This expansion of loss sharing might delay or even prevent disappearance from the market, for example, of insurance to cover losses from criminal acts as discussed earlier in this chapter. If the practice of maintaining separate loss data for theft, arson, vandalism, infidelity, and related acts were discontinued, the need for withdrawal of insurance covering such losses could only be surmised, and actual withdrawal of the coverages would be extremely awkward. Consolidation of loss data to this extent and averaging of losses among so many lines of insurance is not likely to

---

[39]The old age, survivors, disability, and health insurance programs operated by the federal Social Security Administration in the Department of Health, Education, and Welfare are skewed to favor relatively low-income wage earners and low-income self-employees and their families.

occur before the turn of the century. Still, the possibility exists and should not be summarily dismissed. More immediate, however, is the danger that losses from criminal acts will increase faster than loss sharing will broaden, which would threaten the market for insurance covering such losses.

LESS INSURING OF TORT LIABILITY

Still another major change in insurance may occur as population swells and ethics and morality are modified. This change involves the insuring of tort liability. The long-range future may bring a curtailment of insuring for tort liability because such liability itself may become much more limited than it is presently. The word "curtailment" is used here in a relative sense; the dollars of permium for insurance sold to cover tort liability may become a decreasing proportion of the total dollars of insurance premium.

The concerted attention given in recent years to the problems of automobile insurance has emphasized the difficulties of assessing fault and has pointed up the advantages and disadvantages of limiting or abandoning remedies in torts for automobile traffic victims.[40] Two bodies of thought are involved in this debate. One is that any tinkering with the fundamental use of fault as a criterion in determining the incidence of loss is a serious matter.[41] The other is that

---

[40]The literature on this subject is vast and growing. Perhaps the most comprehensive treatment of the problem of compensating automobile traffic accident victims, including a review of earlier studies and current proposals on the subject, is found in Robert E. Keeton and Jeffrey O'Connell, *Basic Protection for the Traffic Victim: A Blueprint for Reforming Automobile Insurance* (Boston: Little, Brown and Company, 1965). The reception accorded the solution proposed by Keeton-O'Connell has been as robust as it has been diverse. While the use of the word "blueprint" in the title might have been somewhat presumptive, there is no question but that it is the standard for change by which most subsequent proposals have been measured and compared. A particularly engaging critical appraisal of the principal issues inherent in any system of compensating traffic victims appears in Walter J. Blum and Harry Kalven, Jr., *Public Law Perspectives on a Private Law Problem* (Boston: Little, Brown and Company, 1965).

[41]Helpful summaries about the rationale as well as the shortcomings of the fault criterion appear in *The University of Illinois Law Forum* (Fall, 1967). One is Spencer L. Kimball, "Automobile Accident Compensation Systems—Objectives and Perspectives," pp. 370-86 (especially pp. 371-80). The other is Guido Calabresi, "Views and Overviews," pp. 600-611.

the tort mechanism, especially as it pertains to negligence, is distressingly less than perfect.[42] Continuing difficulties, fed partly by continued population growth, underscore the relevance of both views.

Negligence, as dealt with in the insurance system, is under sharp attack as the guide for placing responsibility for reparations in *automobile* accidents. The speculation offered in this chapter is that negligence may come under similar attack in numerous other areas of torts. The problem of frequency now centered within automobile claims will surely spread, as population grows, to nonautomobile claims. In the course of time many of the same arguments, pro and con, that are being applied to modification of the automobile reparations system will be applied to other problems of damages not directly related to the automobile. Elaboration about the possible long-range change in the use of insurance can best be made by considering, first, the long-range problem and, second, the long-range alternative solutions.

The problem can be stated simply. By the turn of the century life in the United States may be of such a quality that blame for personal injury or property damage accidents cannot normally be placed with confidence on any individual or group. A rapidly growing population, assuming continued advances in technology, may bring in its wake such crowdedness, such a pace of events, such a multiplication of human contacts, such a spread of dangers, such a profusion of accidents as to frustrate any effort to shift losses and settle disputes by reliance on the traditional tort machinery. The traditional approach might well be further impeded by a growing divergence in concepts of right and wrong.

The difficulties with torts could intensify in at least three ways. First, the American judicial system could be much too slow to keep pace with the magnitude of alleged injustices demanding remedial

---

[42]Perhaps the classic pessimistic pronouncement is that which appeared in the book version of the 1958 Rosenthal Lectures presented at Northwestern University School of Law by Dean Leon Green, *Traffic Victims: Tort Law and Insurance* (Evanston, Ill.: Northwestern University Press, 1958). The book is impressive partly because its author, having experienced a long and brilliant career as a scholar in tort law, urged that the entire time-honored common law apparatus in respect to traffic accidents be discarded in favor of a simple compensation system.

action.[43] No possible expansion of the adjudicatory machinery might be large enough to keep pace with the growth of disputes for which trial is sought even in the absence of population growth.[44] With allowance for the probable sharp increase in the number of situations provoking disputes, the demands on the system may prove overwhelming. Second, the cost of the present system, apart from its necessary expansion, could become higher than society is willing to pay for civil justice, particularly in respect to unintentional torts. We may see a growing willingness to forego justice for expediency at the lower net social cost. Third, and most important, the public may no longer want to consider specific individuals or organizations blameworthy upon the occurrence of certain loss-producing events.

[43]As a hint of what might come, let us note some figures in the *Report of the Administrative Board of the Judicial Conference of the State of New York for the Judicial Year July 1, 1966 through June 30, 1967*, Legislative Document no. 90 (Albany: State of New York, 1968), pp. 118-19, 130-31, 136-37, and 144-45 of the appendixes. Some 267,000 civil cases were filed in the various state and local courts in New York during the period covered by the report. The number averages out to almost 15 per 1,000 population. If the rate for filing civil suits should hold and if the New York State population should increase by about 50 percent by the year 2000, the number of civil cases filed in 2000 in state and local courts in New York without change in the system could exceed 400,000, a substantial portion of which might be based on alleged torts. (Assumption of a 50 percent increase in population is consistent with the "Series C" projection of the Bureau of the Census for the United States as a whole, as discussed in Chapter 3.) With the growing frictions likely to be produced by population expansion, the rate of civil cases per 1,000 population could increase. Suppose that by 2000 the rate had increased one-third to about 20 cases per 1,000. In such a circumstance the number of civil cases filed in the state of New York might reach about 500,000. A proper question is whether the legal system in this country could be and would be expanded sufficiently to accommodate the larger volume indicated by this speculation. The question is made especially appropriate by the waiting time currently required in numerous metropolitan areas for a case to come to trial. For practical purposes, even as the system is now operated, justice is often defeated by being delayed.

[44]Doubtless, a variant of Parkinson's Law operates to expand legal action so as to overtax the capacity of the courts, however large they might grow. Conard and others, on the basis of a large-scale study of reparations for victims of automobile accidents occurring in the state of Michigan in 1958, were led to observe sagely: "For every injury case now reaching trial, there are seven more suits which are settled before trial, and the long delay is one of the reasons for settling. A slight reduction in delay will surely bring additions to the backlog of cases seeking trial. And behind the woodpile of filed cases lies a forest of unfiled cases which might become filed cases if court procedures were more expeditious." Alfred E. Conard and others, *Automobile Accident Costs and Payments—Studies in the Economics of Injury Reparation* (Ann Arbor: The University of Michigan Press, 1964), p. 4, used by permission.

Pursuing the third point a bit further, we can visualize that the crowding and its attendant complications in the society of the future may dilute the ordinary individual's sense of personal responsibility and personal accountability. He may not be nearly so disposed then as he is now to place blame on other individuals. He may develop a growing tendency to view them as he views himself: inescapably a tiny part of and often the victim of a Gargantuan and vexingly complex system. He may be more inclined to vent his frustrations against the system than against the particular individual who chanced to produce the injury.[45]

Departure from the desire to affix individual blame would represent a major shift in ethics and morality. Perhaps the departure will never develop to any appreciable extent. Still, the pressure of population growth may be so strong and incessant as to produce in due time the most fundamental of changes, including this one. A sobering thought is that if this sort of change has not been wrought by the year 2000 it may become a reality before 2100.[46]

If liability in respect to negligence and perhaps other torts is curtailed in the future, the losses are not likely to be left where they fall. The incidence of loss is almost certain to be modified in some fashion. The alternative methods of loss sharing that seem practical are either strict liability coupled with compulsory liability insurance or compulsory first-party insurance coupled with elimination or limitation of liability.[47] From a very fundamental and long-range point of view, these two alternatives may not be essentially different. They contain considerable overlap in long-range effect. Both involve

---

[45]Even today, many victims of tortious conduct not compensated to their satisfaction are as likely to bear grudges against the system and the institution of insurance as against the tort-feasor himself.

[46]At some point, however, a discussion of possible future changes fails to hold our interest. Most of us probably encounter difficulty in being genuinely interested in the nature of mortal life in, say, 2300 A.D. by which time (barring the unforeseen) not only we but also our children, grandchildren, and perhaps even great and great, great grandchildren will have long since "shuffled off this mortal coil."

[47]The transition away from fault and along either of these avenues, if it occurs at all, will not be made without much controversy and rancor. As an example of the truly fundamental nature of the possible transition, one might consider the vendetta between the Defense Research Institute (DRI) and the American Law Institute (ALI) in which the DRI spokesman accused the ALI of using its restatement of the law of torts as a vehicle for attempting to broaden the concept of strict liability of sellers. Thomas L. Dalrymple, who was involved in preparing the DRI monograph *Products*

loss sharing through insurance. In one instance the insurance premium is to be paid directly by the statutory offender and in the other instance by the victim. The ultimate pattern of loss sharing could be about the same, regardless of who pays the premiums directly. To the extent that the same losses are to be shared and the insurance costs are shiftable in a competitive economy, the differences may be transparent.[48]

It is not inconceivable to think that under either alternative the benefits payable could be precisely specified as to type but unlimited as to amount. For example, they may exclude any compensation for pain and suffering or indignities but may be payable without limit for the reasonable cost of necessary medical care and for the continuation during the lifetime of the victim of an income comparable with his ordinary earnings.

The insurance policies in the decades to come may also be couched in terms of providing restoration rather than simply paying money up to certain amounts for certain contingent events. The description of the insuring process in Chapter 2 made reference to specific performance. Over the years, specific performance by the insurer could take increasing precedence over payment. In an environment where the actual treatment, repair, replacement, or substitution may become increasingly difficult to secure and administer, insurers may find themselves much more heavily engaged in the restoration business than they are presently.[49] As society grows

---

Liability—Brief Opposing Strict Liability in Tort (Milwaukee: The Defense Research Institute, Inc., 1966), argues that Section 402 A of the ALI revision is a forecast rather than a restatement of existing law. The DRI brief contains the argument that the restatement has an impact on morality: "There is a moral element to a move from liability for fault to liability without fault. Liability for fault is within the realm of normal expectation of right in our society. Liability without fault is a strange creation which arouses the antagonism of a wrong." The feud is aired in "Law Institute Hit for Urging Concept of Strict Liability," *National Underwriter*, vol. 70 (September 16, 1966), p. 31. Unquestionably, the restatement is related to morality. A debatable point, however, is whether the restatement had a greater impact on morality than morality had on the restatement.

[48]Over the long-range future the insurance costs of employees may be paid increasingly by employers through group arrangements. Costs so paid by employers probably will be shiftable to consumers with about the same difficulty or ease as costs paid by employers for their own liability insurance.

[49]Except, unfortunately, in respect to life insurance, unless cryogenic interment (Chapter 6) or some equally bizarre technique provides a breakthrough.

more crowded, the administrative phases of living may become much more complicated and the need for help in cutting through the maze of formalities much more acute.

If securing admission to a health care facility grows more difficult, or pinning down a repairman grows more irksome, or winning delivery on a replacement part more frustrating, or forcing substitution of a new unit for a defective one more aggravating, the public may no longer be satisfied when the insurer merely pays instead of performing. The nature of insurance could change to a greater emphasis on indemnity as opposed to money. "Servicing" may take on an entirely new concept with insurers finding themselves genuinely involved in servicing the insureds to whom policies have been sold.[50]

To digress even further, we can reasonably expect that this growing pressure on insurers for service may encourage them to establish standard and continuing relationships with numerous other businesses. The aim would be to provide at least some of the variety of services that may be demanded directly or indirectly from the insurers. The growing pressure over the long run might also encourage the linking of insurance with ancillary activities as contemplated in the holding company concept. The meaning of ancillary, however, may become much broader than that regarded in current proposals.[51] Insurers that become operating components of conglomerates conceivably could take advantage of some of the potential of other members of the conglomerate to provide the wider services that may be expected of insurers in the future.

[50]The growing practice of rehabilitation in personal injury cases is perhaps but a miniature of what is to come in the way of insurance company performance when losses occur.

[51]An example of a quite narrow concept, compared to that visualized, can be found in the *Report of the Special Committee on Insurance Holding Companies* (New York: State of New York, Insurance Department, 1968). The committee recommended that insurers be allowed wide freedom to form insurance subsidiaries but no freedom to form noninsurance subsidiaries unless the subsidiaries would be truly ancillary to the insurance enterprise. Types of activities recognized as being ancillary included the management of mutual funds and the provision of investment counsel, actuarial service, loss prevention, data processing, appraisal service, safety engineering, and the like. The day may come when a comparable list would include construction companies, hospital chains, automobile repair chains, psychiatric centers, appliance centers, and numerous other "restorative" establishments.

OTHER POSSIBILITIES

Population growth may affect the ethical pillars of insurance, the resulting moral behavior, and thus insurance itself, in even stranger ways in the future. For example, the crowding may require more regimen in life in order to keep people alive and productive. The necessary regimen, even in a democratic society, may be possible only if imposed by the government. Over several generations, this regimen, although necessary, could eat away at the desire to achieve and to acquire, especially if limitations were placed on what could be done with the acquisitions. In time the regimen could dull the average person's sense of responsibility and his sense of apprehension of the future. One result could be a continuing decrease in personal savings relative to income. Another might be a loss of interest in providing for surviving dependents, attributable in part to the belief that they will be provided for anyway, come what may. Both of these influences could work to the detriment of life insurance. Such a dismal development is only a possibility without any convincing documentation to support it. No meaningful way exists even to gauge its probability because so little is known about how human beings behave under the stresses produced by an expanding population.

A more cheerful speculation is that population growth, in tending to render many personal relations brusk, cold, and hurried, may strengthen family bonds and relationships. The importance of the family may be enhanced as the members seek to escape, within the family setting, from the impersonality that may characterize much of the rest of life. Such a development might generally tend to make the ethical foundation of insurance even stronger and to encourage relatively more savings and greater use of virtually every type of insurance. Here again, of course, the future is unknown.

Another speculation is extremely far-fetched but not to be ignored. As population pressures build from generation to generation, preservation of aggregate human life could become less prominent as a public goal than it now is because of the sheer redundancy of people. This thought is terribly unpleasant but deserves to be considered within the framework of the problems we are discussing. It is distressing to think of the relentless competition for space and sustenance that will surely be produced in due course if population growth is not restrained and ultimately terminated. One result, as far as insurance is concerned, could be a growing importance of insurance on *things* and a declining importance of insurance on *people*. The year 2000, hopefully, is too soon for a development such as this to manifest itself. We observed in Chapter 3 that competition for life within and among the subhuman species, while orderly, is nonetheless severe. In the inexorable stretch of time this sort of change in moral behavior—perhaps amounting to a moral reversion—could be forced upon man by unremitting population growth. Let us hope that the force is never applied.

5

INFLATION

Partly as the result of population overgrowth and partly as the result of other stimulants, inflation could plague our economic life throughout the remainder of this century and beyond. Of course, it is not certain that inflation will occur; for all we know, our long-range problem may be deflation. Assuming, however, that inflation is more probable than deflation, we turn in this chapter to (1) a review of the nature of inflation, (2) an analysis of the possible effects of inflation on the ethical pillars of insurance, (3) an examination of the record of inflation during recent years, and (4) an assessment of the probability of inflation over the long-range future.

As Chapter 4 demonstrated, long-range speculation about ethics and morality is nebulous, particularly since cause-and-effect relationships are difficult if not impossible to verify. We find ourselves, however, again needing to make some guesses about the strength of a major social force over the long-range future and some estimate of its ethical and moral consequences as they relate to insurance. Once again, we can only look to the trends and make estimates about the future, bolstering our observations with as much of what De Jouvenel calls "intellectual scaffolding" as the data warrant.

Before turning to the nature of inflation, we should remind our-selves that inflation probably bears on insurance in many ways that do not involve ethics and morality. It does so, for example, in the modification of investment portfolios, in the introduction of antic-ipated inflation in the insurance rate, in the marketing of fixed dol-lar coverages, in coverage design, and in a squeeze on profits in which benefits inflate faster than premiums.[1]

We are concerned in this study, however, only with the changes brought about by inflation-induced shifts in ethics and morality. We are specifically interested in the effect inflation may have on the ethical pillars of insurance as described in Chapter 2.

NATURE OF INFLATION

Inflation is such a commonly used word that a definition of it might not seem necessary. The very fact that the word is so commonly used, however, is reason in itself that confusion as to its meaning might exist. If anyone doubts the confusion, he can be reminded of it by a passage in *Elements of Modern Economics* by Albert L. Meyers. Meyers writes:

There are perhaps nearly as many definitions of inflation as there are people who use the term. A short list of some of them may prove inter-esting. Inflation is:
1.   Any increase in the quantity of money.
2.   Any increase in general prices.
3.   Any increase in prices not caused by increased consumer preference for the goods or by a decreased physical supply.
4.   Any increase in government debt that may affect prices.
5.   Any increase in the effective quantity of money.
6.   Any increase in the effective quantity of money that is greater than the increase in money work to be done.
7.   Any increase in money and prices that does not result in increased output of goods.
8.   Any increase in prices that occurs after full employment has been obtained.
9.   Maintenance of a constant price level when costs are falling.
10.   Any increase in capital investment that cannot be continued without a continuous increase in the quantity of money.

---

[1]For a discussion of some of these points see Robert I. Mehr and Seev Neumann in their forthcoming publication whose working title is "Inflation, Technology and Growth: Possible Implications for Insurance" (to be published by the Bureau of Business Research, Graduate School of Business, Indiana University).

11.   A situation in which the public loses faith in the ability of money to keep its value and rushes to get rid of money in exchange for commodities or securities that promise to be a better store of value.[2]

Meyer's list is sufficiently long and varied to demonstrate that any discussion of inflation can generate considerable confusion unless the participants involved are in precise agreement on the subject of their discussion.

Perhaps some of the difficulty students have had in understanding John Maynard Keynes's concept of inflation arose from their failure to notice that certain of his propositions have to do only with what he refers to as true inflation, which by implication is different from a less rigid kind of inflation and is close to the eighth definition in Meyer's list. Keynes, in his book *The General Theory of Employment Interest and Money*, says: "When full employment is reached, any attempt to increase investment still further will set up a tendency in money-prices to rise without limit, irrespective of the marginal propensity to consume; i.e. we shall have reached a state of true inflation." Later in the book he expands his statement in the following manner: "When a further increase in the quantity of effective demand produces no further increase in output and entirely spends itself on an increase in the cost-unit fully proportionate to the increase in effective demand, we have reached a condition which might be appropriately designated as one of true inflation."[3]

Keynes's definition of true inflation does not answer the question of whether inflation can exist when only part but not all of an increase in effective demand could manifest itself in higher prices. This weaker—and for our purposes much more useful—concept of inflation can be found to exist in the situation where not only all of the increased effective demand but also any part, however small, manifests itself in higher average prices.

This weaker and simpler concept of inflation is more consistent with popular ideas and is the one used in this book. It is close to the second definition in the Meyers list. It is also consistent with defini-

[2]Albert L. Meyers, *Elements of Modern Economics* (4th ed.; Englewood Cliffs, N.J.: Prentice-Hall, Inc., 1956), p. 348. Copyright © 1956 by Prentice-Hall, Inc. Reprinted by permission of Prentice-Hall, Inc. Meyers classifies definitions seven through eleven as dangerous types of inflation.

[3]John Maynard Keynes, *The General Theory of Employment Interest and Money* (New York: Harcourt, Brace and Company, book not dated, preface dated 1935), pp. 118-19, 303.

tions found in economics textbooks. Paul Samuelson, for example, says: "By *inflation* we mean a time of generally rising prices for goods and factors of production."[4] Gardner Ackley refers to inflation "as a persistent and appreciable rise in the general level or average of prices."[5] Lawrence Abbott says much the same thing in defining inflation as "a persistent rise in the general level of prices."[6] Thus, we rely on good authority when we think of inflation as nothing more than a rise in the general level of prices. We might add that the rise must be sustained long enough to be observable and be large enough to be measurable.

In an effort to gain better understanding and control of inflation, economists classify the phenomenon in various ways. In one classification they distinguish between "demand-pull" and "wage-push" inflations. The former is said to occur because aggragate demand as the result of public deficit financing or other reasons increases faster than aggregate supply. The result is a pulling up of prices and wages commensurate with the enlarged demand and the relatively restricted supply. The latter, or wage-push, type of inflation is said to come from wage increases over and beyond those justified by increases in productivity (output per man hour). These wage increases are forced upon the economy by labor unions that have some monopolistic bargaining power in the sale of labor. The wage increases in turn require that if unemployment is to be avoided compensatory increases occur in the prices of goods and services to which the labor is devoted. The increase in prices may provoke in due course another wage push so as to create the familiar wage-price spiral about which so much is spoken and written.

Another way of classifying the types of inflation is to distinguish between cyclical and secular inflations. Cyclical inflation, followed by cyclical deflation, has characterized much of the history of price movements in this country. Simultaneously, in certain periods of our history prices have tended to trend upward. This movement, very

---

[4]Paul A. Samuelson, *Economics: An Introductory Analysis* (7th ed.; New York: McGraw-Hill Book Company, 1967), p. 258. Copyright © 1967 by McGraw-Hill Book Company. Used by permission of McGraw-Hill Book Company. He adds that in periods of price control the definition may need modification to take into account suppression of price rises that would otherwise occur.

[5]Gardner Ackley, *Macroeconomic Theory* (New York: The Macmillan Company, 1961), p. 421. Copyright © 1961 by The Macmillan Company, used by permission.

[6]Lawrence Abbott, *Economics and the Modern World* (2nd ed.; New York: Harcourt, Brace & World, Inc., 1967), p. 146.

important to our discussion, has been referred to as secular inflation. Martin Bronfenbrenner has written about long-term inflation as follows:

Secular inflation is a condition in which the general trend of prices is intermittently upward, like a flight of stairs. To put it differently, there is a jack or ratchet under the price level . . . which hinders prices from falling although permitting them to rise.

Under secular inflation, the annual rate of price increase is highly irregular. . . . There may be frequent breaks, in the form of periods of stability, or even occasional moderate declines such as occurred in the United States in 1949. These declines, however, do not cancel out the increases which preceded them and are themselves cancelled out by the increases which follow them in the course of secular inflation.

Because of its irregularity, secular inflation cannot usually be discounted adequately in ordinary commercial contracts, although "escalator clauses" in building contracts and "cost-of-living" clauses in wage contracts are important exceptions to this generalization. . . .

To sum up: under a regime of secular inflation, any war, calamity, or business boom causes a sharp rise in the general price level. Any recession or depression, however, results primarily in unemployment. Most costs and prices fall only moderately, if indeed they fall at all.[7]

There are still other ways to classify inflation. Ackley recognizes, in addition to demand-pull and wage-push, the following types: government inflation, credit inflation, imported inflation, and administered price or markup inflation.[8] Our purposes are met, however, by the two classifications described in the preceding paragraphs.

Since inflation has many faces and lends itself to numerous classifications, it also quite reasonably might have many causes. Economic literature is replete with discourses on the causes of inflation, and economists often disagree vigorously on the cause of a particular inflation—for example, that which occurred in this country in the 1955-58 period. One generally, but by no means unanimously, accepted cause of inflation is an increase in the money supply. Some economists consider an increase in the money supply to

[7]Martin Bronfenbrenner, "Some Neglected Implications of Secular Inflation," in Kenneth K. Kurihara, ed., Post Keynesian Economics (New Brunswick, N.J.: Rutgers University Press, 1954), pp. 31-33, used by permission. To the two exceptions mentioned in the third paragraph quoted might be added the variable annuity and the automatic increase in the amount of certain coverages during the period of a homeowner's policy. Bronfenbrenner went on to observe (p. 32) that if we could with certainty discount the secular inflation the results would be chaotic.

[8]Ackley, Macroeconomic Theory, pp. 421-59, used by permission.

be more nearly a symptom than a cause. Others do not necessarily associate inflation with an increase in the money supply.[9]

Despite the lack of unanimity regarding increased money supply as a cause of inflation, the matter is mentioned often enough to justify our making it a principal concern in this chapter. The relevance of money supply to inflation has been summarized pointedly by Gottfried Haberler:

Let us start from the basic fact that there is no record in the economic history of the whole world, anywhere or at any time, of a serious and prolonged inflation which has not been accompanied and made possible, if not directly caused, by a large increase in the quantity of money. This generalization holds for developed as well as underdeveloped countries, for capitalist, precapitalist, and even centrally-planned economies. It is true that the velocity of circulation of money changes. . . . But except in periods of hyperinflation (which could not develop without a sharp and sustained rise in the quantity of money) a rise in velocity by itself has never caused, or substantially intensified, serious inflationary trouble.[10]

Haberler's statement is certainly a strong one, admitting no qualifications. We must notice, however, that he said that a case of inflation was necessarily a case of a large increase in the money supply; he did not say that a case of a large increase in the money supply was necessarily a case of inflation. The reason for his not asserting the latter, presumably, is that an increase in money supply could be, although it is not likely to be, matched by a commensurately large increase in the real production of goods and services which would absorb the increase in the money supply. His statement, however, does alert us to the inflationary dangers that arise from increasing the supply of money.

INFLATION AND THE ETHICAL PILLARS

John Maynard Keynes made an appropriate comment about Lenin's view of inflation:

---

[9]See Alvin H. Hansen, *Economic Issues of the 1960's* (New York: McGraw-Hill Book Company, Inc., 1960), p. 11, where he says that the popular argument of "more money chasing goods" failed to explain any of the postwar inflations. He was writing in 1960.

[10]Gottfried Haberler, *Inflation: Its Causes and Cures* (rev. and enl. ed.; Washington, D.C.: American Enterprise Institute for Public Policy Research, 1966), pp. 61-62, used by permission.

Lenin is said to have declared that the best way to destroy the Capitalist system was to debauch the currency. Lenin was certainly right. There is no subtler, no surer means of overturning the existing basis of society than to debauch the currency. The process engages all the hidden forces of economic law on the side of destruction, and does it in a manner which not one man in a million is able to diagnose.[11]

Debauchery is a strong word which means seduction from virtue or morality. One can feel confident that Lenin was talking about inflation, but one cannot be sure how much inflation for how long constitutes debauchery. In any case the quotation is sobering. If the process loosens "all the hidden forces of economic law" to promote destruction, it stands to reason that the behavioral changes wreaked may be drastic and that even a little bit of debauchery, if there be such a thing, can lead to a deterioration of morality. Let us now attempt to evaluate the damage inflation can inflict upon the ethical pillars of insurance and upon morality as related to insurance.

For one thing, inflation may place an individual under strong pressure to cheat. (Whether he will succumb to the pressure is another matter.) Inflation creates the pressure. The sharper the inflation and the longer it lasts, the greater may be the pressure. In respect to insurance the cheating may take the form of submission of improper claims or of dishonest conduct that causes a loss. Examples of the first are false claims (such as filing for a loss under a valuable papers policy when no loss occurred), exaggerated claims (such as falsifying the amount of a windstorm loss or an automobile collision loss), multiple claims for the same loss without any offset as clearly called for in one or more policies (such as claiming a medical payments expense under two group contracts), or deliberate enlargement of a loss by the insured (such as malingering under a disability income insurance arrangement). Examples of the second may be burglary, robbery, embezzlement or arson.

The extent of the cheating under the first set of examples by its very nature cannot be ascertained. Whatever cheating does exist may stem from many reasons other than the pressures created by inflation. Similarly, losses of the second type can seldom be identified with inflation. Nevertheless, the point here is that inflation can

---

[11]As quoted by Bronfenbrenner, "Some Neglected Implications of Secular Inflation," p. 31, used by permission.

motivate individuals to cheat, which in turn affects claims payments by insurance companies.

One of the motives to cheat stems from the feeling that inflation essentially is unfair, that it does not fall with equal severity on the members of a society, and that the inequality is unrelated to merit or effort. Moreover, people recognize that the ills produced by inflation are not necessarily, or even likely to be, corrected by a possible subsequent deflation. Those who suffer most as an inflation progresses may be beyond the help that a later deflation could bring.

It is common knowledge that inflation penalizes individuals using fixed dollar stored purchasing power and rewards those in a position to enjoy current earnings. It punishes creditors and blesses debtors. It disturbs society's traditional way of providing economic compensation. It causes some individuals to suffer and others to prosper without any necessary regard to their contributions to current or past production. It is a nesting ground for speculations in price movements.

With some prices more stable than others for institutional reasons (such as the prices set by a public service commission), inflation repeatedly alters the relationship among individual prices. Rational planning of conduct becomes increasingly difficult and, as a result, efficiency declines. Maneuvering on the part of vested interests created by the inflation, when those vested interests themselves are unstable and transitory, renders decision making even more difficult.[12]

Willard Thorp and Richard Quandt, in their book *The New Inflation*, mention that individuals may refer to inflation as inequitable, immoral, or as a thief. In somewhat formal fashion the authors set forth three major propositions that include most of the reasons advanced in this discussion as to why inflation is felt to be unfair. The following passage is an excerpt:

---

[12]George Katona of the Survey Research Center at the University of Michigan elaborates on the peculiar nature of inflationary expectations. He says that since they are one-way expectations, they are in sharp contrast to the common forms of business expectations. People generally seem to feel that under given conditions the prices can only go up, not down. Furthermore, the inflationary expectations are usually trend expectations in that people are generally convinced that the process is cumulative with a given price increase not fulfilling the expectations but only signifying that additional increases are imminent. See "Attitudes and Behavior in Inflation," in George Katona, *Psychological Analysis of Economic Behavior* (New York: McGraw-Hill Book Company, Inc., 1951), p. 261.

(a)   Inflation redistributes real purchasing power from those whose incomes rise less rapidly than the prices they pay to those whose incomes rise more rapidly than the prices they pay.

(b)   Inflation redistributes real purchasing power from those whose assets rise less rapidly in value to those whose assets appreciate more rapidly.

As a special case of (b), one may state as the final proposition (c) Inflation redistributes real purchasing power from creditors to debtors.[13]

For these reasons many people apparently feel that inflation is fundamentally and terribly unfair—so unfair as to justify their taking protective measures, even to the point of cheating when in different circumstances they might have an aversion to it.

Another reason why people cheat stems from their conviction that the government is cheating them and that their only defense is to respond in kind. Correctly or incorrectly, a person may become convinced that the government is aiding and abetting the inflation which is hurting him and that the government has the power to halt the inflation or at least slow it without other ill effects. He may believe that government leaders, for their own selfish reasons or because of the pressure placed on them by certain groups, are deliberately letting him suffer the higher prices even though they could easily take corrective action. Whether he is correct does not matter in terms of his motivation so long as he holds this conviction. With such an attitude, he may be motivated to lower his own standards or to feel justified in breaching them in the face of what he regards as the government's breach of good faith with him.

Popular economic literature makes much of the idea that inflation really amounts to cheating by the government, that it is a cowardly form of taxation permitting a government to spend money it dares not attempt to raise by taxation. This literature emphasizes that modern governmental deficit financing through creation of new bank credit need be really no different in effect than the older techniques of getting new money by coining the scrapings from old coins or by simply printing more paper. Couched in emotional terms, these discussions doubtless are quite powerful in causing many persons to conclude that by allowing an inflation to progress a government really does cheat.

[13]Willard L. Thorp and Richard E. Quandt, *The New Inflation* (New York: McGraw-Hill Book Company, Inc., 1959), p. 194. Copyright © 1959 by McGraw-Hill Book Company. Used with permission of McGraw-Hill Book Company. See also C. Lowell Harriss, "Inflation's Hidden Effects," *Tax Review*, vol. 28 (July, 1967), pp. 27-30.

Let us look at three of these popular treatments. The first appears in a highly readable little book entitled *An Inflation Primer*, written by Melchior Palyi. Palyi used to be a banker in Germany. At the peak of Germany's hyperinflation in 1923 he was a college teacher in Berlin. Understandably, he takes an exceedingly negative view of inflation. Among his vivid statements is the following:

This should indicate that [the decline in purchasing power] is what a former French premier, Paul Reynaud, called "legalized robbery." Indeed, it is confiscation without compensation. The victims are deprived of their purchasing power. This is "robbery" on a national scale—a surreptitious levy on liquid income and wealth, raised in a haphazard fashion, with no regard for ability to pay, no respect for rule of law, for equity and justice. It penalizes the saver, especially, and the honest producer, while the lucky operator and the political manipulator may reap unearned rewards. It is legalized, of course, the government itself being the culprit. . . .

"Legalized robbery" is a universal feature of counterfeit money, one created by government fiat. It is the product of deliberate, arbitrary measures. . . . It generates in the political arena, from which the effects spread to the market place. The powers that rule over fiscal and central banking policies determine, in effect, whether there will be inflation, how much, and for how long.[14]

Henry Hazlitt develops much the same point by referring to "the Great Swindle." His "Business Tides" column in *Newsweek* was incorporated into a small book in which appears the following:

Inflation is nothing but a great swindle, and . . . this swindle is practiced in varying degrees . . . by nearly every government in the world. This swindle erodes the purchasing power of everybody's income and . . . savings. It is a concealed tax, and the most vicious of all taxes. It taxes the incomes and savings of the poor by the same percentage as the incomes and savings of the rich. It falls with greatest force precisely on the thrifty, on the aged, on

---

[14]Melchior Palyi, *An Inflation Primer* (Chicago: Henry Regnery Company, 1961), pp. 2-3, used by permission. Palyi's intense feelings about inflation doubtless were strongly influenced by the experience he had in living through Germany's runaway inflation. He begins his book by recounting an episode:

In the summer of 1923, the German inflation was rapidly heading toward the grand finale: total repudiation of the currency. As an instructor in a Berlin college, this writer drew a *monthly* salary that had been raised from an inflated 10,000 marks or so in early 1922 to 10,000,000 marks by July, 1923, and the whole amount was paid twice a month; then, once a week; then once each day. The next step to meet the skyrocketing living costs was to pay us twice a day, in the morning and in the afternoon.

Just after 5 P.M. one day in late August, 1923, I was walking down the staircase of the school, carrying the day's second haul of ten million marks (the day's first paid for a modest lunch), when the professor of physics overtook me. "Are you taking the streetcar?" he asked. "Yes," I said. "Let's hurry. The fare will be raised by 6 P.M. We may not be able to pay it" (p. 1).

those who cannot protect themselves by speculation or by demanding and getting higher money incomes. . . .

Why does this swindle go on? It goes on because governments wish to spend . . . but lack the courage to tax as much as they spend. It goes on . . . because governments wish to buy the votes of some of us while concealing from the rest of us that those votes are being bought with our money.[15]

The third example comes from a book by Graham Hutton. He traces in some detail the history of inflation, showing it to be used often by governments under severe pressure for money. He writes:

The interests of all who save, contribute, build, and create for a long-term future are set against those dependent for profit on the highest "velocity of circulation" of money. No one can trust money or government. Society and its once firm institutions begin to flounder in deepening flux. . . . There can be no justice or equity in a . . . governmental policy which deliberately and arbitrarily injures owners of one kind of savings and investment for the future . . . and favours another . . . which alters the terms of all contracts and other legal arrangements for property rights in the future, which does such things without public justification and explanation, and at arbitrary but secret rates of tax. The ensuing sense of injustice in the many injured groupings of the society, the ensuing social stresses and tensions, rise with formidable, explosive force, the faster and farther inflation goes.[16]

Once again the point is not whether these statements are accurate but rather the extent to which they reflect or shape popular attitudes. They clearly show the possibility that an individual may rationalize what he regards—and perhaps properly so—as a gross breach of good faith on the part of the government into an excuse for his own indiscretions.

Still another motive for cheating produced by inflation is the desire to evade the social controls that inflation eventually brings. Persistent price increases evoke demands for public control of wages and prices. The result can be a governmental attempt at setting wages and prices of goods and services and an attempt at rationing critical goods and services in short supply. In such a circumstance, individuals are placed under extreme pressure to circumvent the system. Black markets, hidden payoffs, complicated reciprocations,

[15]Henry Hazlitt, *What You Should Know About Inflation* (Princeton, N.J.: D. Van Nostrand Company, Inc., 1965), pp. 76-77. Copyright © 1960 by Litton Educational Publishing, Inc., used by permission of Van Nostrand Reinhold Company.

[16]Graham Hutton, *Inflation and Society* (London: George Allen and Unwin, Ltd., 1960), pp. 77-78, used by permission.

and other arrangements including theft are likely to become commonplace. The situation is aptly described by Pierre A. Rinfret:

It [inflation] fosters, condones, necessitates, and rewards dishonesty. Faced with inflation people grasp for ways to avoid the deterioration in their purchasing power. The system goes cash because cash cannot be traced. Bank deposits are siphoned out of the country and end up as numbered accounts. The under-the-table payment, the cash fringe benefit, the payoff for services rendered become part of the inflation-avoidance scheme. Tax returns are phonied and more and more payments are made outside the system. Cash, invisible and untraceable, becomes a way of life. The phony insurance claim, the doctored medical bill, the receipt for services never rendered, the hiding of income become the established norm. . . .

Cheating is an inflation hedge and in the process you corrupt the morals, the mores, and the decency of the people. They cheat each other and their government because their government is cheating them.[17]

The evidence that inflation produces a cheating society is fuzzy at best. By its nature, cheating—especially successful cheating—is difficult to document. Yet, the evidence is at least substantive enough to warrant alertness to the prospect that widespread cheating may occur in face of unchecked and continued inflation, with resulting serious effects on insurance loss ratios.

Inflation causes deterioration of the ethical foundation of insurance in a second way—by promoting loss of incentive. Inflation characteristically produces or at least is accompanied by rising taxes. The combination of rising taxes and rising prices, with the burdens of each perhaps falling quite unevenly over the populace, can insidiously but surely sap incentive.

Hutton gives a historical account of inflation, describing the inflation and taxation during the latter days of the Roman Empire:

Heavy taxes on a minority of taxpayers, plus debasement of the currency, gave the legions [the army] and the bureaucracy an advantage over all other classes, until they broke the Empire to pieces. Only one small privileged class—the senatorial—kept its former advantages . . . by contracting out of its traditional task of government and going "back to the land." Thus it became the forerunner of the feudal barons.

Most taxpayers were urban. All of them were a tiny but economically important and productive minority. As their burdens grew, [they] . . . pre-

[17]Pierre A. Rinfret, "Inflation—So What?" *Institutional Investor*, part 1, vol. 2 (August, 1968), pp. 17-18, and part 2, vol. 2 (September, 1968), pp. 19-20. Quotations from August issue, p. 18 and September issue, p. 19, used by permission.

ferred slavery, flight, or the advent of the barbarians. This killed trade, commerce, capital and cities. Outside the cities, in the countryside, legionnaires in their camps and the biggest senatorial landlords on their *latifundia* were exempt from taxes. So progressive debasement of the currency and penal taxation to secure political power and support ended in degradation and disintegration of the State. It was a vast paradox. Power itself, ultimately, deserted the State . . . and took to the smaller localities. Thus came the Dark and Middle Ages of servitude and status.[18]

One can imagine the fate of insurance in such a disintegrative set of circumstances. Rome, in fact, developed a rudimentary system of insurance that did disintegrate, probably long before the disintegration of certain other less sensitive parts of the apparatus of the state. The difficulties of the Roman Empire, to be sure, stemmed from much more than inflation. Even so, inflation apparently was one of the major problems, and a serious consequence of it was the loss of incentive among the productive elements of the society. Edward Gibbon, noting the degradation into which the Roman society had fallen, wrote: "If all the Barbarian conquerors had been annihilated in the same hour, their total destruction would not have restored the empire of the West; and, if Rome still survived, she survived loss of freedom, of virtue, and of honor."[19] Even though social organization in the United States is vastly different from that of ancient Rome, we might find a lesson here for ourselves, especially in regard to how inflation can enervate a society.

Imagine how a person might feel who has never known any significant price deflation and who has seen very little price stability but who has spent his entire life subject to secular inflation. In the course of a few years, given recent and present price patterns, we could easily have a whole generation of such adults in this country.

These individuals conceivably could have very different attitudes about many things than those of us who have seen prices fall as well as rise. Persons in the inflation generation, for example, could have a much higher positive time preference than that held by other generations. They consequently could be willing to discount the future at a much higher rate than is now customary. They could be much less apprehensive of debt and could find bankruptcy much less repugnant. They could be much more disposed than most people

[18]Hutton, *Inflation and Society*, p. 20, used by permission.
[19]Edward Gibbon, *The History of the Decline and Fall of the Roman Empire* (New York: The Heritage Press, 1946), vol. 2, p. 1,103.

now are to the views of hedonism (as discussed in Chapter 8) that pleasure is the chief end of man. They could be more likely to eschew sacrifice and ambition. They could so despair of realizing goals as to set few; they could have a sense of futility in long-range planning. In short, they could become creatures with much more limited time horizons than the horizons to which we are accustomed.

Should such changes occur, the consequences for our current society could be dreadful. In our discussion of inflation and cheating we considered cheating principally in terms of its effect on insurance losses. The consequences for insurance could be even more serious should widespread loss of incentive to produce occur. As we saw in Chapter 2, insurance requires, among other things, an acquisitiveness, a desire to achieve, an apprehension about the future, and a sense of personal responsibility. If inflation, by undermining one's incentive, leaves one bereft of the qualities just mentioned, inflation then also takes away much of one's enthusiasm for insurance. The possible changes in attitude toward insurance might be only one of many fundamental changes accompanying a major loss of incentive.

Let us visualize how someone might regard the purchasing power of his money assuming that he believed inflation would proceed indefinitely at a particular rate. A helpful technique is to apply the concept of "half life" to a depreciating currency.[20] As we know, the expression is used in nuclear physics to refer to the period of time required, given any starting point, for a quantity of radioactive material to lose one-half its radioactivity. In our context the expression can refer to the period of time required under an assumed average annual rate of inflation for a currency to lose one-half of its purchasing power. The half life under various assumed annual rates of inflation is as follows: for 1 percent, 69.7 years; 2 percent, 35.0 years; 3 percent, 23.4 years; 4 percent, 17.7 years; 5 percent, 14.2 years; and 6 percent, 11.9 years.[21]

It is sobering to think that during the preparation of this book the unadjusted "All Items" Consumer Price Index was rising at an annual rate of more than 4 percent. Thus, the half life[22] of our

---

[20]This interesting application was made by Pierre A. Rinfret in "Inflation Hedges," a two-installment piece appearing in the *Institutional Investor*, vol. 2 (June, 1968), pp. 17-18 (July, 1968), pp. 17-18.

[21]Rinfret, "Inflation Hedges" (June, 1968), p. 17.

[22]In this use of the concept of half life an increase in the intensity of inflation shortens the half life, whereas in the usual meaning of the term an increase in the intensity of radioactivity lengthens the half life.

currency, on the assumption of continued inflation at about this rate, was already down to the vicinity of 16 years.

Serious reflection about such a potentially rapid loss of purchasing power might cause even the most inveterate individual to modify his attitudes rather sharply. His preference for pleasure now as against pleasure in the future, his belief concerning whether long-term goals are really attainable, his sense of responsibility for the outcome of events in the far-distant future could undergo substantial changes—all away from rather than toward use of insurance. The stronger his conviction about the future pace and persistence of inflation, the more his attitudes might be altered.

Let us pause to admit that one could certainly take quite a different point of view about inflation, ethics, and morality than that just discussed. He could argue that inflation, instead of producing cheating and loss of incentive, simply spurs most people to even greater acquisitiveness, apprehension, and responsibility in their zeal to stay ahead of the inflation. He could argue further that many people conceivably could be even more interested in certain types of insurance to cover the increasing value of the things people acquired as they "took flight from cash." Such a pick-up certainly could occur in the intermediate range of time. The growth of insurance premium volume in this country in recent years during intermittent inflation could be used to substantiate such a point of view.

The retort, however, would have to be that secular inflation is still too young to take the toll that it will be able to exact when it matures. Likewise, empirical evidence is too unseasoned to permit us to take comfort in the fact that insurance premium volume appears to be still growing healthily in many lines. The gap in our knowledge prevents us from evaluating what the demand for and the availability of insurance ultimately will be in a modern industrialized society that experiences prolonged inflation at an average annual rate of, say, 4 percent or more. Until these figures are obtained, we can afford little smugness. One could argue forcefully that if inflation persists, even a strong individual will eventually capitulate and demonstrate the attitudes discussed here. Inflation may well be a matter of wearing down one's character and initiative. This discussion should not be construed as a prediction that such deterioration will come to pass. It is merely an effort to recognize the possibility that inflation will erode the ethical foundation of insurance. We cannot make a prediction about moral behavior until we formulate some outlook as to the most probable direction of price trends in the future.

A LOOK AT THE RECORD

As the basis for our speculations, let us cursorily examine (1) the record of price movements in the United States over the long-range past and (2) the record of price movements in other countries during the 1950s and 1960s. Although the data are incomplete, not easily comparable from one period to another, and susceptible to all the weaknesses of index numbers, they are still revealing.

Two series of index numbers can be used to obtain a fairly good perception of the long-term behavior of consumer prices in the United States since 1820. One is the Federal Reserve Bank of New York Cost of Living Index, which covers the period from 1820 to 1913.[23] The other is the familiar Consumer Price Index ("All Items") prepared by the U.S. Department of Labor, giving data from 1913 to the present. Index numbers for selected years are shown in Table 17 and Figure 8.

If all of the limitations of index numbers are overlooked, particularly those that apply to the Federal Reserve Bank of New York Cost of Living Index, the figures can tell us several interesting things:

1.   Not much sustained inflation occurred in this country before World War I. On the basis of the Federal Reserve Bank of New York index the average annual compound rate of increase from 1820 to 1913 was only about one-half of 1 percent. Several fairly substantial fluctuations occurred during this long period of time. For example, an increase larger than the total 1820-1913 spread of 35 index points occurred between 1860 and 1865 when the index jumped from 61 to 102, or 41 index points. During this five-year

---

[23]Although this index is quite useful in suggesting in crude terms the timing and degree of inflation, it should not be relied upon in judgments calling for close tolerances. The index is simply a splicing of several indexes that have been reduced to a common base. They did not cover the same commodities and did not apply to the same locations; furthermore, some of them applied to wholesale rather than retail prices. For the period 1820-59 the index is based largely on Alvin H. Hansen's wholesale price index. It also uses Roland P. Falkner's wholesale price index covering from 1840 to 1891; Wesley C. Mitchell's "necessaries of life" index of 60 items for 1860-79; W. Randolph Burgess's index for 1880-89; Paul Douglas's "Most Probable Index of the Total Cost of Living for Workingmen" for 1890-1909; and the cost-of-living index for the Commonwealth of Massachusetts for 1910-12. The index and explanatory notes pertaining to its construction appear in U.S. Department of Commerce, Bureau of the Census, *Historical Statistics of the United States—Colonial Times to 1957* (Washington, D.C.: U.S. Govt. Printing Office, 1960), pp. 111, 127.

TABLE 17

Consumer Price Index Numbers,
Selected Years, 1820-1969

Year	Index A*	Index B+
1820	65	—
1825	58	—
1830	54	—
1835	60	—
1840	60	—
1845	54	—
1850	54	—
1855	67	—
1860	61	—
1865	102	—
1870	91	—
1875	86	—
1880	80	—
1885	75	—
1890	78	—
1895	73	—
1900	80	—
1905	87	—
1910	96	—
1913	100	—
1913	100	34.5
1915	—	35.4
1920	—	69.8
1925	—	61.1
1930	—	58.2
1935	—	47.8
1940	—	48.8
1945	—	62.7
1950	—	83.8
1955	—	93.3
1960	—	103.1
1965	—	109.9
1968	—	121.2
1969	—	127.7

*Index A is the Federal Reserve Bank of New York Cost of Living Index, with 1913 = 100.
+Index B is the "Consumer Price Index—All Items" as compiled by the U.S. Department of Labor, with 1957-1959 = 100.

Sources: For Index A, U.S. Department of Commerce, Bureau of the Census, *Historical Statistics of the United States—Colonial Times to 1957* (Washington, D.C.: U.S. Govt. Printing Office, 1960), p. 127. For Index B, U.S. Department of Commerce, *Business Statistics, 1967—A Supplement to the Survey of Current Business* (16th biennial ed.; Washington, D.C.: U.S. Govt. Printing Office, 1967), p. 38; and current issues of *Survey of Current Business.*

FIGURE 8

Consumer Price Index Numbers, Selected Years, 1820-1969

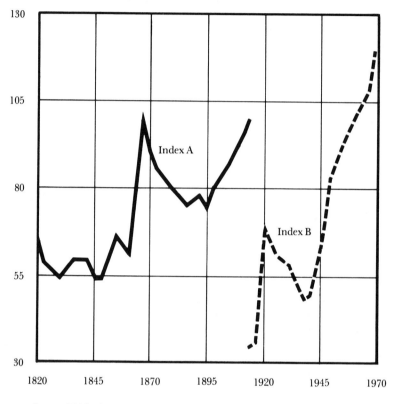

Source: Table 17.

period the average annual compound rate of increase was almost 11 percent. From 1865 to 1870 the average annual compound rate of decrease was about 3.4 percent. Between 1870 and 1913 the average annual compound rate of increase was only about 0.2 percent. The total price rise for the 1820-1913 period was only about 54 percent of the 1820 figure. On the whole, the small amount of inflation that occurred during this period was most unusual.

2.   The end of World War II marked the beginning of the first major postwar period during which prices did not fall significantly upon termination of the fighting. Index A, for example, dropped

from 102 in 1865 to 91 by 1870 to 75 by 1885. The widespread expectation by many economists and others that prices would fall in comparable fashion after World War II was a mammouth error. Probably at no other time have so many economists been so wrong about anything as they were about this.

3.   Between 1940 and 1969 prices increased to about 2.6 times their 1940 level. The average annual compound rate of increase in the 1940s was almost 7 percent; it slowed to about 2.1 percent during the 1950s. It averaged about the same for the 1960-68 period. During the 1960-65 period, however, it was only about 1 percent but moved up to about 3.5 percent for the 1965-68 period. The gain was a bit more than 4 percent for 1968 and more than 5 percent in 1969. Clearly, the pace accelerated in the middle 1960s. For the entire 1940-69 period the average annual compound rate of increase was well in excess of 3 percent.

4.   The table, showing prices only at five-year intervals, hides some of the cyclical and other nonsecular movements. For example, very small declines occurred in 1949 and 1955. In the main, however, the five-year figures depict the overall pattern.

5.   Secular inflation above 2 percent per year is a relatively new phenomenon in this country, manifesting itself in the late 1940s after the removal of World War II price controls and revealing strong tendencies in the second half of the 1960s.

Table 18 and Figure 9 present the long-term behavior of wholesale prices with three indexes used to measure respective periods. The Warren and Pearson index (Index A) shows considerable cyclical and other nonsecular variation, although the degree of yearly fluctuation is not apparent in the abbreviated version given in Table 18. For all of its movement, however, the 1890 figure of 82 stood at only 20.6 percent above its 1749 starting point of 68. In its maximum fluctuation throughout the entire period the index moved from a low of 60 in 1750 to a high of 226 in 1779. The high was about 3.77 times the low. The index dropped rapidly after the Revolutionary War and came to another peak of 112 in 1814 as the consequence of another war. It dropped sharply during the next seven years to 102 in 1821 and then, with numerous oscillations, moved to a low of 75 in 1843. This was the lowest point for the index in the 1800s. It surged again during and after the Civil War, but by the mid-1880s it returned to its midcentury level. From 1749 to 1890 the average annual compound rate of increase was only about 0.1 percent.

TABLE 18

Wholesale Price Index Numbers,
Selected Years, 1749 to 1969

Year	Index A*	Index B+	Index C‡
1749	68	—	—
1750	60	—	—
1755	66	—	—
1760	79	—	—
1765	72	—	—
1770	77	—	—
1775	75	—	—
1780	225	—	—
1785	92	—	—
1790	90	—	—
1795	131	—	—
1800	129	—	—
1805	141	—	—
1810	131	—	—
1815	170	—	—
1820	106	—	—
1825	103	—	—
1830	91	—	—
1835	100	—	—
1840	95	—	—
1845	83	—	—
1850	84	—	—
1855	110	—	—
1860	93	—	—
1865	185	—	—
1870	135	—	—
1875	118	—	—

(Continued)

The twentieth century performance of wholesale prices has been considerably different. The 1969 Department of Labor index number (where 1957-59 = 100; see Index C) was about 2.9 times as large as the 1913 figure. This difference produces an average annual compound increase of about 2 percent. The average rate of increase for the 1940-69 period amounted to about 3.5 percent per year. As with consumer prices, however, much of the increase came in the 1940s, with the average annual compound rate of increase from 1940 to 1950 being about 7.3 percent. As Table 18 and Figure 9 show, wholesale prices were remarkably stable from 1957 through 1964, but they began moving up rather briskly in 1965. Recent yearly figures show that wholesale prices declined slightly in 1949, 1953,

Table 18, continued

Year	Index A*	Index B+	Index C‡
1880	100	—	—
1885	85	—	—
1890	82	56.2	—
1895	—	48.8	—
1900	—	56.1	—
1905	—	60.1	—
1910	—	70.4	—
1915	—	69.5	38.0
1920	—	—	84.5
1925	—	—	56.6
1930	—	—	47.3
1935	—	—	43.8
1940	—	—	43.0
1945	—	—	57.9
1950	—	—	86.8
1955	—	—	93.2
1960	—	—	100.7
1965	—	—	102.5
1968	—	—	109.1
1969	—	—	113.0

*Index A is the Warren and Pearson Wholesale Price Index (All Commodities) for 1749-1890, with 1910-14 = 100. The price data pertain mainly to New York City and were compiled in large part from newspapers and other publications.

+Index B is the U.S. Department of Labor Wholesale Price Index (All Commodities) for 1890-1951, with 1926 = 100. See explanatory note on pp. 103-4 of the source.

‡Index C is similarly a U.S. Department of Labor Wholesale Price Index (All Commodities), this time on the familiar base of 1957-59 = 100.

Sources: For Indexes A and B, U.S. Department of Commerce, Bureau of the Census, *Historical Statistics of the United States—Colonial Times to 1957* (Washington, D.C.: U.S. Govt. Printing Office, 1960), pp. 115-17; see also notes, pp. 102-4. For Index C, U.S. Department of Commerce, *Business Statistics, 1967—A Supplement to the Survey of Current Business* (16th biennial ed.; Washington, D.C.: U.S. Govt. Printing Office, 1967), p. 41; and current issues of *Survey of Current Business.*

1961, and 1963—but not enough in the latter two years to eliminate the likelihood of random reporting errors.

At the risk of redundancy, the following observations can be made about the history of inflation in the United States:

1.   Prior to World War II, the inflation that occurred was not predominantly secular. Rather, it was associated with wars and/or the business cycles. After each rise, the price level declined, although not necessarily to the previous low.

2.   The customary deflation did not occur after World War II. Instead, the inflation progressed rapidly during the late 1940s and then slowed until the mid-1960s when it started moving rapidly again.

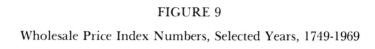

FIGURE 9

Wholesale Price Index Numbers, Selected Years, 1749-1969

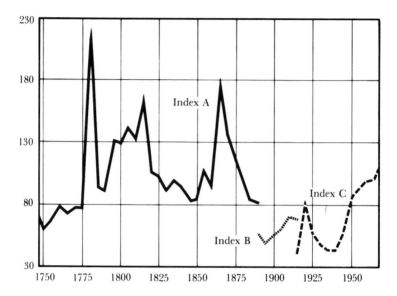

Source: Table 18.

3.   No really significant decline in consumer prices has occurred since 1933, and aside from a minor dip in the 1952-55 period, wholesale prices have followed a roughly similar pattern.

Turning now to the recent price behavior in other countries, we see that, compared to most of them, the United States has fared quite well in avoiding rapid inflation. The fact is that inflation during the last decade or so has plagued most of the countries of the world, just as it has plagued most civilizations since man began to use money. Table 19, summarized from U.N. statistics, shows the recent consumer price history for the United States and 60 other major countries. The appendix provides comparable information about 64 other countries or territories. Table 19 and the appendix are bulky, but they do enable the patient observer to discern a widespread and distinct upsweep of consumer prices since 1953. Although the timing and the degree of the upsweep are not uniform from country to country, the dominant pattern is unmistakable.

The rates for several of the countries listed in Table 19 increased rather briskly in 1963 and 1964.[24] Although the rates of change vary considerably, 19 of the countries outside the Soviet bloc had index numbers within the 101-through-110 range for 1966; 20 fell within the 111-through-120 range; and 16 were above 120. With the exception of the Soviet bloc countries, where officially recognized prices have little necessary significance in the production and distribution of goods and services, most of the countries listed in Table 19 or the appendix show a substantial inflation.[25]

Since Table 19 is so detailed, Table 20 has been prepared to show the total percentage change in the index numbers and the average annual rate of change for each country. Column 1 of Table 20 shows the change in the index for each country from the earliest reported year to the latest reported year, expressed as a percentage of the *earliest* reported index number. This arrangement affords some indication of the magnitude of the price movements in a given country. The table also shows the average annual rate of change in the index numbers (always an increase except for the Soviet bloc countries). The average annual rate of change is expressed in two ways. In column 2 it is expressed as a percentage of the index number for the earliest reported year. The rate was arrived at by dividing the percentage change (column 1) by the number of years involved. The figures have the advantage of showing for the hyperinflationary countries the tremendously large average increases in the price levels in relation to the price level of the earliest reported year. In column 3 the average annual rate of change is given in traditional fashion. Each of these figures represents the average annual rate at which the earliest reported index number would have to grow (or decline) in compound fashion to equal the latest reported index number within the number of years specified. The compounding is annual. As can be seen, the column 2 method produces a rate that is increasingly higher than the column 3 rate as the absolute size of the rate and the length of the averaging period increase.[26]

---

[24]Table 19 shows no column for 1963 since, for most of the countries listed, 1963 is the base year in which the index number stands at 100.

[25]The United Nations data, of course, do not indicate whether black markets existed in the price-controlled countries or, if such markets did exist, the recent price movements in them. One can notice also that no data are available for Red China, Albania, Rumania, Cuba, Nepal, and certain other political entities.

[26]For negative rates of change the column 2 figures, if carried to more places, would be closer to zero than the column 3 figures.

TABLE 19

Consumer Price Index Numbers for 61 Major Countries, 1953 to 1966

	1953	1957	1958	1959	1960	1961	1962	1964	1965	1966
Algeria (1961)*	71	75	84	92	97	100	104	—	—	—
Argentina	9	15	20	44	55	63	81	122	157	207
Australia	81	91	92	94	97	100	99	102	106	110
Austria	—	—	87	88	90	93	97	104	109	111
Belgium	87	93	94	95	96	97	98	104	108	113
Bolivia	—	64	66	79	88	95	101	110	113	121
Brazil	6	13	15	20	27	38	58	187	303	444
Bulgaria	124	96	96	94	94	95	98	100	100	100
Canada	87	92	94	95	96	97	98	102	104	108
Ceylon	93	94	97	97	95	96	98	103	103	103
Chile	5	30	37	51	57	61	69	146	188	231
China (Taiwan)	—	—	68	75	89	96	98	100	100	102
Colombia	40	53	61	66	68	74	76	118	122	146
Congo	—	63	72	77	79	85	89	100	104	110
Costa Rica	80	88	90	91	91	95	97	103	103	103
Czechoslovakia	—	103	103	100	99	98	99	101	102	102
Denmark	—	82	82	84	85	88	95	104	—	—
Dominican Republic	89	93	91	91	88	85	92	102	100	101
Ecuador	85	86	87	87	88	92	94	104	107	113
Finland	67	80	86	87	90	91	95	110	116	120
France	—	—	—	—	—	—	95	103	106	109
Germany, East	—	—	102	100	99	99	100	100	100	100
Germany, West	82	87	89	90	91	94	97	102	106	110
Ghana	76	80	80	82	82	88	96	112	144	151
Greece	—	—	—	94	96	97	97	101	104	109
Haiti	91	103	103	98	93	96	96	109	111	120
Hungary	—	—	100	98	100	100	101	101	103	106
Iceland	58	70	74	75	76	80	89	119	128	142
India	79	82	87	90	92	94	97	113	124	137
Indonesia	—	—	8	10	13	17	46	205	830	—
Iran	57	79	79	87	96	99	100	104	106	106
Ireland	78	87	91	91	91	94	98	107	112	115
Israel	56	75	77	79	80	86	94	105	113	122
Italy	75	83	86	85	87	89	93	106	111	113
Japan	—	—	—	—	—	—	—	104	111	116
Korea	19	67	64	67	72	78	83	129	147	—
Lebanon	80	87	91	94	98	97	98	—	—	—
Mexico	60	81	90	92	97	98	99	102	106	110
Morocco	72	81	83	84	88	90	95	104	108	107
Netherlands	—	—	—	—	94	94	96	106	111	117
New Zealand	76	86	90	93	94	96	98	103	107	110
Nigeria	—	—	—	—	91	96	101	102	107	116
Norway	75	84	88	90	90	93	97	106	110	114
Pakistan	85	91	94	91	97	98	99	104	110	118
Peru	—	—	—	—	83	88	94	110	129	141
Philippines	81	83	85	85	88	89	95	108	111	118

(Continued)

Table 19, continued

	1953	1957	1958	1959	1960	1961	1962	1964	1965	1966
Poland	96	91	94	95	96	97	99	101	102	103
Portugal	86	89	90	91	94	95	98	103	107	112
South Africa	82	90	93	94	96	97	99	103	106	110
Spain	—	—	—	—	—	87	92	107	121	129
Sweden	73	83	87	87	91	93	97	103	109	116
Switzerland	84	89	90	90	91	93	97	103	107	112
Syria	—	—	—	—	—	—	98	106	102	108
Turkey	38	58	65	82	87	90	93	103	107	116
USSR	104	98	100	99	99	98	99	100	99	99
United Arab Republic	99	101	101	101	102	102	99	104	119	130
United Kingdom	75	87	90	90	91	94	98	103	108	112
United States	87	92	94	95	97	98	99	101	103	106
Uruguay	—	—	—	—	—	—	—	143	224	389
Venezuela	92	90	95	99	97	100	100	101	103	103
Yugoslavia	—	68	71	72	79	86	95	112	150	185

*Year given in parentheses is the base year for an index rate of 100. When no year is given, 1963 = 100.

Source: Statistical Yearbook United Nations, 1967 (New York: United Nations, Department of Economic and Social Affairs, 1968), pp. 535-41. Table 177 in the yearbook indicates that for certain countries the index numbers apply only to a specific city or other limited area.

Table 20 elicits three generalizations. First, one cannot help but be depressed by the extreme inflation that has taken place in the major countries of the world. Indonesia, narrowly escaping a communist take-over, is the most conspicuous example. The index number reported for 1965 by Indonesia is over 102 times as large as its 1958 reported index number. While index numbers are not precise—especially at such a fast rate of increase—the numbers leave no doubt that the inflation has been severe. Argentina, Brazil, Chile, Uruguay, and Korea show inflation of runaway proportions. On the subject of Brazil, if 1949 were taken as the beginning year for a measure of price level change instead of 1953, the increase would amount to 87 times the beginning index number instead of 73. One can hardly visualize the violence of such a price movement. E. J. Mann used his experience as a financial analyst in Brazil for the Agency for International Development to write about the mammoth accounting difficulties created by this inflation. He made this comment in 1967:

If an inflation of about 2 per cent a year is troublesome in the United States, imagine an economy where annual monetary inflation over the past ten years has averaged 42 per cent and in the past five years amounted to a staggering 62 per cent (the average annual rate of increase). . . . Trends of

TABLE 20

Total Percentage Changes And Average Annual
Rates of Change in Consumer Price Index Numbers for
61 Major Countries, 1953-1966
(1963 = 100)

	Change Between Earliest and Latest Index Numbers* (1)	Average Annual Rate of Change (2)	Average Annual Compound Rate of Change+ (3)
Algeria (1953-62)‡	46.5%	5.2%	4.3%
Argentina	2,200.0	169.2	27.3
Australia	35.8	2.7	2.4
Austria (1958-66)	27.6	3.4	3.1
Belgium	29.9	2.3	2.0
Bolivia (1957-66)	89.1	9.9	7.3
Brazil	7,300.0	561.5	39.1
Bulgaria	-19.3	-1.5	-1.6
Canada	24.1	1.8	1.7
Ceylon	10.7	0.8	0.8
Chile	4,520.0	347.7	34.3
China (Taiwan) (1958-66)	50.0	6.2	5.2
Colombia	265.0	20.4	10.4
Congo (1957-66)	74.6	8.3	6.4
Costa Rica	28.7	2.2	2.0
Czechoslovakia (1957-66)	-1.0	-0.1	-0.1
Denmark (1957-64)	26.8	3.8	3.5
Dominican Republic	13.5	1.0	1.0
Ecuador	32.9	2.5	2.2
Finland	79.1	6.1	4.6
France (1962-66)	14.7	3.7	3.5
Germany, East (1958-66)	-2.0	-0.2	-0.3
Germany, West	34.1	2.6	2.3
Ghana	98.7	7.6	5.4
Greece (1959-66)	15.9	2.3	2.1
Haiti	31.9	2.4	2.2
Hungary (1958-66)	6.0	0.7	0.7
Iceland	144.8	11.1	7.1
India	73.4	5.6	3.7
Indonesia (1958-65)	10,275.0	1,467.8	93.8
Iran	85.9	6.6	4.9
Ireland	47.4	3.6	3.0
Israel	117.9	9.1	6.2
Italy	50.7	3.9	3.2
Japan (1964-66)	11.4	5.8	5.6
Korea (1953-65)	673.7	56.1	17.0
Lebanon (1953-62)	22.5	2.5	2.3
Mexico	83.3	6.4	4.8
Morocco	48.6	3.7	3.1

(Continued)

Table 20, continued

	Change Between Earliest and Latest Index Numbers*	Average Annual Rate of Change	Average Annual Compound Rate of Change+
Netherlands (1960-66)	24.5	4.1	3.7
New Zealand	44.7	3.4	2.9
Nigeria (1960-66)	27.5	4.6	4.1
Norway	52.0	4.0	3.3
Pakistan	38.8	3.0	2.5
Peru (1960-66)	69.9	11.6	9.2
Philippines	45.7	3.5	2.9
Poland	7.3	0.6	0.5
Portugal	30.2	2.3	2.1
South Africa	34.1	2.6	2.3
Spain (1961-66)	48.3	9.6	9.0
Sweden	58.9	4.5	3.6
Switzerland	33.3	2.6	2.2
Syria (1962-66)	10.2	2.5	2.5
Turkey	205.3	15.8	9.0
USSR	-4.8	-0.4	-0.3
United Arab Republic	31.3	2.4	2.1
United Kingdom	49.3	3.8	3.1
United States§	21.8	1.7	2.0
Uruguay (1964-66)	172.0	86.0	64.9
Venezuela	12.0	0.9	0.9
Yugoslavia (1957-66)	172.1	19.1	11.8
Averages	506.7**	53.5**	8.6**

*Expressed as a percentage of beginning index numbers.
+Average rate at which earliest index number would change to latest index number within the specified period.
‡Years given in parentheses are the years for the beginning and ending index numbers. When no years are given, they are 1953 and 1966, respectively.
§These are U.N. figures.
**Arithmetic average for the figures in the column, except for Bulgaria, Czechoslovakia, East Germany, Hungary, Poland, and USSR.
Source: Computed from data in Table 19.

this magnitude are not easily reversed, and the outlook from the world's fifth largest country which sprawls over half of South America is for continuing inflation. Hopefully, the rate will diminish. . . ."[27]

Second, average annual compound rates of change in Table 20 are noticeably large. Ignoring the Soviet bloc countries and computing an arithmetic average of the remaining figures in column 3—all of which are positive—one can strike an average of about 8.6 per-

[27]E. J. Mann, "Inflation and Accounting in Brazil," *Journal of Accountancy*, vol. 124 (November, 1967), p. 49, used by permission.

cent. If the figures for Argentina, Brazil, Chile, Colombia, Indonesia, Korea, Uruguay, and Yugoslavia (the eight countries with average annual compound rates of increase above 10 percent) are removed from the series, the adjusted arithmetic average is still about 3.6 percent. Since the countries represented in the computation of this average vary so in the size of their gross national product, the meaning of this sort of averaging may be highly questionable. Still, whatever the interpretation of the 3.6 percent average, it is too large to provide any suggestion that worldwide inflation is no problem. A frequency distribution of the average annual compound rates of the several countries further emphasizes the extent and the seriousness of worldwide inflation. This distribution for all the countries in Table 20, except those in the Soviet bloc, appears as Table 21.

Continuing our generalizations about Table 20, we can notice, finally, that no non-Soviet aligned countries except Canada, Ceylon, the Dominican Republic, and Venezuela reported an average annual compound increase of less than 2 percent. Thus, with the exception of Canada, every heavily industrialized nation in the free world has experienced recent inflation averaging at least 2 percent per year at a compound rate.

THE OUTLOOK

We now come to the most difficult part of the chapter, namely, a speculation about prices during the remainder of the twentieth century. If we are to have little additional secular inflation, we need not concern ourselves unduly about the ethical and moral consequences of inflation as they bear on insurance. If secular inflation is to continue over the years, however, the insurance industry and society generally face a fundamental problem that will grow increasingly serious as the inflation grows increasingly long and steep.

Cautioning ourselves at length, as we did in Chapter 1, about the perils of making statements about the future does not obviate the need to make a statement about future inflation. The statement is that indefinitely continuing secular inflation appears to be the most probable behavior of consumer prices in the United States throughout the long-range future. The inflation is likely to continue as long as we live in a society where wage and price decisions are made by individuals or groups rather than by the government. Since the rate of inflation is itself dependent on so many variables, one would appear naive to predict a rate of inflation that will occur from now

TABLE 21
Frequency Distribution of Average Annual Consumer Price Increase for 55 Major Countries, 1953-1966*

Average Annual Compound Rate of Increase	Countries+	
	Number	% of Total
0 —→ 1‡	2	3.6%
1 —→ 2	2	3.6
2 —→ 3	17	30.9
3 —→ 4	11	20.0
4 —→ 5	5	9.1
5 —→ 6	3	5.4
6 —→ 7	2	3.6
7 —→ 8	2	3.6
8 —→ 9	0	0.0
9 —→ 10	3	5.4
10 and over	8	14.5
Total	55	99.7§

*The average is for 1953-66 or for some shorter span within this period. Tables 19 and 20 indicate the relevant periods for the respective countries.

+All of the countries listed in Tables 19 and 20 except Bulgaria, Czechoslovakia, East Germany, Hungary, Poland, and the USSR are included.

‡ —→ is used to mean "up to but not including."

§Due to rounding inaccuracies, this does not add up to exactly 100 percent.

Source: Compiled from data in Table 20.

to the turn of the century. A statement that can be made without naivete, however, is that the average rate could easily be high enough to justify grave concern. Price movements over the last 30 years or so, as we have seen, offer quite a precedent.

Such a bald speculation merits little attention in itself, especially since it is made by one who has little claim to expertise in matters of price movements. Its credulity depends mainly on the arguments that can be offered to support it. Five supporting arguments are presented in the pages that follow.

National Commitment to Full Employment

The die was largely cast for an inflationary economy with the passage of the Employment Act of 1946. The act was passed by a majority vote of both parties in both houses of Congress. One part of the act reads as follows:

> The Congress declares that it is the continuing policy and responsibility of the Federal Government to use all practicable means consistent with its

155

needs and obligations and other essential considerations of national policy, with the assistance and cooperation of industry, agriculture, labor, and State and local governments, to coordinate and utilize all its plans, functions, and resources for the purpose of creating and maintaining, in a manner calculated to foster and promote free competitive enterprise and the general welfare, conditions under which there will be afforded useful employment opportunities, including self-employment, for those able, willing, and seeking to work, and to promote maximum employment, production, and purchasing power.[28]

Time has demonstrated that the act's avowed objectives of promoting the maximum employment, productivity, and purchasing power are not necessarily compatible. The name of the act suggests the national sentiment and order of priorities in the event of conflict. Arthur F. Burns has suggested that the act be amended to include explicitly the objective of maintenance of reasonable price stability;[29] he argues that making the statement explicit would create a moral force for price stability. The fact that the proposed amendment has not been made is some evidence that price stability is not really considered by the public and the policy makers to be as important as full employment.

The nature of the incompatibility between full employment and price stability has been summarized succinctly by Michael E. Levy, manager of the Fiscal and Monetary Department of the National Industrial Conference Board.[30] In early 1966 the seasonally adjusted percentage of the unemployed civilian labor force dropped below 4 percent after having been as high as 5.7 percent for 1963. By the end of 1968 the seasonally adjusted rate of unemployment was about 3.3 percent of the civilian labor force.[31] The drop in 1966 came after nine years of unemployment above 4 percent. After commenting on the progress in reducing unemployment, Levy states the issue as follows:

Within this changed environment [of reduced unemployment], one of the most important questions confronting the policymakers is: how far can expansionary economic policies be pursued in the United States as a means

---

[28]*Employment Act of 1946, United States Code Annotated* (1963), Title 15, Section 1021, p. 529.

[29]Arthur F. Burns, *Prosperity Without Inflation* (New York: Fordham University Press, 1957), p. 71.

[30]Michael E. Levy, "Full Employment and Inflation: A 'Trade-Off' Analysis," *Conference Board Record*, vol. 3 (December, 1966), pp. 17-27.

[31]*Monthly Labor Review*, vol. 92 (February, 1969), Table A-2, p. 94.

of reducing unemployment, before they encounter serious structural bottle-necks and trigger cost and price increases? Once this crucial "trade-off" range has been reached, the further pursuit of expansionary policies will mainly push up costs and prices, rather than reduce unemployment.[32]

Levy recounts that the Council of Economic Advisors and others adopted the deficient demand thesis[33] and asserted that unemployment could be reduced below 4 percent by fiscal manipulations without producing price inflation. He said that others, holding to a structural view, doubted if expanding total demand through monetary or fiscal means would reduce unemployment much below 5 percent without creating bottlenecks and structural imbalance and without unleashing serious inflation. The record clearly shows that unemployment was reduced below 4 percent for a long enough period

[32]Levy, "Full Employment and . . . ," p. 17, used by permission.
[33]This thesis of deficient demand goes back at least as far as Keynes, who in his *General Theory of Employment Interest and Money,* held that a tendency existed for the supply of savings to exceed the demand for investable funds and that demand should be bouyed by massive public spending. Sumner H. Slichter in a book published in 1961 made these comments about the Keynes's demand theory. [Keynes] constructed a theory which gave little hint of the great and growing capacity of advanced industrial countries to increase the demand for goods. His theory of consumption . . . assigned a far too passive role to industrial consumers, and his theory of investment exaggerated the disposition to hoard and gratuitously assumed that the economy possesses only a meager capacity to discover or to create investment opportunities. Indeed, Keynes believed that there was an inevitable tendency for the capacity of economies to produce goods to outrun their capacity to increase the demand for goods. Thus, he held that highly developed economies suffer from a chronic deficiency of demand and that, as the economies become richer, the deficiency of demand becomes greater. This is the essence of the stagnation thesis of which Keynes was the most brilliant champion. Hence, Keynes concluded that as wealth increased, the principal economic function of the state should be to cure the chronic deficiency of demand—partly by changing the distribution of income and partly simply by spending huge amounts of money.
Keynes's theory of demand may have validity for some undeveloped economies in which consumption cannot be financed out of accumulated resources or by credit, in which forms of consumption are kept rigid by custom, and in which there is little capacity to discover investment opportunities or to develop or finance them. Certainly, his theory of demand does not fit the economies of advanced industrial countries and, in particular, it does not fit the economy of the United States, where consumption is highly competitive, where consumers possess abundant credit and other resources, and where industry possesses huge technical resources that give it a large and growing ability to create investment opportunities. The problem of advanced economies is precisely the reverse of the Keynes diagnosis. It is the problem of preventing excessive demand from producing chronic inflation. There is irony in the fact that Keynes announced his theory of chronically deficient demand at the birth of the atomic age, when the economy was just beginning to acquire new powers to increase demand. [*Economic Growth in the United States* (Baton Rouge: Louisiana State University Press, 1961), pp. 84-85, used by permission.]

Slichter's comments about Keynes are interesting indeed. It is in no way disrespectful of Keynes to observe that his demand-deficiency thesis is inapplicable to problems of 1970. Were he alive today, he doubtless would not attempt to apply it. While his preoccupation with demand deficiency strikes many today as ill-advised, we might pause to realize that time may bring such changes as to make our preoccupation with inflation seem equally ill-advised.

of time to demonstrate that it can be done. The question is whether the reduction was accomplished only at the price of quickened inflation that now will be difficult to control. After reporting on the results of a fairly large-scale study undertaken at the National Industrial Conference Board, Levy concludes:

> With the present structure of the U.S. economy, the lowest unemployment rate compatible with sustained "price stability" appears to fall somewhere within the range of 4%-4½%.
>
> Unemployment rates below this range can presently be achieved and sustained without significant price inflation only through measures directly addressed to structural unemployment and other structural bottlenecks and regidities within the economy.[34]

Assuming that the National Industrial Conference Board study is credible, the problem resolves itself into a question of whether specific attacks on structural unemployment can succeed in keeping unemployment under 4 percent. If not, there will be intense political pressure on whatever party is in power to use general measures to push up demand so as to keep unemployment below 4 percent even at the price of continued inflation.

We should note explicitly a point about the "new economics" of the 1960s. This brand of economics, which calls for managing the economy through use of fiscal and monetary tools, does *not* call for further enlargement of total demand without enlargement of supply. Rather, it calls for restraint. The 1968 surtax represented an effort at restraint as did the attempt during the following years to contain the upsurge in demand. The idea of full employment, however, may now be so politically popular that no individual or group can head off secular inflation. The public commitment to full employment is strong. As a result of the demonstration in the 1960s that unemployment can be pushed under 4 percent, the popular concept of full employment probably now presumes unemployment of less than 4 percent. This rate of unemployment is below the NICB trade-off range of 4-4.5 percent.

In short, the idea of full employment may well be addictive and the politically acceptable criterion as to what is full may rise with each success we enjoy in pressing the unemployment rate down. Perhaps there is a ratchet effect at work in our rising concept of full employment. The people in this country may have developed a

---

[34]Levy, "Full Employment and . . . ," p. 27, used by permission.

strong affinity for a more stringent definition of full employment and may have modified their attitude toward maximum tolerable unemployment. Unemployment is easier to visualize and understand than is inflation. Public opinion in a trade-off is likely to opt for reducing unemployment.[35] In the words of *Fortune* writer Gilbert Burck, "The greatest economic problem of industrial civilization still frustrates us. How can a free nation simultaneously achieve reasonably stable prices and reasonably high employment? Decades ago the solution seemed closer than it does today."[36] The odds are that we cannot simultaneously achieve reasonably stable prices and reasonably high employment; the odds are for secular inflation not only in this country but in the free world generally.

Public Tolerance of Chronic Deficits

Another argument to support a forecast of continued secular inflation is the apparent public willingness to tolerate huge government deficits year after year for reasons that are beyond the mere objective of maintaining full employment. We have already discussed the probable willingness of the public to prefer very high employment to price stability and have noted that the resultant deficit spending would probably be inflationary. We move now to an allied point, namely, the high probability of public spending for direct accomplishment of certain objectives other than merely for the maintenance of full employment.

One is not hard put to compile a list of urgent social and individual needs that could be met in the public sector. The recent neces-

---

[35]John Kenneth Galbraith put the point quite straightforwardly when he said:

First of all, let me lay down the primary economic and political condition which controls any useful discussion of this problem. This is the overriding importance of high employment. The opportunity for a job and the income that goes with it come first in our thinking on economic policy. . . it follows . . . that no policy designed to promote the stabilization of prices has any chance of permanent success if it depends, either directly or indirectly, on deliberately continued unemployment. It is my own hope that sooner or later, we will do something to remove both the stigma and the economic penalties which are associated with involuntary unemployment. When this is done we shall be committed to less stringent goals of economic management and full employment may well cease to be such a social imperative as now.

Statement submitted to Subcommittee on Anti-trust and Monopoly, Committee on the Judiciary, United States Senate, March 11, 1959, and reprinted as "Administered Prices and Monetary-Fiscal Policy," in Lawrence S. Ritter, ed., *Money and Economic Activity* (3rd ed.; Boston: Houghton Mifflin Company, 1967), p. 320, used by permission.

[36]Gilbert Burck, "Must Full Employment Mean Inflation?" *Fortune*, vol. 74 (October, 1966), p. 120. Courtesy of *Fortune* Magazine.

sity of giving priority to war-related public expenditures has increased the pressure for massive outlays of federal money in other areas. The space program, new kinds of public welfare, efforts to harmonize race relations, inner-city reconstruction, highway construction, airport construction, intra- and inter-urban transportation, new hospital and school facilities, antipollution activities, park development, and national defense are high on the list of urgent public needs. Most of us would like to have all these and other projects undertaken in the public sector because we have seen increasing manifestations of the public squalor about which Galbraith wrote several years ago.[37]

Without taxing our imaginations we can also see that these needs, if unmet, can only grow more acute in the years to come. Directly or indirectly, the need for highways, schools, hospitals, improvement in race relations, airports, slum clearance, depollution of air and water, and so on arise largely because of a growing population. As the population grows, the clamor for increased public spending doubtless will increase with the likely result that growth in spending in the public sector may outstrip growth in the gross national product.

Further, it stands to reason that much of this increase in public spending may be inflationary because it will come not from increased taxes or noninflationary public borrowing but rather from federal creation of bank credit, which amounts to monetization of the additional debt so created. The chairman of the board of governors of the Federal Reserve System spoke a few years ago on the danger of expecting too much from government.

Inflation is no longer just a threat—it is a reality. Its pervasive effects are now spreading through many aspects of our economic life. The advance in prices has been rapid and widespread. Wage increases continue to be far in excess of productivity gains. Financial markets have become heavily congested . . . our balance of international payments has continued in substantial deficit. Inflation is jeopardizing attainment of both our domestic and our international objectives. . . . We must recognize also that we cannot keep on calling upon our governments—Federal, State, or local—to do things we are unwilling to pay for. If we are to achieve in fact the public goals we feel most useful and desirable, then we must, as a self-governing people, be willing to accept and adhere to some sensible order of priorities among them in accord with the national preferences.[38]

[37] John Kenneth Galbraith, *The Affluent Society* (Boston: Houghton Mifflin Company, 1958). See especially Chapter 18 for a discussion of the theory of social balance.

The problem is not that theorists fail to agree on the type of remedy which a stabilizing budget policy calls for when the economy is hyperactive. The outline of the stand and cure for hyperactivity is a matter of substantial agreement. Frazar B. Wilde, as chairman of the Committee for Economic Development, stated it recently as follows:

Whatever a stabilizing budget policy may mean to others, here is what it means to us. . . . We believe that the impact of the budget should vary directly with the conditions of the economy as a whole, being more expansive when the economy is depressed and more restrictive when the economy is booming or inflationary.

We emphatically believe, as a corollary of this, that policy should produce a budget surplus to be used for debt retirement under conditions of high employment and full utilization of resources. This is important primarily because the surplus would add to the funds available for private investment, ease the pressures on monetary policy, and thereby promote economic growth with price stability.

We have said many times that a stabilizing budget policy is achieved when *the government sets its expenditure programs and tax rates so that they would yield a surplus under conditions of high employment and price stability.*[39]

Wilde's emphasis on the necessity for draining some of the exuberance from an overly active economy is shared to a greater or lesser degree even by champions of the new economics, although some of them might prefer tax cuts to the creation of a surplus for debt retirement.[40]

The problem, then, is not what constitutes the standard cure for a prolonged inflation but, rather, whether public opinion will permit the cure to be applied. The willingness of Americans and thus their policy makers to limit public spending to what can be matched by taxation and noninflationary borrowing would be a tremendous exercise in public self-control. If the control is not forthcoming, the consequences could be dismal. A democracy is vulnerable to large numbers of persons developing vested interests in public expenditures. The pressures that have developed already—not

[38]William McChesney Martin, Jr., "Statement to Congress," *Federal Reserve Bulletin,* vol. 53 (December, 1967), pp. 2,031-34.

[39]*Managing a Full Employment Economy* (New York: Committee for Economic Development, 1966), p. 7, used by permission.

[40]See, for example, the statement of Walter W. Heller, who recommended that the boom be dampened by imposition of an income surtax; *Managing a Full Employment Economy,* pp. 19-20.

to mention the pressures that may develop later—make it totally inexpedient for political leaders to take bold stands for public economy. Political history over the last few decades suggests that such a stance is quite likely to produce a resounding defeat at the polls. If the majority of voting Americans in the years to come is not willing to expect less of the government, particularly the federal government, there is little prospect that public expenditures will be contained sufficiently to avoid inflation.

Although the evaluation is clouded by the Korean and Vietnam wars, the record since World War II provides little comfort to one who is looking for evidence of anti-inflationary budgetary management. Much of the spending, of course, has been war-related. Even so, there is room for wholesale doubt about the ability and desire of a modern, industrialized democracy to produce a federal budgetary surplus in periods of even the highest employment. Table 22 gives the federal cash budgets from 1946 through 1969. As can be seen from the figures, the federal net cumulative deficit from 1945 through 1969 has run to well over $60 billion, and almost all of this has occurred since 1960. The gross cumulative deficit of about $90 billion has been offset by a cumulative surplus of about $30 billion, but nearly $14 billion of the surplus appeared before 1950. Assuming that these trends are relevant, the outlook for a balanced budget over the long-range future is certainly gloomy.

Some economic theorists have reconciled themselves to this deficit by declaring that the budget need only be balanced over a decade or a cycle or that it does not need to be balanced at all as long as the annual deficit is smaller than the growth in real GNP. They hold that debt retirement is not necessarily a high-priority objective.[41] Given the urgent needs for public expenditures as previously discussed, many economists doubtless would not want a federal budgetary surplus in any foreseeable situation.

Growing Supply of Money

We have already recognized that federal deficits are not necessarily inflationary. Only when the deficit is accompanied by an increase in the effective money supply is inflation likely to occur. When the

---

[41]See the discussion in Samuelson, *Economics: An Introductory Analysis*, Chapter 19, pp. 335-58.

TABLE 22

Federal Government Net Cash Transactions with the Public (Except Borrowing), 1946-1969

Year	Receipts from Public	Payments to Public	Difference
1946	41.449*	41.399*	0.050*
1947	44.270	38.613	5.657
1948	44.917	36.893	8.024
1949	41.340	42.637	-1.297
1950	42.413	41.962	0.451
1951	59.266	58.034	1.232
1952	71.334	71.982	-0.648
1953	70.232	77.384	-7.152
1954	68.598	69.676	-1.078
1955	71.450	72.176	-0.726
1956	80.332	74.737	5.595
1957	84.520	83.396	1.124
1958	81.729	88.950	-7.221
1959	87.553	95.559	-8.006
1960	98.287	94.733	3.554
1961	97.919	104.734	-6.815
1962	106.206	111.875	-5.669
1963	112.577	117.151	-4.574
1964	115.031	120.340	-5.308
1965	123.376	127.920	-4.544
1966	145.136	150.868	-5.731
1967+	149.562	158.352	-8.790
1968+	153.676	178.833	-25.157
1969+	187.792	184.556	3.236

*Figures in billions of dollars.
+Figures for 1967, 1968, and 1969 were taken from current issues of *Survey of Current Business* (p. S-18) and are not strictly comparable to figures for earlier years.

Sources: U.S. Department of Commerce, *Business Statistics, 1967—A Supplement to the Survey of Current Business* (16th biennial ed.; Washington, D.C.: U.S. Govt. Printing Office, 1967), p. 94. The following note, from pp. 94-95 of the source, defines the figures: "The totals represent, in effect, a summation of all Federal transactions with the public, other than borrowing and debt repayment. . . . The figures shown include not only those receipts and expenditures counted in the Federal administrative budget, but also the transactions of trust and deposit funds held by the Federal Government and certain transactions of Government-sponsored enterprises [such as the FDIC] that are not considered a part of the Government in the conventional budget data."

economy is operating near capacity with an adequate money supply for the existing price level, further increases in money supply are not likely to be offset by increases in production. Instead, the major impact is likely to be on prices.

Since we do not have to worry unduly in this country about debasement of coins or rampant printing of new paper money, we need concern ourselves principally with the effect of federal borrowing on the volume of credit. Table 23 shows the magnitude of the money supply in recent years.

Differences of opinion as to what properly constitutes the effective money supply causes Table 23 to be more detailed than might otherwise be necessary. Economists used to say that the money supply consisted only of currency outside of banks plus bank demand deposits (excluding interbank deposits). Increasingly, the view has been adopted that bank time deposits also are a part of the money supply because bank credit can be and often is moved back and forth between demand and time deposits, especially since interest rates have risen. There is also a widespread and growing belief that time deposits in mutual savings banks and savings and loan associations as well as in commercial banks are a part of the money supply. Some monetary scholars even go so far as to include savings in credit unions, life insurance cash values, and U.S. savings bonds in the total. The prevailing opinion, however, seems to be that, while these holdings are "near money," they probably should not be included in the definition of money supply.

Thus, Table 23 shows three totals to permit examination of the behavior of three possible combinations of the money supply. The column 4 total relates only to currency and commercial bank demand deposits; the column 6 total includes these plus time deposits in commercial banks; and column 9 includes deposits in mutual savings banks and savings and loan associations. The grand total for 1965 and later years is about three times the total of currency and demand deposits. At the end of 1969 the grand total was about 3.4 times its 1947 size.

It is easy to see that the absolute figures in all three totals have grown rapidly. The significant relationship, however, is that between the rate of growth of the money supply and the rate of growth of real GNP. Assuming that the velocity of circulation of money remains the same from one period to another, no effective increase in the money supply occurs until the supply grows at a rate faster than that for real GNP. Table 24 and Figure 10 show the rate of growth for each of the three totals given in Table 23.

Table 24 and Figure 10 show that if money supply includes deposits in mutual savings banks and savings and loan associations, demand and time deposits in commercial banks, and currency outside of banks, the rate of increase in money supply has exceeded the rate of increase in real GNP from 1952 to 1969 with the exception

TABLE 23

U.S. Money Supply, 1947-1969*

Year	Currency (1)	Demand Deposits+ (2)	U.S. Govt. Demand Deposits (3)	Total, Columns 1, 2, & 3 (4)	Bank Time Deposits+ (5)	Total Columns 4 & 5 (6)	Deposits Mutual Savings Banks (7)	Deposits Savings-Loan Ass'ns. (8)	Grand Total, Columns 6, 7, & 8 (9)
1947	26.6	85.2	2.0	113.8	34.2	148.0	17.8	9.7	175.5
1948	26.1	86.2	2.1	114.4	35.8	150.2	18.4	18.4	187.0
1949	25.5	85.7	2.5	113.7	36.3	150.0	19.3	12.5	181.8
1950	25.1	89.1	3.1	117.3	36.7	154.0	20.0	14.0	188.0
1951	25.6	93.7	4.0	123.3	37.2	160.5	20.9	16.1	197.5
1952	26.7	98.5	4.8	130.0	39.7	169.7	22.6	19.2	211.5
1953	27.7	100.6	4.4	132.7	42.8	175.5	24.4	22.8	222.7
1954	27.5	102.8	4.4	134.7	46.9	181.6	26.3	27.3	235.2
1955	27.6	106.8	4.1	138.5	49.3	187.8	28.2	32.2	248.2
1956	28.0	108.0	3.9	139.9	50.8	190.7	30.0	37.1	257.8
1957	28.3	108.5	3.5	140.3	55.1	195.4	31.7	41.9	269.0
1958	28.4	110.0	4.3	142.7	62.8	205.5	34.0	48.0	287.5
1959	28.9	113.9	4.6	147.4	66.8	214.2	35.0	54.5	303.7
1960	29.0	111.9	5.3	146.2	69.1	215.3	36.3	62.1	313.7
1961	29.1	114.0	4.8	147.9	78.5	226.4	38.3	70.9	335.6
1962	30.1	116.1	6.0	152.2	91.1	243.3	41.3	80.2	364.8
1963	31.5	119.0	5.9	156.4	105.5	261.9	44.6	91.3	397.8
1964	33.5	122.8	5.8	162.1	119.4	281.5	48.8	101.9	432.2
1965	36.3	130.5	4.6	171.4	146.6	318.0	52.4	110.4	480.8
1966	38.3	132.1	3.4	173.8	158.1	331.9	55.0	114.0	500.9
1967	40.4	140.9	5.0	186.3	183.5	369.8	60.1	124.5	554.4
1968	43.4	149.6	4.8	197.8	204.3	402.1	64.5	131.6	598.2
1969	46.0	153.6	5.5	205.1	194.1	399.2	66.5	134.4	600.1

*All figures are in billions of dollars.
+Excluding interbank and U.S. government deposits.

Sources: *Federal Reserve Bulletins* for all data after 1964 plus mutual savings bank and savings and loan association data before 1965; U.S. Department of Commerce, *Business Statistics, 1967— A Supplement to the Survey of Current Business* (16th biennial ed.; Washington, D.C.: U.S. Govt. Printing Office, 1967), p. 100.

of 1955, 1959, 1966, and 1969. During several years the excess was sizable. If the definition of money supply is restricted to currency outside of banks and demand plus time deposits in commercial banks, the same generalization holds except that the excesses are not as large, and 1956 and 1960 must be added to the years of exception. If the money supply is narrowly defined to include only currency outside banks and demand deposits, its rate of growth exceeded that of real GNP only during five years of the 1952-69 period.

TABLE 24

Rate of Increase in U.S. Money Supply
Compared with Rate of Increase in Real GNP, 1948-1969

	Rate of Increase from Previous Year			
Year	Money Supply* (1)	Money Supply+ (2)	Money Supply‡ (3)	GNP in 1958 Dollars (4)
1948	-0.3%	0.8%	1.7%	4.5%
1949	-0.6	-0.1	1.2	0.1
1950	3.1	2.7	3.4	9.6
1951	5.1	4.2	5.0	7.9
1952	5.4	5.7	7.1	0.3
1953	2.1	3.4	5.3	4.5
1954	1.5	3.5	5.6	-1.4
1955	2.8	3.4	5.5	7.6
1956	1.0	1.5	3.9	1.8
1957	0.3	2.5	4.3	1.4
1958	1.7	4.9	6.9	-1.1
1959	3.3	5.2	5.6	6.4
1960	-0.8	0.5	3.3	2.5
1961	1.2	5.1	7.0	1.9
1962	2.9	7.5	8.7	6.6
1963	2.7	7.6	9.0	3.8
1964	3.6	7.5	8.6	5.0
1965	5.7	13.0	11.2	7.0
1966	1.4	4.4	4.2	6.4
1967	7.2	11.1	10.7	2.4
1968	6.2	9.0	6.2	5.0
1969	1.3	-2.0	-0.6	7.7

*Currency outside banks plus demand deposits.
+Column 1 money supply plus time deposits in commercial banks.
‡Column 2 money supply plus deposits in mutual savings banks and savings and loan associations.

Sources: Table 23; U.S. Department of Commerce, Business Statistics, 1967—A Supplement to the Survey of Current Business (16th Biennial ed.; Washington D.C.: U.S. Govt. Printing Office, 1967), p. 4, for GNP data; and current issues of Survey of Current Business.

Because of the high interest rates payable on savings as opposed to demand deposits during recent years, considerable shifting of deposits back and forth between demand and savings accounts has occurred to put idle money to work even for short periods. For this reason, the inclusion of savings deposits in the definition of money supply seems preferable to omitting such deposits. On this basis the conclusion is clear that money supply adjusted for the real growth in the economy has increased, especially in the 1960s, to such an extent as to add a powerful force to inflation.

FIGURE 10

Rate of Increase in U.S. Money Supply Compared with
Rate of Increase in Real GNP, 1948-1969

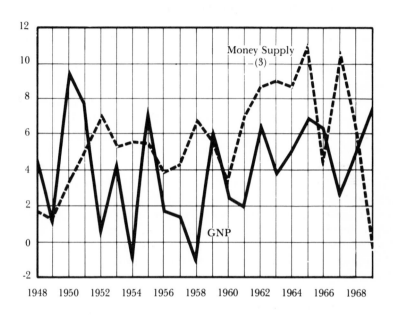

Source: Table 24.

The effective money supply depends not only on the quantity of money but also on the velocity with which the money is used. Good figures on velocity are hard to obtain. One bit of evidence that the velocity might have increased is the fact that the size of U.S. government demand deposits as reported in Table 23 is much greater in relationship to federal payments to the public (Table 22) in 1947 than in 1969. An implication is that in the public sector the turnover might be faster now than earlier. The case need not rest on this point, however. We only need to make what seems to be a very reasonable assumption that the velocity of money has not declined to offset the increase in the quantity of money during recent years. If this assumption is valid, then the effective supply of money (defined to include commercial bank time deposits, currency, and bank demand deposits) has clearly increased. As we have noted already, the

167

pressures for public spending in an increasingly populated and urbanized society are likely to grow sharply over the long-range future. The consequences in regard to inflation will depend on the reaction of the voting public to these pressures.

An appropriate way to conclude this discussion is to consider the comments of two distinguished economists. Martin R. Gainsbrugh, senior vice-president and chief economist of the National Industrial Conference Board, in speaking about the currently fashionable constructive budget deficit and constructive international deficit theses, has said: "Time will test the validity of these present-day theories as they did that of the mature economic philosophy. But sufficient time has already elapsed to reveal creeping inflation as the Achilles heel of the new economics."[42] Walter W. Heller, speaking in 1966, stated the challenge in dramatic fashion when he said: "Can we manage high-pressure prosperity without a price-wage spiral? No country in the free world has ever done it. This country has not done it. Can we do it?"[43]

Thus we are left uneasily wondering whether public opinion in this country will sanction restraining public expenditures over the long-run future in order to permit the new economics to control inflation successfully. Unfortunately, the possibility of successful inflation control is unlikely.

Two Additional Arguments

There are two remaining arguments to support our conjecture of sustained inflation between now and the turn of the century. The first is that deflation substantial enough to discount future price rises is unlikely to occur. Rather, the price rises are likely to be built permanently into the price structure to make long-range inflation even more potent. Such has been the record since the 1930s.[44] The principal reason for the unlikelihood of future compensatory deflation in price behavior lies in the power of organized labor in collective bargaining. In the late twentieth century, organized labor in the

---

[42]Martin R. Gainsbrugh, "Inflation and the New Economics," *Conference Board Record*, vol. 4 (August, 1967), p. 5, used by permission. He also referred to inflation as the soft underbelly of the new economics.

[43]*Managing a Full Employment Economy*, p. 16, used by permission.

[44]We have already taken notice of the apparent ratchet effect that characterizes modern price movements.

United States will not likely be disposed to tolerate even small wage reductions unless the country's very economic system is threatened— and perhaps not even then. The tendency, rather, will be for nego- tiated wage increases to exceed productivity gains and therefore to be inflationary in themselves. The current pattern of wage increases in the 6 percent or 7 percent range as against productivity gains in the 2 percent to 3 percent range may well continue. This stickiness of wages on the downside is aggravated further by the existence of minimum wage laws. To the extent that low-productivity workers are kept on the payroll, these laws maintain wages at levels in excess of productivity. Gottfried Haberler, writing in 1966, commented as fol- lows about the relationship of minimum wage laws and inflation:

The planned increase in the minimum wage and extension of the coverage of the minimum wage law to categories of workers not now covered should be dropped. The best policy would of course be to abolish the minimum wage laws altogether. It should be realized that minimum wages cannot raise the overall *real* wage level. All they do is to cause unemployment of marginal workers, mainly teenagers; they may raise somewhat the wages of the lowest categories of workers at the expense of those who lose their jobs and they do exert an upward push on *money* wages in general, thus intensi- fying inflationary pressures.[45]

The other argument has to do with the growing importance of ser- vice enterprises. We can observe that since the end of World War II the services portions of the Consumer Price Index have increased in importance relative to the consumer goods portions. Hospital and medical care, transportation, and personal services are examples. Services are likely to become even more important as the future un- folds. If so, we may experience a bias in the economy toward prices that are higher than those that would prevail if the accent were on goods. The reason is that production of services does not show as much promise for economies of scale as does production of goods because of the degree of human energy and skill required to provide many of the services. With services already constituting more than a third of consumer purchases and with the proportion possibly rising, we find a fairly substantial additional inflationary pressure.

Some economists argue that the highest priority in curing infla- tion should be to increase production rather than to restrain govern- ment expenditures or raise taxes. Arthur A. Thompson, for example,

[45]Haberler, *Inflation, Its Causes and Cures*, p. 30, used by permission.

writes: "When society consistently wants more output than can be produced, corrective policy calls not so much for tax increases (or lower government expenditures) to curtail aggregate demand as for actions that will *increase aggregate supply* in the long run."[46] The suggestion is most worthy. It is mentioned here only to point up the fact that a significant outward movement of the production possibilities curve may be more difficult for consumer services than for consumer goods. Even if wholesale prices were stabilized, troublesome problems might remain in attempting to stabilize consumer prices. The services components might prove more resistant than the goods component to the curtailment of aggregate demand solution proposed by Thompson.

The speculations set forth in this chapter can be summarized in the following propositions:

1.   Extended secular inflation can produce widespread cheating and loss of incentive.

2.   Price behavior in the United States and many other parts of the world since World War II appears to have taken on the quality of secular inflation.

3.   Several types of evidence suggest that secular inflation will characterize price behavior in the United States and perhaps throughout the democratic parts of the world during the next several decades.

4.   If these statements prove accurate, moral behavior may deteriorate in the United States over the long-range future so as to expose insurance to destructive forces previously unknown.

[46]Arthur A. Thompson, "The Control of Demand-Pull Inflation: A Policy Suggestion," *Quarterly Review of Economics and Business*, vol. 8 (Spring, 1968), p. 54, used by permission.

6

ENERGY AND LEISURE

If, as we have speculated, population over the next several decades is likely to grow faster than the production of basic goods,
then the resulting overgrowth will probably contribute to a general scarcity of necessities that in turn will encourage crime, inflation, and extensive human suffering. The recent history of population growth and inflation, as we have seen, lends strong support
to this type of outlook.

Many people, however, as we have also observed, take a different point of view. They believe that over the long-range future
productivity will grow in many parts of the world significantly
faster than population. Consequently, they visualize not increasing
scarcity but rather increasing abundance. With the increasing abundance they foresee a decreasing workweek and more time on the
part of large masses of people for nonoccupational pursuits. They
worry more about future constructive use of free time than about
the Malthusian positive checks on populations. A large part of their
hope for future abundance rests on an expectation that the real cost
of a unit of energy needed to produce goods and services will decline substantially during the next few decades. They hope, for
example, that drastic reductions in the cost of electricity will enable productivity gains to be made easily. They recognize that without lower-cost energy, mankind will be hard pressed to produce

goods and services fast enough to keep pace with, much less gain on, population.

At this stage in our study we cannot help but ask ourselves what will happen if our earlier speculations are wrong and relative future abundance is made possible by lower-cost energy. This chapter considers this question in relation to the theme of this book. Specifically, the chapter consists of (1) a brief review of the recent history of productivity in this country; (2) a crude assessment of the likely future real cost of energy, particularly in the United States; (3) a sketchy examination of the nature of leisure; and (4) a few long-range speculations about the possible implications for insurance of ethical and moral problems that might result from increased leisure on the part of large numbers of people.

Consideration of this question is not intended as a repudiation of the speculations made earlier. In the author's judgment the evidence to support them is too persuasive to be ignored. Treatment of the new question here is merely a prudent effort to recognize a new set of problems that could arise in case increasing abundance, contrary to the stronger present evidence, does become a way of life in the future. This chapter, in a sense, is a hedge and reflects an attempt to "cover all bases." Let us look briefly, therefore, at the recent history of productivity and at the average number of hours of work per worker per week in this country in recent decades to gain some perspective.

RECENT PRODUCTIVITY AND THE WORKWEEK

Productivity is a troublesome concept to define. The basic idea is simple enough and embraces merely the output per unit of input. The difficulty arises in defining and measuring specific outputs and inputs. Take, for example, telephone service. The output is not simply the number of telephone calls made or even the total time consumed by calls or number of instruments in service. Many qualitative changes occur over time including speed, clarity, reliability, and convenience of service. The qualitative differences are not really quantifiable. Similar problems arise with the input. One has difficulty in comparing the current input involving elaborate equipment with the simpler input of a few years ago involving relatively more human effort. Even if we restricted ourselves to considering human effort, we would have to face the fact that such effort varies markedly in its skill and intensity.

Still, if generalizations are to be made at all about productivity, some tolerably consistent expression is required. The most widely accepted expression is output per man hour. This expression is far from perfect for its purpose. It treats a unit of input as strictly an hour of on-the-job time of a human being without regard to his skill, strength, or zeal. It requires that all output be expressed in equivalent monetary units, even though some of the output is extremely difficult to evaluate. With all its shortcomings the expression is extremely useful and enables rough comparisons to be made over time and between productive organizations. The usefulness of the expression probably increases as the number of periods under study and the size of the organization increase. Thus, it is especially useful for the study of long-term national trends.

By using "output per man-hour," we can say that average productivity for the United States for a given year is that year's total output of goods and services, expressed in arbitrarily selected constant dollars and divided by the total number of man-hours required to produce that output. A man-hour is thought of roughly as 60 minutes of time worked by any human being for whom payroll records are kept.

By this measure, the pace of productivity gain in the United States has been brisk during this century. From Table 25 we can deduce that from 1900 through 1955 productivity in the United States increased by nearly 270 percent of the 1900 figure; from 1955 through 1969 the increase was about 49 percent of the 1955 figure. This record is indeed impressive and stands as a testimony to American ingenuity and enterprise. It is all the more impressive when contrasted to the reported population growth in this country for the same two periods. From 1900 to 1955 population increased by about 115 percent of the 1900 figure and from 1955 to 1969 by roughly 25 percent of the 1955 figure.

The productivity figures are reasonably consistent with those reported in a recent study, *Technology and the American Economy*. The first volume of this publication constitutes the summary report to the President and Congress by the National Commission on Technology, Automation, and Economic Progress. Although the commission was created to deal principally with the problem

TABLE 25

Index of U.S. Output per Man-Hour, 1900-1969

Year	Real Gross Private Domestic Product Per Man-Hour, Total Economy*	Output Per Man-Hour, Total Private Economy+
1900	55.6	—
1905	59.9	—
1910	64.4	—
1915	67.2	—
1920	78.3	—
1925	91.6	—
1930	97.5	—
1935	108.0	—
1940	124.0	—
1945	159.0	—
1950	175.4	—
1955	204.8	93.9
1956	206.5	94.1
1957	211.7	96.9
1958	—	99.8
1959	—	103.4
1960	—	105.0
1961	—	108.6
1962	—	113.8
1963	—	117.9
1964	—	122.5
1965	—	126.3
1966	—	131.4
1967	—	134.3
1968	—	138.7
1969	—	139.9

*1929 = 100.
+1957-59 = 100.

Sources: Real gross private domestic product per man-hour (total economy) for 1900-1957 from U.S. Department of Commerce, Bureau of the Census, Historical Statistics of the United States— Colonial Times to 1957 (Washington, D.C.: U.S. Govt. Printing Office, 1960), Table W-1, p. 599; Output per Man-Hour (Total Private Economy) for 1955-1965 taken from U.S. Department of Labor, Handbook of Labor Statistics—1968 (Washington, D.C.: U.S. Govt. Printing Office, 1968), Table 71, p. 123; for 1966-1969 taken from current issues of Monthly Labor Review.

of unemployment, it has compiled considerable data on many aspects of employment. In respect to productivity the commission reports:

In the 35 years before the end of the Second World War, output per man-hour in the private economy rose at a trend rate of 2 percent a year. But this period includes the depression decade of the 1930's. Between 1947 and 1965 productivity in the private economy rose at a trend rate of about 3.2

percent a year. If agriculture is excluded, the contrast is less sharp, with the rate of increase 2 percent a year before the war, and 2.5 percent after. . . .[1]

As with productivity, measurement of the average length of the workweek is not precise. Part-time workers and moonlighters influence the figures. Even so, the decline is plain to see. An article in a 1964 issue of the Chase Manhattan Bank's *Business in Brief* contrasted the fairly common twelve-hour day, six-day week as of the mid-nineteenth century with the typical eight-hour day, five-day week of the 1960s. The following excerpt from the article emphasizes the unevenness of the decline:

> The big change to our current [1964] 8 hours a day, 5 days a week did not come all at once, of course. Nor did it come at a smooth, even pace. . . . The average workweek fell fairly steadily from 1850 to 1900 at a rate of around 2 hours every 10 years. At that juncture the decline picked up speed, with the workweek shrinking roughly 4 hours each decade between 1900 and 1940.[2]

World War II interrupted the decline. In fact, as Table 26 shows, the rate jumped slightly. It returned to about its prewar level and has remained close to the 40-hour week since then. We should not overlook the fact, however, that an increase in the number of paid holidays and an average lengthening of paid vacations has provided additional free time.

An increase in productivity can result in an increase in total output, a reduction of working hours, or some combination of the two as in the United States. Column 5 of Table 24 gives us an idea of the extent of the increase in output. Some of this increase is due to increased productivity and some of it to an expanded work force. Table 26 shows the decline in the average number of hours worked per week by employees in manufacturing in the private sector of the economy since 1909. Aside from the figure for 1935, which reflects heavy unemployment and curtailed production schedules, the drop has been from 50 to 40 hours, approximately.

Clearly, our data indicate that productivity during this century in this country has grown faster than has population. The interesting

---

[1]U.S. National Commission on Technology, Automation, and Economic Progress, *Technology and the American Economy* (Washington, D.C.: U.S. Govt. Printing Office, 1966), vol. 1, p. 2.

[2]"Leisure in America," Chase Manhattan Bank *Business in Brief*, no. 57 (July-August, 1964), p. 2, used by permission.

175

TABLE 26

Average Weekly Hours of U.S. Manufacturing Employment,
1909-1969

Year	Average Weekly Hours of Work*
1909	51.0
1914	49.4
1920	47.4
1925	44.5
1930	42.1
1935	36.6
1940	38.1
1945	43.5
1950	40.5
1955	40.7
1956	40.4
1957	39.8
1958	39.2
1959	40.3
1960	39.7
1961	39.8
1962	40.4
1963	40.5
1964	40.7
1965	41.2
1966	41.3
1967	40.6
1968	40.7
1969	40.6

*Figures are for production or nonsupervisory workers on private, nonagricultural payrolls, total manufacturing sector.

Sources: Average weekly hours of production or nonsupervisory workers on private non-agricultural payrolls (total manufacturing) for 1909-1967 from U.S. Department of Labor, Handbook of Labor Statistics—1968 (Washington, D.C.: U.S. Govt. Printing Office, 1968), Table 63, p. 112; for 1968 and 1969 from Monthly Labor Review, vol. 93 (May, 1970), Table 17, p. 106.

question is how long this trend will continue. One factor may eventually prevent production from continuing to grow faster than population. As population grows, and assuming no lowering of the age of entry into the labor force, an increasingly large portion of the population will be too young to work. Assuming no reduction in the standard of living and no increase in the workweek, productivity must increase sufficiently to meet the needs of this group. If, as in our society, the average age of entry into the work force is progressively raised, then the problem is compounded.

Actually this problem of growth of productivity is the same thing that Malthus wrote about, except that he was especially concerned with food production. We wonder now as he wondered then how many times production can be doubled; we cannot help but be impressed with exponential growth. Sooner or later, production, and thus productivity, will encounter difficulty in keeping pace with the exponential growth of population. In the meantime, we may be as confused as he apparently was about when the encounter will take place.

OUTLOOK FOR ENERGY SUPPLY

The behavior of productivity over the long-range future probably will be related very closely to the cost of a unit of energy needed to generate the power to run the American economy. Therefore, attention is given here to the likely need for energy and to the forms in which energy may be supplied between now and the turn of the century.

Our future standard of living and the average weekly working time required to maintain this standard will depend heavily on the availability of raw materials needed to produce the required goods and services. Abundant resources make the task easier; scarcities add to the difficulty. Abundance and scarcity are peculiar concepts in the sense that the earth contains an enormous quantity of minerals and other substances. The rub is that extraction and processing of these materials require prodigious force, especially as the relatively accessible deposits are consumed. Whether scarcity or abundance prevails is partly influenced by the cost of the force required for extraction and processing. Therefore, the real cost of energy lies at the root of the abundance or scarcity issue.

Harrison Brown and his coauthors made the point vividly by writing as follows:

> Ordinary igneous rocks contain most of the elements necessary for the perpetuation of a highly industrialized society, and in proportions which are not unreasonable from the point of view of industrial needs. One hundred tons of average igneous rock contain, for example, about 8 tons of aluminum, 5 tons of iron, 180 pounds of manganese, 40 pounds of nickel, 20 pounds of copper, and 4 pounds of lead. Many of the elements which are not found in sufficient quantity in igneous rocks, such as chlorine, bromine, and iodine, can be found in the oceans. Other elements, such as nitrogen

and oxygen, are readily available in the atmosphere. Still others can be found in the practically inexhaustible supplies of limestone (a source of carbon), gypsum (a source of sulphur), and phosphate rock (a source of phosphorus). Given the brainpower and the energy, the people of the world could, if need be, support themselves entirely with the leanest of ores, the waters of the oceans, the rocks of the earth's crust, and the very air around them.[3]

Seemingly, then, we do not face any immediate and actual physical shortage on the earth of most of the ingredients necessary to expand production of life-sustaining goods and services. The practical limitation, given a sophisticated technology and the will to work, comes in the availability of sufficiently low-cost energy to extract and use these vital ingredients. No larger proportion of total human efforts need be devoted to extracting resources as long as the real cost of energy declines commensurately with the rising force required to extract and use a resource. However, if the real cost of energy rises, we will face increasing scarcities and the prospect of increasingly harder and longer work, except as relieved by improving technology.

To pinpoint the matter, let us assume that nothing changes so as to affect productivity except the cost of energy. If the real cost of energy declines in a society with a stable population, that society faces the pleasant prospect of raising its material standard of living, increasing its leisure time, or choosing some combination of the two. Conversely, if the real cost of energy rises, the society faces the unpleasant prospect of decreasing its material standard of living, increasing the time spent in occupational pursuits, or choosing some combination of the two.

The energy requirements for a world society of more than 3.5 billion people are vast; the requirements for a world society of more than 6 billion are almost incomprehensible. The quantity of energy used in 1960 has been estimated at about the equivalent of 4.2 billion metric tons of coal.[4] About 1.56 billion metric tons (equivalent) were used in North America.

Energy demands in the future, naturally, will depend partly on the rate of technological development. Fisher and Potter made the

---

[3]Harrison Brown, James Bonner, and John Weir, *The Next Hundred Years* (New York: The Viking Press, 1958), p. 91, used by permission.

[4]Joseph L. Fisher and Neal Potter, *World Prospects for Natural Resources* (Baltimore: The Johns Hopkins Press, 1964), p. 47. The study was done at Resources for the Future, Inc.

following projections of energy (as multiples of the 1960 quantity) needed by the world during the year 2000:[5] if the trend in world consumption from 1950 to 1960 continues, 5 times the 1960 quantity will be needed; if world consumption is at the 1960 U.S. per capita level, 13 times; if world consumption is at the 1960 Western European per capita level, 4 times; and if North America, Western Europe, USSR, and Oceania are at the 1960 U.S. per capita level and the rest of the world is at the 1960 Western European per capita level, 6 times.

Perhaps none of the estimates is on target in view of the fact that U.S. per capita energy consumption may also change. Energy consumption in the United States was about 17 times as large in 1955 as in 1850, a period during which population increased to only about 7 times its 1850 size.[6] What the total future energy needs in the United States will be is anybody's guess. One estimate is that, given numerous assumptions as to the size and nature of the economy, electricity generation by 2000 may need to be about 3.5 times its 1960 level; use of petroleum about 2.5; and use of natural gas about 1.8.[7] The essential point, however, is that the quantity of energy used may be strongly influenced by the real cost of the energy available.

The uses to which energy is put vary drastically over time and from one area to another. In the United States in the 1950s, roughly 40 percent of the nation's commercially produced energy was consumed in industrial production, while transportation, households, and other uses consumed 20 percent each.[8] This mix, of course, may change over the future.

The cost of a unit of energy has also varied over time and from one source to another. In fact, relative costs have been the principal determinant of the changing mix. Over the years an increasing proportion of the total energy has been used for generation of electricity. Assuming that this trend is likely to continue, the cost of a

[5]Adapted from Fisher and Potter, *World Prospects for Natural Resources*, Table 13.

[6]Sam H. Schurr and others, *Energy in the American Economy, 1850-1975* (Baltimore: The Johns Hopkins Press, 1960), p. 35. The study was done at Resources for the Future, Inc.

[7]Hans H. Landsberg, Leonard L. Fischman, and Joseph L. Fisher, *Resources in America's Future* (Baltimore: The Johns Hopkins Press, 1963), pp. 837, 848, and 850. This study was done at Resources for the Future, Inc.

[8]Schurr and others, *Energy in the American Economy 1850-1975*, p. 1.

TABLE 27

Sources of Energy as Percent of Total
U.S. Requirements, 1920, 1947, and 1958

	1920	1947	1958
Oil plus natural gas liquids	15%	33%	45%
Natural gas	—	10	25
Coal	75	50	25
Hydroelectric, wood, and other	10*	7	5+

*Wood constituted the bulk of this figure.
+Hydroelectric power constituted 80 percent of this figure.
Source: Sam H. Schurr and others, *Energy in the American Economy, 1850-1975* (Baltimore: The Johns Hopkins Press, 1960), pp. 1, 2.

unit of delivered electricity is a useful benchmark for our speculation. An approximation based on 1966 aggregate data relating to electricity sold to all types of ultimate consumers suggests that the average price was roughly 1.5¢ per kilowatt hour.[9]

Another problem in the use of energy is determining the source that is the most efficient for the particular use involved. Coal, oil, natural gas, wood, and flowing streams of water are important sources of energy. The choice of a particular source is influenced by technology and vice versa. The more advanced the technology, the greater are both the need for energy and the ability to obtain it. The sources of the energy used in the U.S. economy have changed substantially over time, and the figures given in Table 27 should help to reflect this. These figures are rough estimates only but are useful in reflecting the change. Several other more glamorous sources of energy and several potential sources will be mentioned later. In a geological sense the sun is the ultimate source of energy on this planet in that it has sent potential heat to the earth and stored it in wood, coal, oil, natural gas, and other fuels. It is continuing the process, but at its own geological pace.

Currently our major sources of energy are fossil fuels. Such fuels are finite no matter how large the supplies may be. If we continue to use them, we are bound to exhaust the supply sometime unless we learn how to replenish the fuels at least as fast as we use them. Since

[9]Computed from data in *Survey of Current Business*, vol. 49 (February, 1969), p. s-26.

Nature provides our geological capital at an exceedingly slow pace, we are not likely ever to reach the point of a self-sustaining yield. Charles Galton Darwin, thinking in the perspective of a million years, has commented as follows:

Coal and oil have been accumulating in the earth for over five hundred million years, and, at the present [1952] rates of demand for mechanical power, the estimates are that oil will be all gone in about a century, and coal probably in a good deal less than five hundred years. . . . We are squandering our energy capital quite recklessly; it will very soon be all gone, and in the long run we shall have to live from year to year on our earnings.[10]

Darwin's comments, against the backdrop of a million years, are in interesting contrast to those of Brown and his coauthors, previously quoted, who wrote in a thought span of a hundred years. Whether, even with unlimited energy, mankind in large numbers actually could sustain itself forever on the earth as Brown implies is an interesting question. However, in our relatively short perspective of thinking only to the turn of the century, we can be concerned more with the real cost of energy than with the complete exhaustion of fossil fuels. On the basis of the conclusions drawn in the three Resources for the Future studies cited in this chapter, the following generalizations seem to be warranted:

1.   Enough coal, our resource of last resort, is extractable at present real costs to dwarf any conceivable demand during the present century. Landsberg, Fischman, and Fisher have estimated that the earth contains perhaps 1.7 trillion tons and that at least 200 billion tons could be mined at current prices. Demand for the 1960-2000 period was projected at about 25 billion tons.[11] While this reserve of minable coal is huge, we must remember that much of our present energy conversion equipment (for example, automobiles, ships, and residential furnaces) is not adaptable to coal. Adaptation would be painfully expensive and, coupled with the relatively inefficient use of coal for transportation, would mean increases in real cost of energy. Hence, economic availability of other sources of energy is of critical importance.

[10]Charles Galton Darwin, *The Next Million Years* (Garden City, New York: Doubleday & Company, Inc., 1953), p. 63. Copyright © 1952 by the author. Reprinted by permission of Doubleday & Company, Inc.

[11]Landsberg, Fischman, and Fisher, *Resources in America's Future*, p. 414.

2.   The supply of oil may be so limited or be so stubbornly deposited that it will meet a decreasing proportion of our growing needs for energy between now and the turn of the century. The fact is that no one knows the extent of the oil contained in the earth. Furthermore, no one knows what proportion of the unknown quantity may prove to be economically recoverable. Recognizing these difficulties but attempting a speculation anyway, Landsberg, Fischman, and Fisher have cited an estimate that the total crude oil base of the United States might have been about 400 billion barrels of which about 60 billion by 1960 may have already been recovered. Recovery in the United States in 1960 was about 2.5 billion barrels. By contrast, world production of crude oil in 1960 was about 7.5 billion barrels.[12] The extent of crude oil deposits outside the United States is even more uncertain. The recoverability of the residue of oil still in the earth is problematical.[13] It is possible that the United States may not be able to meet its growing energy needs with domestically produced or imported oil and by the turn of the century will have to increase its relative use of coal or find a major substitute energy source such as atomic fission.

3.   Natural gas and natural gas liquids, being closely related to crude oil resources, are probably subject to the same generalizations as made about oil.

Energy is potentially available from numerous sources other than fossil fuels. The sources include wind, tides, direct solar energy, thermal flows from within the earth, fuel cells, vegetation converted into alcohol or other burnables, cryogenic fuels (low-temperature liquids into which gas, such as hydrogen, has been converted), thermonuclear fusion, and atomic fission. Additionally, the prospect exists of imparting superconductivity to certain metals by cooling them to near absolute zero. They could be used to conduct elec-

[12]Landsberg, Fischman, and Fisher, *Resources in America's Future*, pp. 389, 390, 403. The huge Alaskan discovery announced in 1968 illustrates the uncertainty associated with the supply of oil. See *Time* (June 13, 1969), p. 100, for a relevant discussion.

[13]We should not be misled by the highly publicized proved reserves, often expressed as a ratio to current annual production. These reserves are really working inventories and should not be construed as the total resource base, the ultimately recoverable resource base, or even the total of the resource recoverable at current costs. Such reserves are merely the known and fairly reliably measured inventory awaiting recovery. The size depends in part on the lead time desired in exploration activities.

tricity much more efficiently so as to expand current energy supplies. Finally, more efficient use of heat producing electricity may be achieved through thermionic or thermoelectric direct conversion (generation of electricity by use of heated and cooled metal conductors) and magnetohydrodynamics (generation of electricity through interactions between a magnetic field and superheated ionized gas).

With the exception of atomic fission, none of these sources is likely to be developed for efficient production by the turn of the century. Major technological breakthroughs, however, are seldom envisioned far in advance of their appearance. A major advance in respect to any one of these potential sources might give mankind a giant boost by providing incalculable quantities of controlled energy. The literature of energy is rife with accounts that express both the excitement and the frustration inherent in current development projects.[14]

One of the potential sources of energy mentioned is so stupendous that it warrants further comment. The quantity of energy that would be made available through controlled thermonuclear fusion is astronomically large. If a controlled fusion reaction could be achieved, man would find himself with an energy supply having no practical limit.

In fusion, light atomic particles are forced to unite and form a heavier atom. In the process they release tremendous quantities of energy. A type of hydrogen atom, known as deuterium, is usable in this process. Deuterium, found in ordinary water in the ratio of 1 part deuterium to about 6,500 parts hydrogen, can be isolated when heavy water is made.[15] Because the nuclei in deuterium repel each other with strong positive charges, they can be forced together (into fusion) only under extremely high temperatures—running to several million degrees. In the process the deuterium turns into a plasma. Because of its electrical properties the plasma creates for itself a kind of magnetic shell or "magnetic bottle." This magnetic bottle is

[14]Two examples are "Economics and Future Energy Sources" in Robert W. Prehoda, *Designing the Future* (Philadelphia: Chilton Book Company, 1967), pp. 119-30, and the article, "Energy," by Charles A. Scarlott in Foreign Policy Association, *Toward the Year 2018* (New York: Cowles Education Corporation, 1968), pp. 114-25.

[15]The May 13, 1967, issue of *Business Week,* pp. 164-68, carried an account of a new plant being built in Nova Scotia to make deuterium oxide for about $18 a pound. The substance is also usable in atomic fission reactors.

highly unstable and can be destroyed by even slight disturbance. The technological problem arises in finding a container in which fusion can occur. All known materials melt at temperatures far below that required for the fusion. Here, then, is the peculiar situation where the lack of proper containment stands between man and the benefits that would flow from the practically limitless energy that could result from controlled thermonuclear fusion. Perhaps someday a method of containment will be found.[16]

Presently, atomic fission, which is something quite distinct from thermonuclear fusion, offers the chief hope for a major new source of energy in this century. In fact in 1967, 15 electricity generating plants in the United States and more in Europe were equipped to secure their heat by atomic fission rather than by burning fossil fuels.[17] By early 1968, utilities in the United States had placed orders for 61 additional atomic fission plants to be operable at the latest by 1974. About 40 percent of the new orders placed by utilities in 1967-68 for electricity generating plants called for atomic fission reactors. The average size of the new plants is to be well over 500 megawatts electrical (MWe), considerably larger than the average size of fossil fuel plants, and 14 are to exceed 1,000 MWe. The first fossil fuel plant with a capacity of 1,000 MWe was built only a few years ago. The relevant point is that the present technology of atomic fission calls for large installations. Even the power plants in the aircraft carrier *Enterprise* and in other naval vessels are quite large.

[16]Coincidentally, at about the time of this writing an Associated Press news release written by Frank Carey reported that Lev A. Artsimovich, director of the Soviet Union's work in controlled thermonuclear fusion research, and his colleagues had succeeded in heating hydrogen gas (presumably deuterium) to 20 million degrees and sustaining the heat in a magnet field for one-fiftieth of a second. This combination of heat and duration apparently represented the best result thus far attained. While American, Soviet, and other scientists reportedly have routinely obtained temperatures exceeding 50 million degrees, they have not been able to sustain the heat for as long as one-fiftieth of a second. The release quotes Amasa Bishop of the U.S. Atomic Energy Commission as saying that recent successes definitely opened the prospects for having hydrogen powered reactors "well before the turn of the century." The recent Soviet accomplishment, however, is still far below the current goal of maintaining 300 million degrees for at least one-third of a second without any escape of the plasma. "Soviets Stride in Tapping H-Power," *Bloomington* (Ind.) *Daily Herald-Telephone* (April 11, 1969), sec. 2, p. 11.

[17]Numerical data in this paragraph come from Milton Shaw and Merrill Whitman, "Nuclear Power: Suddenly Here," *Science and Technology*, no. 75 (March, 1968), pp. 22-34.

Atomic fission comes about through the splitting of heavy atoms. The split releases tremendous energy as well as radioactivity. Disposal of the radioactive wastes poses a troublesome but not unmanageable problem. Only certain materials contain the heavy atoms—the "fuels," as it were—that release the energy upon being split. Therein lies the rub. Given short-run technology, the earth's crust may or may not contain enough fissionable material to satisfy long-range needs. Uranium is the principal fissionable material. Known supplies are primarily in the United States, Canada, and South Africa.

The economics of atom fission as a major future source of energy rests in part on the cost of uranium. U^{235}, the fissionable part of uranium, constitutes about 1 percent of the magnitude of uranium, the remainder being nonfissionable U^{238}. Recently, a process has been developed that may permit fissionable plutonium (Pu^{238}) to be derived from U^{238}. Thorium (Th^{232}) may also be convertible into U^{235}. Each of these developments would have the practical effect of relieving the atomic fission fuel problem. A prospect exists that new reactors can be developed and put into use, perhaps by 1980, to produce and use these fissionable materials. Some U^{235} is likely to be required to feed the conversion. In an expression of hope and optimism, the new type of converting reactor has been named a "breeder" because in converting U^{238} and Th^{232} into fissionable U^{235} or Pu^{239}, it might be able to create more fissionable material than it consumes. If so, the hopes for peaceful use of atomic fission may be realized at long last.

Sir William Penney, as chairman of the United Kingdom Atomic Energy Authority, recently expressed confidence in this new process. He wrote: "If, as seems justified by present knowledge, the fast-breeder system is completely successful, both technologically and economically, the world reserves of uranium can be a source of cheap electricity on a world scale for a century or more."[18] He likened the scale of nuclear power as a source of energy to that of fossil fuel.

---

[18]William Penney, "The Future of Nuclear Power as Seen from the United Kingdom," in Edward and Elizabeth Hutchings, eds., *Scientific Progress and Human Values* (New York: American Elsevier Publishing Company, 1967), p. 57. Copyright © American Elsevier Publishing Company, Inc. Used by permission.

Estimates have been made that certain of the breeder reactors may permit electricity to be generated at a cost as low as 2 or 3 mills per kilowatt hour.[19] This estimate, so far below the current average costs cited earlier, may be more of a fond wish than a forecast. Yet the odds are good that man will soon have, at least for a few decades, huge quantities of energy at a real unit cost that is lower than ever before. Shaw and Whitman predict that by the year 2000 atomic fission may be used in the production of at least half—perhaps more—of the nation's electricity. The Resources for the Future scholars make a similar projection.[20]

In summary, our hopes for lower-cost energy to support future production clearly seem to lie with atomic energy. The first alternative, attainment of controlled thermonuclear fusion, would be an event of major social and scientific importance; however, there is scant evidence to indicate when, if ever, such an attainment will be reached. The second alternative is atomic fission. Here, the critical development, given the uncertainty in the quantity of recoverable fissionable materials, is the breeder reactor. If this type of reactor is highly successful, the unit cost of energy may decline significantly. If it is not, our fond expectations for atomic fission may not be realized. If neither controlled thermonuclear fusion nor breeder-reactor atomic fission is a working reality by the turn of the century, we may face higher rather than lower real costs of energy in the event huge new supplies of recoverable petroleum are not discovered and developed.

At best, speculation about supply of energy over the long-range future is clouded with uncertainty. Assertions that new energy sources will be available to meet fully the expanding needs of a growing and increasingly industrialized society seem to have a somewhat hollow ring. Similarly, however, assertions that the real unit cost of energy will move upward before the turn of the century could be to sell man much too short in terms of his ability to gain new knowledge and apply it for his own benefit.

For the purposes of this chapter a prudent course of action seems to be to postulate decreases in the real cost of energy in such magnitude as to allow large numbers of individuals in this and per-

---

[19]Shaw and Whitman, "Nuclear Power: Suddenly Here," p. 34.
[20]Landsberg, Fischman, and Fisher, *Resources in America's Future*, p. 841.

haps several other industrialized nations to cut back significantly on the average weekly hours required to earn a living. This postulate puts us in the position to think about some of the long-range consequences of a substantially reduced workweek for large segments of society. In pursuing these speculations, however, we should remember that future population may grow so fast as to render our speculations useless.

THE ETHICS OF LEISURE AND THE ETHICS OF WORK

Suppose for the sake of discussion that significant numbers of people in this country over the next few decades really will have more free time than people generally have had. The consequences for insurance will depend on how people use their additional freedom from occupational demands. We recognize immediately that if nonoccupational activities are generally more dangerous than occupational activities, we can expect more accidental bodily injuries and deaths and more accidental damage to property. These accidents will have direct repercussions for life, health, and property-liability insurances.

Our concern in this book, however, is a bit more roundabout and fundamental. It pertains to how people may behave generally, how their ethics and morality may change, what their attitudes toward insurance may be, and how any change in ethics and morality may affect the availability of insurance. To gain a fix on the subject, let us briefly consider the concepts of leisure and work.

In his *Politics* Aristotle makes the point that the Spartans were orderly, efficient, and generally secure while they were at war. He says that their society disintegrated as soon as they built an empire and stopped fighting. They did not know how to use the free time that came with the peace they won.[21] The record over the centuries of how others who gained free time used it has been similarly appalling. Free time in large blocks has been mainly at the disposal of small privileged minorities supported by large and often enslaved majorities. One can find no uglier and more spine-chilling accounts of the depravities of man than those contained in the Old Testament and other records of the affairs of kings, queens, and others of privi-

---

[21]Ernest Barker, trans., *The Politics of Aristotle* (Oxford: Oxford University Press, 1961), p. 79.

leged power and station. Free time is one thing; genuine and edifying leisure is something else.

Our concept of leisure, as opposed to mere free time, has been derived largely from the Greeks who wrote about it. Whether the leisure about which we read was really a way of Athenian life is subject to some question. At any one time perhaps no more than 25,000 free adult Athenian males were eligible for the amenities of leisure. Slaves performed most of the work. How many of the free males pursued leisure how often and in what fashion is left to our fancy; how the women who were associated with the free males spent their time is also a matter of surmise. In our esteem of the Greeks we may exaggerate what really happened.

Be that as it may, we do have the statements of Plato, Aristotle, and others about Greek life and leisure. Sebastian de Grazia, in his Twentieth Century Fund study of work and leisure, has summarized some of the Greek thinking on the subject. De Grazia makes much of the Greek word *schole* as having to do with the peace and quiet that comes with halting or ceasing purposeful action. He says that this word contains the root meaning of leisure. He finds importance in the additional fact that one of the Greek words for work is *ascholia,* which suggests in our context "unleisure."[22] In this sense, work is the sort of thing done out of necessity and perhaps but not necessarily with reluctance or with discomfort. It is done for a purpose other than itself. It is a costly means, not an end. Leisure, by contrast, is activity or lack of it freed from necessity; it constitutes the end in itself. In general the Greeks regarded work with disdain and honored leisure as positive and virtuous.

According to De Grazia, Aristotle in his *Ethics* brings out that something pursued for the sake of something else is not final; only that which one truly seeks is one's final goal. Leisure by definition is final. Both Plato and Aristotle conceived that the highest form of leisure, and thus ultimately the most satisfying activity, was contemplation of the good. They asserted that when man was contemplating he was engaging in the activity that best distinguishes him from all other species. Music, conversation, and allied activities were regarded as valuable chiefly because of the aids they lent to contemplation.

[22]Sebastian de Grazia, *Of Time, Work, and Leisure* (New York: The Twentieth Century Fund, 1962), pp. 11-25.

The early Christians apparently also allowed room for contemplation. Many of Jesus' parables and examples provided fertile material for contemplation. The early Christians added one highly significant new dimension to contemplation when they insisted that it not be merely of the good but rather of God through Jesus Christ and that the ultimate of contemplation was to see God.

The Romans modified the Grecian concept somewhat in regarding *otium,* leisure, as being important not only as an end in itself but as having some use in improving the efficiency of *negotium,* the negative of *otium. Negotium* is close, indeed, to our concept of work.

Perhaps the Roman modification of the classical Greek concept of leisure helped to open the way centuries later for the Protestant ethic (also referred to in literature as the Calvinist ethic, the Puritan ethic, the prosperity ethic, and the work ethic). The concept of work and leisure espoused by some of the theologians of the Reformation was notably different from that of the Greeks. Luther and Calvin in particular succeeded in endowing work with an aura it has retained to this day. Their writings were very influential in causing people to change their minds about work and to stop viewing it strictly as a curse from which one should try to escape through religious isolation or war. Spencer D. Pollard, professor of economics at the University of Southern California, condensed the preachments of Luther and Calvin into six doctrines that he feels pertain to what he calls the prosperity ethic. He summarizes one of the six doctrines, "vocation," as follows:

All honest work is sacred if done well and with a sense of service to others. This replaces the older view that only certain holy vocations in religious service are sacred and that ordinary work is a curse put upon mankind as a punishment for sin. Far from being a curse, the Protestant Ethic says, ordinary everyday work is essential and natural and pleasing to God and we must continue it to our last days.[23]

Pollard also quotes Luther to show that Luther emphasized the sacredness of all work. Luther wrote:

Since it is God's will that everyone should serve his fellows here in his respective station, in the office committed to him, we shall do what-

---

[23]Spencer D. Pollard, *How Capitalism Can Succeed* (Harrisburg, Pa.: The Stackpole Company, 1966), pp. 105-6, used by permission.

ever is enjoined upon us. We will serve our subjects, our neighbors, our wives and children so long as we can; we would not relax our service even if we knew we had to depart this very hour and leave all earthly things.[24]

Pollard calls attention to a Calvinist extension of the idea of work, namely, that while eternal life is not the reward for work, success in one's calling can be construed as evidence that the individual is preordained for salvation.[25] This success, according to Calvinist thinking, is deemed the outward evidence of progress toward the salvation that God may grant.

It is hardly an oversimplification to say that in the Reformation the ethics of work and the ethics of leisure were simply reversed from the classical Grecian pattern. The justification for leisure came to rest almost exclusively in the renewability for work. With so much needing to be done in God's world and with men being God's instruments for accomplishing His purposes, work became glorified instead of being regarded as a curse. Idleness and even nonoccupational activity were regarded as wasteful and dangerous because of opening the way to temptation. The idea of idleness being the devil's workshop fits neatly into this view.

Coupled with the glorification of work was a growing reluctance to depend on mere contemplation for divining the truth. During the Renaissance, for the first time in Western culture, nature was studied directly to discern the truths that God had chosen to reveal to man. Perhaps St. Thomas Aquinas was the last great spokesman of the movement of Scholasticism to propound the contemplative pursuit of truth. This substitution of study for contemplation further detracted from the wholesomeness of leisure.

For many of us—perhaps for the overwhelming majority of us who are adults—the work ethic is thoroughly ingrained. We cannot help but feel that work is virtuous, that the roster of honorable callings is long and varied, and that any sort of activity completely free from necessity is somehow suspect and devoid of meaning. We are prone to look for "the necessity" with which to grace any activity

[24]Pollard, *How Capitalism Can Succeed*, p. 109, used by permission.
[25]Pollard, *How Capitalism Can Succeed*, pp. 112-13. An informative discussion of the Calvinist ethics of piety, thrift, and work and a contrast with the Judeo-Christian welfare ethics can be found in Richard N. Farmer, "The Ethical Dilemma of American Capitalism," *California Management Review*, vol. 6 (Summer, 1964), pp. 47-58.

we plan to pursue. We generally feel more comfortable with work than with leisure. We probably still endeavor to instill the work ethic into our children despite warnings that the ethic has or may soon become obsolete.[26] How our children currently respond and how they will respond in the future to such teaching is another matter.

Having been nurtured on the work ethic, we may have some difficulties in loosening our ties to it, should such become necessary. Accommodation to leisure may prove frustrating. If more free time does become available, many people may initially choose to work at a second job and impute to it real or feigned necessity.[27] If and as productivity continues to increase faster than population, moonlighting sooner or later may lose its appeal, and workers by and large will have to confront the reality of additional nonoccupational time. Whether people can adapt is the central question. Kahn and Wiener summarize their feeling on the matter by stating that "unless an American has taken an ideological and moralistic stance against the work-oriented value system, he cannot abandon work."[28]

As mentioned previously, leisure traditionally has been associated with the elite, a small minority of people who by training should be best prepared for it. In the future, however, free time may become available first and in largest blocks to those people who have thought least about it and who may be the least equipped to use it. The free time is more likely to come to the workers than to the managers. Donald N. Michael refers to this possibility as a social inversion. He writes:

As to the leisure classes of recent history, even this small elite, trained from childhood in self-indulgence and use of free time, for the most part either was bored or preoccupied with intrigue, the pursuit of love and

---

[26]For example, Stuart Chase cites, but does not categorically endorse, Gerard Piel, who argues that the "Horatio Alger ethic of working hard for a living . . . is as far out of date as the *Arabian Nights.*" See Chase, *The Most Probable World* (New York: Harper & Row, Publishers, 1968), p. 147, used by permission. Chase, p. 146, recounts Piel's lament that American education unfortunately is still wrongly directed toward getting a job and that it should be directed deliberately toward preparation for "no-jobs," including leisure.

[27]For that matter, "necessity" is subject to degree over a wide domain.

[28]Herman Kahn and Anthony J. Wiener, *The Year 2000* (New York: The Macmillan Company, 1967), p. 214. Copyright © 1967 by The Macmillan Company. Used by permission.

license, and given various forms of violence. . . . And, too, the masses worked and the elites had the free time. Now we are faced with a social inversion, with the masses leisured while the elites work.[29]

The result, assuming that the potential productivity gains are not merely a mirage, could be free time on a mass scale. Mass leisure is a distinctly new phenomenon that troubles futurologists. For example, Dennis Gabor, professor of applied electron physics at the University of London, speculates that the working minority may become so small as to be recruitable from volunteers. He offers the thesis that society, faced with the prospect of mass leisure, is already at work preparing defenses against it.[30] He suggests that the dream of leisure may turn into a nightmare in the absence of a knowledge and a fortitude for using the free time.

The frustration to which Gabor points could be even worse than he describes. If highways are likely to become congested, recreational areas overcrowded, and health care facilities inadequate, these scarcities may prove troublesome. People may have more free time and money than formerly but may face genuine difficulty in using their extra free time and extra funds for goods and services they really want.

IMPLICATIONS FOR INSURANCE

Three types of possible changes in behavior have important insurance implications. Let us look briefly at each type, recognizing all the while that our speculations are extremely tenuous.

First, the free time may bring a growing variety of new human conflicts. With leisure not being something that can be provided on a mass scale, as some authors imply, but rather something each must find, it could prove to be quite elusive. Many people may be totally unable to find it. In their search for it individuals may find them-

[29]Donald N. Michael, "Free Time—The New Imperative in Our Society," in William W. Brickman and Stanley Lehrer, eds., *Automation, Education, and Human Values* (New York: School & Society Books, 1966), pp. 300-301, used by permission. As if to bear out the point, the July 18, 1969, issue of *Time* (p. 15) observes that the average workweek is declining for laborers but is increasing for executives. The magazine reports a study by Daniel D. Howard Associates which showed that for a group of Chicago businessmen the average workweek for chief executives was 63 hours.

[30]Dennis Gabor, "Inventing the Future," in Morris Philipson, ed., *Automation: Implications for the Future* (New York: Vintage Books, 1962), pp. 153-54.

selves embroiled in new types of human conflict. The conflicts may be person-to-person, group-to-group, race-to-race, and nation-to-nation. The new relative freedom from economic pressure may allow many individuals to become emotionally concerned with numerous causes that in leaner times would be of subordinate priority. Older people, upon finding themselves with more free time, may pursue values that theretofore they had to ignore. Young people, growing up in relative abundance, may adopt value systems quite inconsistent with the value system that produced the abundance that frees them to devote themselves to cultivation of leisure.

Doubtless, race relations are a case in point. As material conditions improve generally, many people among all races have more time to recognize, object to, and attempt to solve racial problems. The result, strangely enough, is likely to be increased bitterness and human conflicts as opposing points of view clash. The emotions are not less intense by virtue of the fact that they have grown out of problems not always accorded primary priority in the affairs of men.

Campus unrest, not completely distinct from racial problems but extending beyond them, is perhaps another example of the new types of human conflict. The dilemma of higher education is not that the educational opportunities are poorer than they traditionally have been. Although the huge size of some institutions is definitely a handicap to quality, educational opportunities generally are far better in this country and in certain other parts of the world than in prior times. The unrest probably stems largely from a significant difference between the recent and current generations of students on the one hand and earlier generations of students on the other. The current generation probably has a much larger proportion of students who have never had to face the threat of real economic deprivation and who have had to devote relatively little effort to maintain their own material well-being. By and large many of these students have more time than did most of their predecessors to plunge into causes which formerly were of lower priority.

One such cause célèbre—and perhaps at the root of much of the campus disorder—is student participation in the management of educational institutions. Undoubtedly, this cause has been exploited by organized extremists, who, with varied motives, actually want to wreck the system of education in this country. More importantly, the cause is lent considerable support by large numbers of students with time to devote to such a pursuit. They have the time because society as a whole is sufficiently productive to afford them the freedom to indulge themselves in such problems.

The possibility exists that large numbers of students have been and will be manipulated, or even duped, by clever extremists. Still, the manipulation would not be as easily accomplished without the masses of students having the time to devote to such activities. The same point might be made in respect to some of the extremists themselves. Without relatively high material well-being, they might not, for example, have the time nor the enthusiasm to pursue the political aims of the New Left.

This new dimension of relative freedom from necessity and the ensuing conflicts was commented on meaningfully by R. L. Cutler, special assistant for urban affairs at the University of Michigan. In moderating a recent discussion published in the *General Electric Forum,* Cutler said:

For more than 20 years now the American middle class has enjoyed an affluence that would have been unimaginable to most youngsters in the 1930's. Today's young people are surrounded by enormous material wealth and I think they generally take it for granted. . . . They're used to getting what they want. They demand immediate solutions to problems and their key word is "now." The strain and frustration that result when they do not get what they want can be deadly.[31]

We are moved to wonder what will happen to individuals and to society if these young people discover as they grow older that they still have relatively more time free from occupational pursuits than did their elders. The result could be traumatic. A common complaint among many young people today, as well as among many oldsters, is that they are not really involved in the main business of life. With free time in a sense plaguing them throughout their lives, they could grow horribly frustrated in their inability to accept and pursue the leisure thrust upon them. Contemplation of the good in either the classical Greek or early Christian sense is likely to hold little appeal. Being action oriented, they are likely to act, even precipitously. Perhaps Dennis Gabor is justified in his apprehension that people generally are unable to embrace the concept of mass leisure.

Considering the rather ugly history of those who have tasted

---

[31]R. L. Cutler, "Industry's Responsibility in a Young Society," *General Electric Forum,* vol. 12 (Spring, 1969), p. 22, used by permission.

ease and plenty, we may have very little ground for supposing that relative abundance will ever promote peace and tranquility. On the contrary, if it should come about, it might be likely to produce such human conflict as to be self-limiting or even self-defeating. Perhaps the sad turn of events in the Garden of Eden was more prophetic than most of us care to admit.

In any case the current social unrest on the part of disenchanted youth bodes ill for the supposition that relative prosperity engenders goodwill, loyalty, gratitude, and respect toward the persons and institutions identified with the underlying prosperity. Perhaps the nature of man is to criticize, to challenge, and to repudiate the existing social order. If so, the criticisms, challenges, and repudiations may be all the more vicious and tumultuous if and as men are freed increasingly from the pressures of livelihood and afforded time to give attention to subordinate priorities.

George R. Vila, chairman and president of Uniroyal, Inc., has observed a curious irony. He points out that

... what we have already achieved in prosperity and freedom from drudgery has resulted, not in contentment, but in an enhanced selfishness and feeling of either alienation or rebellion in many sectors of our society. . . . It is indeed paradoxical that as we have relieved ourselves of our economic frustrations and increased man's scope and range, we have at the same time precipitated aggressions against our society and the system which created such abundance.[32]

Paradoxical or not, these precipitations, fed by the increasing freedom from necessity on the part of young people, strike at the ethical pillars of insurance and threaten the institution. Insurance markets, as we have already observed, are keenly sensitive to social turbulence. If the current social unrest is attributable even partly to young people attempting to adapt themselves to a leisure ethics, we can only shudder at the prospects of what might come if and when relatively more people find additional time on their hands. What is now referred to as a generation gap may then constitute a major social schism. We are forced to recognize in the words of De Grazia that "Poverty brings one kind of corruption; prosperity another." He also reminds us: "Peace and

---

[32]George R. Vila, "The Wages of Leisure," *Conference Board Record,* vol. 5 (March, 1968), p. 27, used by permission.

prosperity are dangerous if a country doesn't know what to do with leisure."[33]

Insurance consequences of such conflicts can be illustrated by a problem that is current at the time of this writing. Multiple-line underwriters are anxious to eliminate or greatly restrict the vandalism and malicious mischief coverage that applies to university and other public buildings. This coverage, when coupled with 90 percent coinsurance, historically has been sold in certain areas for a few mills per hundred dollars of insurance. One can understand the underwriters' wariness. One can also understand the growing need for this type of coverage where in large concentrations of property such losses over short periods can accumulate into hundreds of thousands of dollars. Increasing human conflict over the future decades can intensify problems of this type and ultimately destroy the market not only for vandalism and malicious coverage but also for direct damage insurance generally on many types of properties.

A second type of change in behavior with troublesome insurance implications pertains to gambling. Futurologists seem to feel that an indolent society is a society attracted to if not obsessed with gambling. Perhaps they simply take their cue from George Orwell. We recall from Orwell's *1984* that gambling was a way of life for the proles, those people so low on the social scale as not to be involved at all in the political activities. For whatever reason, gambling is a recurrent theme in futurologists' speculations. An example is as follows:

But on the whole the next twenty years will see mainly a vast increase in unthinking, uncritical leisure based on activities which depend upon random chance and the satisfaction of mathematical probability, like bingo, roulette, and certain card games, and on forms of gambling sports—football pools, horse-racing, greyhound-racing. . . . I believe . . . gambling . . . is likely to occupy the large mass of the population, cutting across all divisions of intellect, occupation, age, and sex.[34]

This prospect is not encouraging. A gambling society is likely to be an enervated society. The companion ills of shirked responsibilities, loss of zest to achieve, and dishonesty are likely to be evi-

---

[33]DeGrazia, *Of Time, Work, and Leisure*, p. 6, used by permission.
[34]H. M. Finniston, "Gadgets, Games, and Gambles," in Nigel Calder, ed., *The World in 1984* (Baltimore: Penguin Books, 1965), vol. 2, pp. 96-97, used by permission.

dent. These qualities are at fundamental odds with the ethics on which insurance depends.

A third behavioral change potentially troublesome for insurance, and the last one to be discussed in this chapter, has to do with profligacy. A productivity high enough to offer a majority of people in the United States substantially more time free from occupational demands could engender profligacy. Perhaps profligacy is not necessarily a sin in a society of plenty. What is wasted can easily be replaced. Nevertheless, insurance depends on a generally prevailing distaste for loss, a propensity to preserve rather than to squandor. A danger exists in a free-time society that the public, after a generation or two, could develop an extreme "easy-come, easy-go" attitude.

In such a case one of two possible consequences is likely to emerge: either the frequency and severity of insurance claims are likely to increase or interest in using insurance is likely to wane. In a purely utopian society of abundance and leisure, insurance probably is redundant. It is not needed for income replacement, for handling large expenses, for indemnity, or for defense against and payment of liability judgments. About the only imaginable need might be to cover the economic consequences of losing the utopia, and such a loss doubtless would be uninsurable anyway.

Thus it would appear that insurance, at least in certain types and amounts is needed less and desired less the closer one approaches his utopia. In such a situation an individual probably can afford increasing waste and is interested in insuring only a decreasing portion of his affairs. In the face of profligacy the insurance that is used is likely to be placed under increasing pressure from insured losses. Fundamentally, waste is repugnant to insurance. If our society really does become prosperous enough for waste to become a virtue, the institution of insurance will be in trouble. In the long run a waste ethic is incompatible with insurance.

In summary, some persons suggest that in the United States, at least for a few decades, productivity may grow so much faster than population as to generate much more time freed from occupational labors. Under several rather tight assumptions having to do with availability of cheap atomic energy such a condition is possible. The problems then would be quite different from those alluded to in earlier chapters as arising from scarcities. Reared on the belief that work is righteous and leisure suspect, Americans might have considerable behavioral difficulty in case they were required to reduce their work schedules substantially. Particularly troublesome insurance problems might arise in new types of human conflict brought about by increased time free from occupational demands, in tendencies toward gambling with its threat to the ethical pillars of insurance, and in the waste arising out of profligacy and running against the grain of the ethics of insurance.

7

TECHNOLOGY

Whatever the resolution of the abundance-scarcity issue, advances in science are virtually certain to yield new technologies that will change our lives. We turn now to consider some of the ways new technology over the long-range future may produce changes in ethics and moral behavior that, in turn, may create difficulties in the insuring process. No effort is made in this chapter to survey and catalog all of the improvements recently made and all of the truly remarkable potentialities that seem to lie just beyond the horizon. Technology is extensively treated in other studies, a few of which are cited in this chapter. Attention is given, however, to the details of several developing technologies that promise to be highly relevant to the theme of this book.

We read and hear so much about dramatic advances in science and the resulting improvements either recently made or about to be made in technology that we can easily become inured to the statements. The heavy repetition of these statements fosters a tendency on our part to shrug them off as melodramatic exaggerations. Perhaps some of the statements are overdone. Yet, the potential of science and technology over the next several decades is nothing short of astounding. We cannot be complacent about what is taking place technologically.

Technology is a word with a vague meaning. It conjures in our minds massive machinery, delicate instruments, electronics, mysterious phenomena such as laser beams and nuclear reactors, and laboratories where strange medicines are made. Technology is all these things and more. It is the totality of the means employed by a society to provide itself with the goods and services that comprise its material culture. It is knowledge about the universe put to work to satisfy material wants. It is application of know-how in making things that people want to consume directly, want to use in making other things, or want to use in performing services that other people desire. Indisputably, the quality of our lives depends largely on the state of technology. We have a vitally urgent interest in the pace of technological development.

Since this book pertains to insurance, we have occasion to focus on the relationship between technology and insurance. One is not hard pressed to see numerous aspects of this relationship. Technology will yield new products for which insurance is needed. Existing insurance contracts will have to be extended or new ones designed to apply to the new property. Similarly, technology will bring about new ways in which losses can occur to persons and things, and if the new perils are to be subject to insurance, then changes again will have to be made in insurance coverage. Technology will also render some of the present coverages obsolete because the property or the peril will no longer be pertinent to current modes of life. Technology is almost certain to permit tremendous economic growth that will enlarge the base of insurance. Premiums, even discounted for inflation, are virtually certain to be larger and will probably grow at an increasing rate. Technology will even affect the insuring process itself, and while it is not likely to add to the steps enumerated in Chapter 2 or to eliminate any of them, it may drastically change their manner of execution.

These statements indicate that the relationship between technology and insurance is intimate and detailed. In fact, insurance reflects changes in technology so accurately and so promptly that one can almost read the history of a society by tracking the changes in the insurance documents used in that society. One need only consider the changes in objects treated, the perils insured against, the nature of the exclusions in the contracts, the size of the premium, the method of settling claims, the principal sources of dispute, and the matters of current concern to the insurance regulatory authorities to perceive the major social developments. Insurance faithfully mirrors the technology and the social concerns of the society it serves.

With such a plenteous overplay between a society's technology and its insurance we could easily obscure the principal theme of this book and transgress its limited domain. Another reminder, therefore, may be in order that we are concerned only with the insurance consequences of possible changes in moral behavior produced over the long-range future by developments in science and technology. As was the case in our speculation about population growth and inflation, we are probing especially for signs of possible erosion of the ethical pillars of insurance and for signs of possible moral aberrations that may occur independently of any change in ethics.

Such an endeavor necessarily takes on a decidely negative tone. We pass over or give only scant attention to the remarkable and encouraging potential of our society to develop for the better. Many of the technological changes that may appear before the turn of the century have the potential of improving our lives immeasurably. They are a source of immense promise and hope; they may permit the people of this country to upgrade their moral behavior uniquely. Our treating such prospects lightly is not an indication of pessimism. The specific purpose of this study is to call attention to areas of stress and possible future difficulty, not to underscore the tremendous moral strength that our society has and is likely to retain. Hopefully, early attention to potential moral difficulties may contribute to their being avoided.

TECHNOLOGY AND HUMAN NATURE—A SPECULATION

To make progress in our study of technological advances and their ramifications, we need generalizations about the effects of technology on human behavior. Unfortunately, those generalizations cannot be documented. Some or all technological advances may be ethically and/or morally neutral; some may reinforce prevailing ethics and morality; others may undercut tradition. Of those technological advances that do create a pressure for change, some may tend toward one direction; some toward another.

One can argue with Tolstoi that human nature is basically unchangeable, the "great constant" running down through the ages. In such a circumstance scientific knowledge and technological advance are hardly likely to make much difference in the way people behave.

Their ends and means are likely to remain fundamentally the same. Whether one regards this human nature as fundamentally good or fundamentally bad is immaterial to the argument that it is not likely to change significantly. What appear to be changes over time may, in this view, be merely different expressions of permanent characteristics. The differences may arise because of changes in the environment that permit people to do what they would like to have done all along or that prevent them from continuing to do what they still want to do. The view sometimes takes the form of the assertion that God made man in His own image and that the image is eternal.

A distinctly different view, as previously discussed in Chapter 4, is that man is on a long, uneven ascendancy to a high plateau of ethics and morality. Whether this plateau constitutes a utopia, the "millenium," or something else, it is the destination—at least in an intermediate sense—toward which man is ascending.

Numerous other possible views about human nature offer themselves. One is that man is undergoing a gradual but steady moral descent. Another is that moral behavior is subject to recurring swings throughout time. The discussion cannot be final because the matter is indeterminate. Even if a historical relationship could be documented, no assurance would exist that the relationship would hold in the future. Technological advance in the future may contain an altogether different mix of ethical and moral influences than it has in the past. How the technological advances that are likely to come during the remainder of the century will influence ethics and morality in this country are matters that we cannot settle.

Inability to affix causality between changing technology and human nature does not preclude our making a speculation. The speculation offered in this chapter is that the particular mix of technological advances that appears to be in store in this century because of increasing scientific knowledge may contribute to a widespread weakening of the sense of the unique dignity of a human being. Over the decades to come, technological events may occur in such a way as to shake man's faith in his own capabilities and superiority. He may see himself increasingly at the mercy of large-scale events and processes. He may come to feel that the progress of events is increasingly beyond his control to the point that he loses confidence in himself and others and in his purpose in the universe. In such a perspective he could lose the feeling of fundamental worth that over the centuries has given man the air and feeling of unique dignity among all creatures. Out of this loss could grow a feeling of resignation and futility that could fundamentally alter his beliefs concerning what men ought to do, with a resultant change in his behavior. The fact that no such change has occurred before is no guarantee that it will not happen in the future.

The implications for insurance are profound because a widespread sense of futility is incompatible with the ethical foundation of insurance. It works directly counter to each of the ethical pillars on which insurance rests. In futility men are prone to stop trying as hard and to stop caring as much. Insurance is especially sensitive to such a change. For this reason we are justified in speculating about the possible effects of technological change on insurance if for no other reason than to be better able to prevent some of them from taking place.

In each of the following three major sections of this chapter attention is given to a particular aspect of scientific development and the new technology likely to follow in its wake. The science and technology are examined in terms of the way they may eventually undermine in people their feeling of human dignity. Such a speculation is not intended to detract from the wonders that the new technology holds nor from the progress that it may bring. Rather, the speculation is to give attention to what may be the dangerous, unwelcome, and perhaps unnecessary by-products of technology in the years to come.

NEW DIMENSIONS IN SCIENCE AND TECHNOLOGY

A highly impressive trend in science is the increasing breadth and precision of scientific measurements. As the dimensions of science, both maximum and minimum, are extended, the dimensions of technology will show similar characteristics. Something about these developments causes one to pause.

A search is under way to find the most elementary particles that constitute the fundamental building blocks of the universe. The studies call for extremely small measurements.[1] Recent research

---

[1]This discussion is based in large part on an article by Murray Gell-Mann, professor of theoretical physics at the California Institute of Technology, entitled "The Elementary Particles of Matter" in Edward and Elizabeth Hutchings, eds., *Scientific Progress and Human Values* (New York: American Elsevier Publishing Company, Inc., 1967), pp. 3-14. Copyright © 1967 by American Elsevier Publishing Company, Inc.

203

suggests that the numerous textbook statements asserting that neutrons and protons are the elementary building blocks are unfounded. Physicists working in the mysterious and microscopic realm of quantum theory are identifying and classifying numerous types of particles believed to serve as carriers in transmitting force between objects. One type of classification is based on the range and the strength of the force or interaction exerted. The physicists find themselves working with dimensions such as 10^{-13} of a centimeter or 10^{-40} on an arbitrary scale of strength. Such smallness is difficult to conceive. Even more strange is the fact that these numbers do not constitute the minimum to which measurement or calculation need go in the search for the ultimate, indivisible, stable particle of matter. The minimum apparently has not been and may never be reached.

Some of the particles are characterized by what the physicists call a "strong (nuclear) interaction." Others are not. Among the former are leptons, including electrons and neutrinos. Among the latter are the hadrons, including neutrons, protons, mesons, and baryons. Within both the leptons and hadrons nature seems to have created a strange symmetry between the respective particles and their opposites or antiparticles. A few types of antiparticles have been discovered recently in the laboratory. Because of reciprocal electrical properties, a particle and its antiparticle will annihilate each other on contact. What happens to them is not altogether clear.

Another unsettled point has to do with the composition of the several types of hadrons. Scientists are wondering of what the hadrons are made and if all or some of them might be composed of still more elementary particles. Conceivably they are. Some physicists are working with hypothetical particles called quarks and are presuming that these are the fundamental building blocks of the universe. Quarks are presumed to have an extremely small mass and electrical charge. In fact, three kinds are assumed to exist. Yet none has been found. If quarks are the fundamental form of matter in the universe, it is strange that none has been found. Yet, with the qualities and measurements imputed to them, they obey numerous predictions made about them, and they help to explain the behavior of the hadrons.

An even more engaging thought is that quarks, if they do exist, may be divisible. The particles into which they are divisible may in turn be divisible. If quarks do not really exist, the hadrons may be divisible into something else, still unknown. The point of this discussion for our purposes is to ask ourselves where, if at all, the subdivision of matter stops. As the scientists have learned to detect successively smaller masses, shorter ranges, and weaker forces, they have carried their inquiries closer to the infinitesimal. One wonders what the ultimate limit of their inquiries and measurements is. Could it be that there is no limit? If there is no limit, is everything theoretically divisible into nothing?

At the other extreme scientists with the aid of radioastronomy are now studying distances estimated not as 10^{-13} centimeters but rather in millions of light-years. The universe is composed of gigantic galaxies, perhaps a billion or more. While the galaxies vary in size, the figure of 100,000 light-years in breadth is not an unusual measurement. With light traveling at a rate in excess of 186,000 miles per second, the human mind has difficulty comprehending the distance measured by 100,000 light-years. Even so, the average distance between galaxies is thought to be about 3 million light-years. The galaxies extend at least to 5 billion light-years from the center of the cluster of galaxies and perhaps far beyond. Within the range of observation there are about 1 billion galaxies. Our own galaxy, the Milky Way, has perhaps 200 billion suns. For all we know, some or all of these suns may have planetary systems of their own. The systems could exist but be too small to be detected. The earth and the other planets in our own solar system are probably too small to be detectable at such a distance with our current technology. The galaxies may average 100 billion planetary systems per galaxy. If so, the combined total of planetary systems within the known universe could be at least a 100 million million million, or 1 trillion.[2]

What lies beyond the known universe is a matter of speculation and fantasy. Some evidence exists that the universe is still expanding. The expansion literally may be in the nature of an explosion with matter moving outward at the periphery with explosive force and speed. Perhaps the explosions are sustained for centuries or thousands of years with the outward movement continuing through space all the while.

---

[2]The figures and concepts in this discussion of astronomy have been taken from estimates made by Fred Hoyle, Plumian Professor of Astronomy at Cambridge University, and Jesse L. Greenstein, professor of astrophysics at the California Institute of Technology. See Fred Hoyle, *The Nature of the Universe* (rev. ed.; New York: Harper & Row, Publishers, Inc., 1960), especially pp. 93-115; and Jesse L. Greenstein, "The Speculations of Science about the Universe," in Hutchings, *Scientific Progress and Human Values*, pp. 15-26.

Within the known universe some of the stars are much hotter than our sun. They are so hot at their surfaces that instead of emitting regular light and heat they emit shortwave radiation (X rays). Other stars are larger than our sun, so large as to occupy all the space used by our entire solar system. Were the center of such a star located where the center of our sun is now, the earth would be deep inside the larger star. Our solar system is apparently about 5 billion years old but still much younger than most of the other suns in our galaxy.

If life does exist elsewhere in this galaxy, such life-forms could have had a head start on earthling man of a few billion years and thus could be considerably more advanced intellectually than we are. Greenstein perhaps spoke for all of us when he said:

> If intelligence succeeds in communicating with foreign intelligence the consequences will be tremendous. It was emotionally destructive to find that man was only clinging to the thin skin of a slag heap, revolving about a middle class star—one of two hundred billion—located in a remote suburb far from the center of our own Milky Way. Even worse, the larger universe revealed hundreds of millions of other galaxies, each with their stars and possibly with forever undetectable planet systems, and with inhuman time scales of billions of years. But more violent in emotional impact than the number and scale of mechanical things is the question of the possible presence somewhere else in the universe of life and mind vastly more advanced than ours.[3]

Greenstein did not indulge in speculation about what might be beyond the farthest galaxy. One can only be perplexed by thinking about what the outermost limit of the universe might be, what the maximum measurement is. Such thoughts, actually, are self-defeating. If the universe is "contained" in any other thing, then that container, itself, would have to be "in" something. One would have to think about the limits of the thing that contained the container, and so on. The only conceivable answer is that there is no limit and that beyond the farthest galaxy lies nothing—but plenty of it!

These diverse frontiers of science are amazing. Already, technology is moving in the wake of science. Computer and medical technologies, for example, are making use of exceedingly small dimensions. The measurements are still large compared to a quark but are small relative to minimum measurements of the past. At the

---

[3]Greenstein, "The Speculations of Science about the Universe," pp. 22-23, used by permission.

same time, the technology required for extraterrestrial travel uses measurements that, while minuscule on the scale of the universe, are gigantic compared to earlier maximum measurements.

This extension of the boundaries of measurement is sure to have a humbling effect on the human personality. No thinking individual can comprehend these activities without wondering about man's role in a universe vastly more complicated than earlier concepts held it to be. One reaction, and a highly satisfying one, is for an individual to feel all the more convinced that man is the product of an omnipotent God who keeps track of the objects of his creation, including human beings. This view is not merely deistic but is also theistic. It does not stop with the assumption that a powerful being created the universe. It proceeds to the conviction that God is personal, that he is running the universe, that he is sensitive to needs of those whom he has created, and, most importantly, that he is approachable by human beings whom figuratively at least he created in his own image. For Christians this access is through Jesus Christ who has the power to bestow eternal life to those who claim it through his name.

With this sort of concept of the universe and of man's relationship to God, one can take small and large dimensions in stride. Each step toward infinity and each new marvel simply provides for the believer more evidence of the majesty of God, who is the believer's own creator, protector, and friend. With such a view, one need never lose his sense of the dignity of a human being. Each advance in science and technology is a confirmation of his fellowship with God and his dominion over his environment as promised in this life.

The difficulty is that relatively few people on the earth hold to the conviction of a loving, involved, merciful, and personal god. Without such a conviction, contemplation of the ultimately small or the ultimately large can be decidedly unsettling; the sense of futility can be profound. Perhaps many people, upon thinking about these matters, have the same feeling of abject frustration that Hoyle expressed in the following lines:

It seems to me that religion is but a desperate attempt to find an escape from the truly dreadful situation in which we find ourselves. Here we are in this wholly fantastic Universe with scarcely a clue as to whether our existence has any real significance. No wonder then that many people feel the need for some belief that gives them a sense of security, and no wonder that they become very angry with people like me who say that this security is illusory. But I do not like the situation any better than they do. The difference is that I cannot see how the smallest advantage is to be gained from deceiving myself.[4]

Perhaps many individuals, not being so articulate as Hoyle, prefer not to ponder over such matters at all. Yet, the publicity attending each new step in science or technology calls to their attention the new dimensions and raises new questions about the nature of the universe and the function of man in it.

A further point needs to be treated. One might argue that even without religious faith, man need not feel insignificant. After all, man is doing the measuring, and he created the technology to which the measurements are related. The net result, so the argument goes, is more likely to be exhilaration than depression. Perhaps the argument is valid. One snag, however, is that only relatively few men do the measuring and develop the technology. The mass of humanity, about whom we are concerned, does not necessarily impute to itself the accomplishments of a few. Perhaps people generally do not feel a vicarious personal triumph as each scientific frontier is penetrated and each new technology is developed. The feeling is more likely to be a mixture of awe and confusion.

If large numbers of people begin to feel abjectly insignificant, ethics and moral behavior could be affected over the long run. Some people, with a feeling of resignation at the complexity and uncertainty of it all, may react with a stronger positive time preference. They may want more things immediately and grow increasingly impatient with obstacles, lead time, and prerequisites of work and merit. Positive time preference, when overdone, is inconsistent with the ethics on which insurance is based. It is at odds, particularly, with the ethical pillars of apprehension, tradition, and responsibility.

DEVELOPMENTS IN BIOLOGY

Let us turn now to the realm of biology and speculate a bit concerning the influence of advancing technology on the ethical pillars of insurance and on man's general sense of the dignity of a human being. The potential for advancement of knowledge concerning the nature of life and of living organisms is nothing short of astounding. The potential for health, comfort, pleasure, and relief from pain is, with-

[4]Hoyle, *The Nature of the Universe*, p. 121, used by permission.

out exaggeration, the most exciting development in the progress of mortal man. Nothing should obscure from our vision the benefits that these new technologies hold. They have the potential to change our manner of living drastically for the better, provided we are wise enough to use them to accomplish such an objective.

At the same time, and in keeping with the spirit of our inquiry in this book, we should also be mindful of possible adverse accompaniments of the technological advances in biology over the next several decades. The advances may occur so fast, may be so remarkable, and may affect so many people as to bring about a significant change in moral behavior.

We find that much publicity is being given to such exotic developments as regeneration of organs in certain living creatures, hibernation, removal of a living brain without disruption of its functioning, erasure or transfer of memory, linking of brains with computers, test-tube fertilization of human eggs and implantation of the fertilized egg in a womb, delay of aging, multiple production of identical living organisms, choice of sex of offsprings, and numerous other medical feats. Doubtless, some of the speculations are built on sheer fantasy; doubtless, others are much more substantial. Perhaps in the course of time all of them and even more startling advances will occur. Presently, however, we can easily grow confused in attempting to separate fact from fiction and the highly probable from the remote.

The point of acute relevance to our study is that the speculations recited above have to do with life itself. Holding life dear, as we do, we are emotionally vulnerable to any technology that changes our concepts of life and our adaptations to it. We think of Joyce Kilmer's well-known line "but only God can make a tree," and then we read of living tissues being created and grown in an unnatural habitat. We cannot help but wonder about the limit to which man will be able to go in learning about the mysteries of life.[5] Our reaction is a mixture of excitement and bewilderment.

Some people are already wondering if biologists and other scientists are going too far too fast in probing the secrets of life before

[5]For example, the December 18, 1967, issue of the *National Observer* carried a report of the work of Arthur Kornberg, professor of biochemistry at Stanford University and a 1959 Nobel prize winner, who, with colleagues, assembled from inert chemicals an artificial gene that can reproduce itself. It was reported as being an almost lifelike substance, pp. 1, 7.

humanity in general is ready to use the results. Gordon Rattray Taylor, author of a recently published book for laymen dealing with biology, has written:

> It seems quite possible that the rate of biological innovation may be so high as to destroy western civilization, perhaps even world culture, from within, creating a disoriented, unhappy and unproductive society, unless it is brought under deliberate control. . . .
> I am therefore forced to the conclusion that society will have to control the pace of research, if it can, and will certainly have to regulate the release of these new powers. There will have to be a biological "ice-box" in which the new techniques can be placed until society is ready for them.[6]

Taylor's concern may or may not be entirely justified. The fact that he would make such a strong statement in what is a generally dispassionate account of technological developments and outlook in biology is, itself, impressive. Still, his suggestion that the pace of research be controlled is out of order. In the first place, given the present organization of the world community, the pace cannot be controlled. Second, even if the pace were controllable, man would lose an inestimable potential for good by denying himself the knowledge that he might acquire. Surely man should learn all he is capable of learning about everything, including the phenomenon of life itself. Yet, he must also give full attention to the new problems that result. One of these new problems could be that, strangely enough, his growing knowledge about himself and other living things may detract from his sense of his own dignity. More precisely, what a few men learn and publicize about the heretofore mysterious aspects of life, growth, and death may disturb and confuse many other people unlettered in biology. This result need not necessarily occur. If it does occur, however, it may add to the erosion of the ethical pillars of insurance.

In the way of illustration let us look at three areas of likely remarkable advancement in biological science and in the associated technologies. In the process of this brief examination we will be particularly alert for possible ethical and moral implications of the developments that are likely to come to pass, many probably before the end of this century.

---

[6]Gordon Rattray Taylor, *The Biological Time Bomb* (New York: World Publishing Company, 1968), pp. 20, 21. Copyright © 1968 by Gordon Rattray Taylor. Reprinted by permission of the World Publishing Company.

Transplantations and Implantations

In recent years we have witnessed interesting advances in the technology of transplanting organs from one human to another. We have also seen development and use of artificial instruments that serve outside the body as substitutes for the heart, kidneys, and lungs. Relatively few of the efforts have been successful in the sense of restoring the patient to a normal life. Widespread criticism of motives, methods, and timing has accompanied this pioneering as, indeed, it accompanies most pioneering. Almost certainly, however, transplant and implant techniques will be refined and used on a gigantic scale in the future. Such techniques, despite setbacks and complications, are likely to be routine by the turn of the century. Let us sketch some of the prospects, recognizing in the process some of the major problems that may arise.

Living tissue transplanted from one member of a species to another member of the same species is referred to as a homograft and the process as homografting. So much attention in recent years has been given to transplantation of human hearts as to obscure in the public mind the work that is proceeding in respect to other organs. The fact is that kidney, liver, spleen, eye, limb, endocrine gland, and other transplantations have been undertaken. The surgical techniques, except perhaps for the liver, seem to be fairly well understood. Once the difficulty with the rejection of transplanted tissue is overcome, we can expect rapid increase in the use of transplanted organs.

Little doubt exists that the immunity barrier eventually will be overcome. By coincidence, at the time of this writing a United Press International news story appeared announcing that the structure of the key immunoglobulin molecule in human body chemistry has been ascertained. The news release states that the knowledge provides scientists with a way to learn how to assist the body in defending itself against bacterial, viral, and other harmful invaders and how to prevent the body from attacking vital organ transplants.[7] When biologists better understand the structure, they probably can

[7]Delos Smith, "Pure Antibody Structure 'Spelled Out'," as appearing in the *Bloomington* (Ind.) *Daily Herald-Telephone* (April 14, 1969), Sec. 2, p. 13. Gerald M. Edelman of Rockefeller University made the announcement in a paper delivered at the annual meeting of the Federation of American Societies for Experimental Biology.

rather quickly learn how to control the body's rejection apparatus so that it can resist bacteria and viruses while not resisting transplanted tissue.

Another avenue of inquiry and experiment builds on a technique long used in blood transfusions, which in a way are like transplantations. Efforts are being made to classify and match tissues in somewhat the same fashion that blood has been typed and matched in recent years. The aim is to seek maximum compatibility (or minimum incompatibility) between the tissues of the donor and the transplantee.[8]

Assuming that the immunity barrier to homografts can be overcome, we are likely to see a dramatic increase in transplantations. Despite all the perplexing legal and ethical questions that may arise, the demand for hearts, kidneys, lungs, livers, spleens, eyes, ears, fingers, hands, feet, whole limbs, glands, and other "replacement parts" is likely to become enormous.[9] The day may come when people, in the interest of delaying senescence, may routinely want preventive replacement organs even before malfunctioning becomes apparent in the "original equipment."

One needs little imagination to foresee frightfully difficult problems with supply. The present inability to store living organs is a decided constraint, although it may be overcome in due course. Storage banks may become operable, provided scientists learn how to keep the organs alive during the storage period. Perhaps cryogenics, the science of behavior of materials at extremely low temperatures, offers a possibility for successful organ storage.[10]

---

[8]Some of this work has been done by British biologist Sir P. B. Medewar, who was awarded a 1960 Nobel prize for medicine and who is the author of *The Future of Man* (New York: Basic Books, Inc., 1960). For a description of his work in tissue classification see Taylor, *The Biological Time Bomb*, pp. 59-60.

[9]Experiments are in progress that may lead to transplantations of ovaries and gonads. Concern is already being registered as to troublesome legal and moral questions of parental identity if and as the transplanted organs function in producing offspring.

[10]Some people, perhaps only because of wishfulness or desperation, are taking quite seriously the idea of freezing entire human beings who are near death. The hope is that when medical technology advances to the point of offering a cure for their disease or regeneration of their aged bodies they can be revived and cured or regenerated. Several corporations have been created to perform the low temperature storage. Numerous individuals have been frozen. The concept and hope attached to it are spelled out in Robert C. W. Ettinger, *The Prospect of Immortality* (rev. ed.; New York: Macfadden-Bartell Corporation, 1966). Since no hard evidence exists that cryogenically interred persons can ever be revived, much less cured or regenerated, the subject is not pursued further in this book.

Whether or not a way is found to store body organs, society may accept the idea that no organ that might be useful to sustain another's life should be buried or burned. We may see the establishment of a custom and the facilitating social machinery whereby organs are systematically and immediately removed from those for whom recovery is impossible. The legal, ethical, and moral problems latent in such a custom are readily apparent. We have already observed the discussions and the disagreements among authorities as to precisely when death occurs. We can expect the debate to focus on the precise identification of a patient's deterioration to the point of constructive death slightly in advance of the inevitable total death. The debate will be stirred by the widespread recognition that removal of organs from the dying individual after he has passed the point of no return but before he has reached the point of total death may mean that the life of another may be sustained. Removal of organs from the dying to provide longer life for the living may become a socially sanctioned practice. Even so, the question of just whose organs are to be removed, by whom, under what circumstances, when, by whose authority, and for what purposes will defy categorical answering for some time to come.

Since organs may become increasingly valuable as their transfer becomes easier, we can also expect a commercial market in human organs to develop. It may be legal or illegal. The value of a particular organ will depend in part on the simplicity and the reliability of homografting that organ. Any one of us might become willing to pay a considerable sum for a compatible organ necessary to prolong one's own life. Even though the idea of a market in human organs somehow seems repugnant, all of the market ingredients may be present, provided the immunity barrier is overcome. Joshua Lederberg, professor of genetics and biology, School of Medicine, Stanford University, and 1958 winner of a Nobel prize for medicine, has written:

> The medical revolution should begin to arouse anxieties over its orderly process. We must recall that the homograft "barrier" has preserved the personality of the body. We have not hitherto had to think deeply about the technology and ethics of allocating precious organs for lifesaving transplantations. The potential dehumanizing abuses of a market in human flesh are fully anticipated in imaginative literature. . . .
> . . . we cannot overlook what medical progress has already done for the species in the name of humanity—for example, the catastrophic leap in world population through the uncompensated control of early mortality. We must try to anticipate the worst anomalies of biological powers. To antici-

pate them in good time is the first element of hope in developing institutional and technological antidotes.[11]

The practice may develop where wholesalers or retailers in human organs will pay an individual during his lifetime for the right to his body, or certain parts of it, at the point of his constructive death. If demand for human organs does continue, the practice of selling one's organs in advance of delivery could become so commonplace as to develop into a new industry.

Even if we would grant the widest possible development of organ storage and the attendant creation of organ markets, whether public or private, commercial or charitable, supply may still fall far short of demand. Moreover, homograft transplantation is at best a cumbersome process. Other and better technologies may be developed.

One alternative technique is heterografting, or transplanting into a human the living tissue from a member of some nonhuman species. If the immunity barrier can be overcome for homografting, it probably can be overcome eventually for heterografting. The problem of supply could be enormously simplified by making transplants from nonhuman creatures.

Lederberg recommends that a vigorous eugenics program be launched with the objective of developing a particularly useful type of creature especially for supplying spare-part organs for humans. Obtaining a genetically constant inventory of organs in creatures bred solely for this purpose might simplify defeat of the rejection process in the transplantation.[12] Given the possibility of cloning (the production of identical or nearly identical offspring in large numbers), as discussed later, the organs perhaps could be fairly well standardized.

Some heterografts have already been made; kidneys from chimpanzees and baboons reportedly have been transplanted into human beings.[13] Although each reported that the donee died soon after the heterograft was made, death in at least one of the cases resulted from pneumonia two months after the operation rather than from

---

[11]Joshua Lederberg, "Biological Future of Man," in Gordon Wolstenholme, ed., *Man and His Future* (Boston: Little, Brown and Company, 1963), p. 268, used by permission.

[12]Lederberg, "Biological Future of Man," p. 268.

[13]D. S. Halacy, Jr., *Cyborg: Evolution of the Superman* (New York: Harper & Row Publishers, 1965), p. 77.

rejection of the organ, which seemed to be functioning well. The patient had been released from the hospital.

Successful heterografting, assuming it comes to pass, will result in what biologists call chimeras. In Greek mythology the term "chimera" refers to a she-monster vomiting flames and having a lion's head, a goat's body, and a dragon's tail. Biologically, this term refers to an individual, organ, or other part made up of tissues of diverse genetic origin or, loosely speaking, something made of incongruous parts. In the future many people may be able to live as chimeras whereas they would otherwise quickly die. If the immunity reaction problem is solved, the world within a few generations may contain millions of people each with one or more heterografts from commonly known animals or from uncommon animals developed, as just mentioned, to supply replacement organs for humans in need of them.[14]

A chilling postscript is that the creation of chimeras can work both ways. Human limbs someday perhaps can be grafted onto non-human creatures. While it is almost inconceivable now, the time may come when all or part of a human brain may be transferable into, say, a dog. One is hard pressed to decide what such a creature would then be.

An even more reliable source of replacement parts for human beings in the distant future may be artificial devices rather than living tissues. The concept of a prosthesis, such as a wooden leg or a hearing aid, is nothing new. What is new is the likelihood of implantation of devices in the human body to substitute for or supplement a natural organ and to operate automatically or even to be controlled by the individual's own brain. Such individuals could become increasingly machinal and decreasingly organic.

Credit is given to Manfred Clynes for coining the word "cyborg" to mean a hybrid human. The term is an abbreviation for "cybernetic organism," or for an artificially extended homeostatic control system that functions unconsciously. Clynes referred to man-made devices that, rather than being external or attached protheses, are implanted and *incorporated* into the regulatory feedback chains.[15]

---

[14]If the practice of homografting and heterografting grows so large as to cause death rates to decrease, the problems of population overgrowth, as speculated upon in Chapters 3 and 4, may become much more severe.

[15]Halacy, *Cyborg: Evolution of the Superman*, pp. 8, 9.

The concept of the cyborg has arisen from the new body of thought referred to as "bionics," a branch of cybernetics fusing biology and engineering. The pacemaker to assist in the regularization of the heartbeat is perhaps but an early and crude hint of what is to come. Artificial hearts and kidneys implanted in the human body, each with its own power source and feedback system, may be workable long before the turn of the century. Already, external machines have been used in lieu of human hearts and kidneys. Artificial limbs, controlled by the person's nervous system just as natural limbs are, may be commonplace within a few decades. Conceivably, an individual may have several artificial limbs capable of quite different purposes. The several limbs would be detachable, and the individual would put on whichever one best suited the particular purpose he had in mind. Halacy treats some of the novel implications of this possibility in the accomplishment of sustained hard work and in athletic contests. The cyborg in certain circumstances may be able to resist fatigue and perform in definitely superior fashion compared to an ordinary human being.

Much attention has been given recently at General Electric to the concept of "Cybernetic Anthropomorphic Machines" (CAM) that are robots with a feedback system. The feedback causes the robot to use its limbs to duplicate actions performed by the controlling human, although the robot is not made in the image of man. The machine, really an amplification of the man, can perform tasks calling for extreme delicacy or immense strength.[16]

The developments that have occurred and those that are probable make us wonder what the ultimate may be in the process of substitution, what such beings will be, and how they will behave. Mindful of Psalm 8:5 that man was created only "a little lower than the angels," we wonder what a human being really is. How much adaptation can take place without destroying the identity of the particular human being? How much can take place without causing the resultant being to lose his humanity? What is the minimum residue required for a human being? Is this minimum residue the brain? Is the mind something above and beyond the matter of which the brain is composed and the electrical and chemical actions and re-

---

[16]Taylor, *The Biological Time Bomb*, p. 83. Also, a United Press International release on April 9, 1969, described the work of Ralph S. Mosher at General Electric; he demonstrated the operation of his "Handyman."

actions that take place?[17] If a human brain could ever function outside the human body, would the functioning entity be a human? A serious question has to do with the ethics and morality to be expected of a homograftee, heterograftee, or cyborg. Another question is how the behavior of ordinary human beings will be affected by widespread contact with these adapted human beings. Early evidence suggests that, upon being rescued from the brink of death, homograftees may be likely either to develop an extraordinarily keen sense of appreciation of life or to become psychotic. Perhaps over the decades the answers to these questions will depend largely on the way the adapted beings are treated as they attempt to resume normal behavior. Surely a safe generalization is that the possibility of profound changes in the composition and perhaps the appearance of large numbers of people may alter prevailing attitudes about the dignity of a human being, with the result that a human might be considered to have less dignity than before and to be worthy of less respect.

Molecular Biology

By the turn of the century other advances in changing the nature of man may have been made in the field of biology. Recent understanding of deoxyribonucleic acid (DNA) has pointed up the possibility of direct alteration of many observable qualities of a human being. The development is at once so grand and so ominous as to warrant a brief explanation.

In 1859 when Charles Darwin published *The Origin of Species*, the prevailing theory of heredity was that parental qualities were blended in the offspring and that a thorough mixing occurred over the generations. Gregor Mendel's *Versuch uber Pflanzenhybriden*, published in 1866, led to the concept that heredity was based on a combination of particles and, thus, that a particulate and not a fluid theory was needed to explain heredity. The science of genetics and its subdivision of eugenics developed. Animal husbandry, embodying the idea of selective breeding so as to give desirable qualities the best chance of appearing in the offspring, became the accepted way of improving the stock of a species. In respect to humanity,

---

[17]J. B. S. Haldane, late British biologist, argued for a distinction in a discussion entitled "Future of the Mind," in Wolstenholme, *Man and His Future*, pp. 326-27. Numerous scholars engaged in the discussion. Haldane's comments were in retort to an assertion that the distinction between mind and matter led to a mistaken dualism.

where social restraints understandably hinder the practice of animal husbandry, progress in eugenics has been slight, having been largely confined to the discouragement or prohibition of procreation among the most eugenically inferior individuals.[18] Even in respect to animals and plants, genetics is a frustratingly tedious process.

Progress in molecular biology, including an understanding of DNA, within a decade or two may permit technicians to change the development of an embryo by interfering directly with its genes. If so, a change can occur within one generation instead of requiring many. The new process, referred to as "human engineering" or "euphenics," literally contemplates an interference with nature in order to redesign an embryo by removing undesired characteristics and substituting desired ones.

In the simplest terms we might say that the genes consist of DNA and that the genes perform four tasks: (1) they carry detailed instructions, or specifications, as to how the organism is to be manufactured; (2) they duplicate themselves when the cell divides; (3) they occasionally err in copying so as to permit a mutation (on balance, a copying mistake in a human gene occurs no more than once per million years); and (4) they send developmental instructions to the growing organism.[19]

Biologists can now read and substantially understand these developmental instructions. They also have a general idea of how the copying takes place and how ribonucleic acid (RNA) is used to transmit the instructions to control development of the organism. Surprisingly, they have found that the same basic language is used in the DNA of such diverse organisms as viruses, bacteria, tobacco plants, and man. They suspect that the code is universal! James F. Crow, chairman of the Laboratory of Genetics at the University of Wisconsin, has described the DNA structure as follows:

> The DNA molecule is a double coil. I think of it as a ladder with flexible uprights twisted so as to make a complete 360 degree turn every ten steps. (It is perhaps easier to visualize if we think of the ladder as

---

[18]In fact, eugenicists express grave concern that the efficiency of modern medicine in sustaining eugenically inferior individuals works against improvement of the human race. Since these individuals live long enough to procreate, qualities that would disappear under conditions of natural selection persist over the generations, perhaps even on an expanding scale.

[19]This discussion is based in part on information in James F. Crow, "Heredity and Evolution," in Hutchings, *Scientific Progress and Human Values*, pp. 80-94. For further details readers are invited to consult this lucid source.

straightened out, thereby brushing under the rug a number of topological difficulties) [sic]. The steps are each composed of two parts, a pyrimidine and a slightly larger purine. The space between the uprights is sufficient for one of each, but too small for two purines and too large for two pyrimidines. There are two purines, A and G, and two pyrimidines, T and C. (A stands for adenine, G for guanine, C for cytosine, and T for thymine.) The rules of chemical binding specify that A can bind only to T, and C only to G. Thus there are four kinds of stairsteps A-T, T-A, C-G, and G-C; if half the step is known, the other half is uniquely determined.

There is nothing in the chemical structure that specifies that the steps need be in any particular order. This immediately suggest that the information is carried in the sequence of stairsteps. There are 4^{1000} permutations in a gene 1,000 units long; clearly there is no shortage of information-carrying capacity.[20]

He explains further that the two complementary vertical halves of the ladder split easily because they are held together by a hydrogen bond much weaker than the chemical bond holding together the rest of the DNA structure. The ladder or a part of it has a tendency to split up the middle. Each split part then has a tendency to pick up a complement like that from which it split.

The basic idea of euphenics is that the instructional code can be directly altered, in the embryo or elsewhere, to produce a different being than would otherwise have resulted. The process is limited only by man's knowledge of how to rewrite the genetic code and by his inclination to intervene. This knowledge is virtually nil at the present but is likely to grow rapidly now that the basic instructional pattern is understood. Lederberg, who suggested use of the term "euphenics," has speculated as follows:

From principle to detail is still a big step. We do not in fact yet know the actual nucleotide sequence of any gene. Only in micro-organisms, whose DNA content is from a millionth to a thousandth of man's, can we momentarily substitute one DNA molecule for another in the genetic composition of a cell, and then inferentially judge the chemical differences between them. But a little inspiration and reasonable effort will be rewarded by detailed knowledge of genetic structure, very soon for microbes, no more than a decade or so away for parts of the human genome.[21]

[20]Crow, "Heredity and Evolution," p. 87, used by permission. The parenthetical expressions are those of Crow.

[21]Lederberg, "Biological Future of Man," p. 264, used by permission. He also observes: "Most predictions of research progress have proved recently to be far too conservative," p. 266, used by permission. Taylor, *The Biological Time Bomb*, p. 202, estimates that as of 1968 there were about 200,000 biologists in the world. Even if a small proportion of this number addresses itself to this problem, the efforts may be massive and the progress fast.

If and as euphenics does yield a practical technology, the possibilities for altering the qualities of man become fantastic. Perhaps within a few decades certain qualities can be eliminated from and other qualities built into large segments of the human race. Some qualities that are now relatively rare, such as photographic memory, conceivably can be introduced on a much wider basis. Over a period of a few centuries virtually the whole human race might be redesigned.

Another interesting thought is that if euphenicists can remold one embryo to a new design perhaps they can also learn to remold another to the same design. If they can produce two such organisms, perhaps they can produce many. Thus, the prospect of cloning becomes something more than an idle thought. "Clone" comes from the Greek word meaning twig or slip. In biology it refers to a genetically uniform mass of cells asexually reproduced. Cloning of identical cells has already been accomplished in respect to carrots.[22] No similar experimentation with animal or human cells is reported in the sources cited in this chapter. Such experimentation may not be in progress and in fact may never be undertaken. Yet, the concept is quite consistent with euphenics. We must remember that the relatively recent deciphering of the genetic instructional code represents a truly major advance in knowledge. In the context of such a discovery, precedents mean little. Similarly, earlier estimates of what is possible and what is not have been rendered suspect. Thus, some day a large number of absolutely identical or closely similar beings (human or otherwise) may live at the same time. Perhaps they may even be engaged in designated occupations. In the long run the process might even lead to a categorizing of society, or parts of it, in the manner of the Epsilons, Deltas, and others in Huxley's *Brave New World*. On the other hand, cloning may never proceed to such an extent. Here as in numerous other parts of this book we find ourselves speculating about truly stupendous potentials in the face of tremendous uncertainties.

The obvious threat that accompanies the obvious blessing of euphenics is that the knowledge of how to control the design of

[22]The science and technology of cloning as of the middle 1960s is described in Taylor, *The Biological Time Bomb*, pp. 23-30. The discussion is in the context of growth of organisms in vegetative fashion, with the growth starting without normal fertilization.

human beings could be misused. The technology may prove simple compared to the problem of how to use it. The question of who is to say what traits and physical characteristics are desirable in whom appears almost impossible to answer. The answer comes down to ethics and theology. Perhaps relatively little difficulty might be encountered in reaching agreement to eliminate certain characteristics, such as a propensity for epilepsy. Much more difficult, however, might be decisions as to size, shape, sex, intelligence, coloring, pugnacity, strength, memory, ambition, compassion, stubbornness, and so on, assuming that any of these would come within the euphenicist's control.

The knowledge of how to interfere need not necessarily lead to interference with normal development of embryos. It is hard to visualize, however, that the knowledge would be acquired but never used. Another possibility is that the knowledge might be directed simply to a reinforcement of the basic ethics on which insurance depends, as discussed in Chapter 2. Such an outcome, however, seems no more likely than any other. If moral behavior really does become subject to considerable change over the next several decades, no assurance exists that euphenic decisions would necessarily be compatible with long-run availability and use of insurance. If such decisions are left to parents, we can expect that they will cover the spectrum of possibilities. If sooner or later society as a whole or a segment of society takes a hand in making the decisions, there is no telling what the outcome of the public decision making may be. If euphenics technology does develop, humanity in the years to come may find itself divided into groups, each group representing a particular value judgment as to the *desiderata* in a human being. Ultimately, euphenics could replace national and ethnic criteria for classifying human beings.

Whatever the way of making the decisions, assuming euphenics develops to the point of rendering such decisions important, the result might be a further loss in the sense of the unique dignity of a human being. The knowledge that an individual could, in a sense, be tailored to specifications could prove to be immensely disturbing and could upset traditional ways of approving virtue or disapproving the lack of it. One's outlook in regard to the possible consequences of euphenics doubtless is shaped by his faith or lack of faith in the innate, unalterable long-run wisdom and goodness of man. Lederberg's caution, quoted earlier, that we should anticipate the worst in the hope of preventing its coming to pass is sound advice.

In this spirit, then, we are justified in at least recognizing the possibility that euphenics may lead to changes in ethics and morality incompatible with the long-run availability and use of insurance. Hopefully, the evidence as to which ethical pillars of insurance are to be challenged will become apparent early enough, euphenically speaking, for something to be done about the challenge.

Behavior Induced by Drugs or Surgery

Finally, in this discussion of biology, we need to speculate about ethics or morality being altered over the long-run by drugs, surgery, or some combination of the two. Evidence understandable to a layman as to what has happened and what may happen in this regard is elusive. The specter of mind control looms, but its dimensions are not at all distinct. Yet, one thing is clear: whereas drugs and brain surgery traditionally have been thought of merely in terms of restoring the organism to its normal functioning, they are becoming increasingly able to change behavior compared to the norm. Let us examine very briefly one aspect of this potential and then consider its implications for ethics and morality.

By the turn of the century man may have learned much more about how to control his behavior through the use of drugs and through brain surgery. These potentialities are simultaneously wonderful and frightening. If such technologies become realities, two consequences will result: (1) an individual may consciously and willingly alter his own behavior or (2) an individual's behavior may be controlled or at least influenced by another without his permission or even his knowledge.

Behavioral influence is nothing new. Hudson Hoagland, professor of biological psychiatry at Boston University and former president of the American Academy of Arts and Sciences, points out that we control each other through cajolery, seduction, and incitement. To the list can also be added threat, intimidation, duress, and coercion. Human beings in virtually all types of societies and cultures have developed effective ways of countering many of these attempts at behavioral controls. The future may disturb this balance. Hoagland repeats a warning made earlier by psychologist B. F. Skinner, who says a real danger exists that new technologies of behavioral control may come so fast that effective countercontrol measures will not keep pace. Hoagland expresses his own concern by adding: "Despite objections, science will increasingly facilitate control of human behaviour and it must be used wisely if we are to avoid disaster."[23]

One of the ways that behavior may be influenced, if not controlled, is through the use of mind-affecting drugs. Psychopharmacology during the last two decades or so has already produced new stimulants, antidepressants, and tranquilizers. These drugs primarily affect the subject's mood or disposition. No doubt other drugs can be developed to alter behavior even more strikingly. As Taylor points out, "It would be absurd to suppose . . . that the discovery of new mind drugs will stop at this point. As the chemistry of the brain is gradually unravelled, an increasingly extensive and precise intervention in mood will surely become possible." [24] Among the possibilities are antiaggression drugs (and presumably their opposite, aggression drugs) and more refined aphrodisiacs and anaphrodisiacs. Little imagination is needed to visualize the discovery and production of pharmacological agents to influence the level of compassion or hostility, to sharpen or confuse one's recognition of traditionally held values, to add to or detract from one's slowness to anger or despair, and to increase or decrease one's susceptibility to suggestions from another.

Equally interesting is the possibility of altering behavior by means of surgery. The surgery may consist of tiny lesions in the brain or it may involve implantation of devices for electrical stimulation, perhaps remotely controlled. Experimentation has been done already on animals. Minor lesions in certain areas of the brain of normally vicious animals render them docile. Conversely, certain normally gentle animals, subjected to relatively minor brain surgery, are turned into raging, vicious beasts. In other experiments pecking orders and other hierarchical relationships have been changed after brain surgery on the subjects. Microelectronic instruments even now can be and have been implanted in the human brain to control pain. They have been used in animal, bird, and fish brains to control sleep, hunger, thirst, sexual desire, alertness, aggression, and other responses.

[23]Hudson Hoagland, "Potentialities in the Control of Behaviour," in Wolstenholme, *Man and His Future*, p. 304, used by permission. Skinner expressed his concern in an article, "The Control of Human Behavior," published in *Transactions of the New York Academy of Sciences*, vol. 17 (1955), pp. 547-51.

[24]Taylor, *The Biological Time Bomb*, p. 129. Reprinted by permission of the World Publishing Company.

Hoagland speculates that in time chemical agents may be found that will selectively accomplish what is now done by surgery. Already, cats exposed to certain substances for potential use in chemical warfare can become terrified at the sight of mice.[25] The additional results of a few more decades of experimentation are likely to be sensational—even incredible.

If an individual in the future can expose himself fairly routinely to drugs or surgery that will alter his behavior, or if technologies develop by which others can influence or perhaps even manipulate him, the prospects are overwhelming. Both situations, should they become commonplace, would hold tremendous potential for good or evil. Possibly, behavioral alteration might develop to the point where a particular kind of ethics can be infused into human beings. Even with fabricated ethics and morality, however, many of today's fundamental problems would remain, having only been moved from one place to another in the decision chain. For example, if an individual *could* fashion his own behavior in advance, he would still have to decide *how* to fashion it. If others could do it for him, with or without his consent, a massive problem would arise in regard to who should make the decision about the type of ethics and morality to be instilled. Whether such infused ethics would include those necessary for insurance to function is problematic. Also problematic is the question of whether life would be tolerable at all in a society where even morality was deterministic, resulting strictly from controlled electrical and chemical actions in the brain.[26]

Still, if the technologies are developed, they are likely to be used. The way in which they are used could have a powerful influence on what man feels he ought to do and on his consistency in

[25]Hoagland, "Potentialities in the Control of Behaviour," p. 309.

[26]Some persons might argue that such a deterministic system has always operated and that the concept of "free moral agency" is illusory. They go so far as to insist that crime is largely attributable to faulty genetic or other physical composition rather than to controllable choice. In her March 9, 1969, syndicated column Flora Lewis reports a case of a lawyer arguing that his client should not be punished for robbery. The premise was that the accused had an extra Y (male) chromosome and that the extra chromosome, according to certain scientists, disposed the individual toward criminality and removed the act from the individual's own realm of responsibility. *Indianapolis Star*, Sec. 2, p. 3. If judges and juries begin to honor such defenses before scientists develop the technologies for preventive control, whether or not the argument has any merit in the first place, crime frequency may increase drastically. Removal of fear of punishment could destroy a powerful deterent to criminal action.

following his convictions. In any case the growing awareness that human psyche can be manipulated could detract from the sense of human dignity even on the part of those whose behavior is not altered. F. H. C. Crick, recipient of a 1962 Nobel prize for medicine, articulated a speculation shared by many when he said, "The development of biology is going to destroy to some extent, our traditional grounds for ethical beliefs, and it is not easy to see what to put in their place."[27]

CYBERNETICS

Still another scientific and technological development, cybernetics, is likely to exert major influences on our way of life over the next several decades. We could be just at the threshold of an extensive advance in knowledge. The potential advance is not completely distinct from the developments in biology already discussed. In fact, it doubtless will contribute to those developments. Since it is primarily a methodology rather than a subject, however, it goes beyond biology to embrace every division of human knowledge. The probability of cybernetics producing major changes in our society by the turn of the century seems high enough to warrant our considering a few of the fundamentals of this relatively new phenomenon. Let us look first at the nature of cybernetics and then at some of the possibilities cybernetics holds for bringing change. Finally, let us speculate about some of the ethical and moral implications of such changes, especially as they pertain to the availability and use of insurance.

The Concept of Cybernetics

As a scientific discipline cybernetics is closely identified with Norbert Wiener, who, before his death in 1964, was professor of mathematics at the Massachusetts Institute of Technology. He pioneered its early theoretical development during and after World War II. Since Wiener's death, cybernetics as a science and a technology has advanced far beyond its earlier state, and the coming decades are likely to see his vision for this science fulfilled and even surpassed.

[27]F. H. C. Crick, "Ethical Considerations" in Wolstenholme, *Man and His Future*, p. 364, used by permission.

Since Wiener is often thought of as the father of cybernetics, it is fitting in our brief consideration of the subject that we look to his writings among others for conceptual substance. Wiener defines cybernetics as control and communication in the animal and the machine.[28] Numerous other writers have either adopted or modified this definition. For example, Stafford Beer, head of the Department of Operational Research and Cybernetics of The United Steel Companies Limited in Great Britain, says simply that "cybernetics is the science of communication and control."[29] On the other hand, two Czechoslovakian authors, Jiri Klir and Miroslav Valach, regard the Wiener definition as expressive but unnecessarily restrictive. They present a compilation of sixteen variations and finally settle on a fairly involved definition that contains several terms to which they have given specific mathematical meanings.[30] Most of their definitions, however, embrace in one fashion or another the idea of control of some sort of system through the communication of information. Thus, the basic concept of cybernetics clearly seems to be the use of information to produce the desired output on the part of some entity capable of performing in an environment that changes over time. The entity is controlled in such a way that it adapts its performances to the changes it detects in its environment.

Although the term cybernetics has been traced back to Plato, Wiener is credited with giving it a modern use. As Wiener has written:

> Until recently, there was no existing word for this complex of ideas, and in order to embrace the whole field by a single term, I felt constrained to invent one. Hence "Cybernetics," which I derived from the Greek word *kubernetes*, or "steersman," the same Greek word from which we eventually derive our word "governor." Incidentally, I found later that the word had already been used by Ampere with reference to political science, and had been introduced in another context by a Polish scientist, both uses dating from the earlier part of the nineteenth century.[31]

---

[28]Interestingly enough this definition is found in the title of his classic book, *Cybernetics or Control and Communication in the Animal and the Machine* (2d ed.; New York: The M.I.T. Press and John Wiley & Sons, Inc., 1961).

[29]Stafford Beer, *Cybernetics and Management* (New York: John Wiley & Sons, Inc., 1959), p. 7.

[30]Jiri Klir and Miroslav Valach, *Cybernetic Modelling* (London: Iliffe Books Ltd., 1967), pp. 65-69. This book resulted from the translation into English, by Pavel Dolan, of a manuscript published in 1965 in Czechoslovakia.

[31]Norbert Wiener, *The Human Use of Human Beings* (Boston: Houghton Mifflin Company, 1954), p. 15, used by permission.

Plato used the term to refer to the science of steering ships. The Latin word meaning "governor" apparently is a variation of the Greek word for "steersman."

To understand cybernetics one must understand the concept of a system. A system is a set of related elements or connected parts. The universe is a system; so is an atom or a basketball team. Other examples are a state high school athletic association, a political party, a manufacturing association, a machine, a human being, a country club, and an automobile. The choice of the type and size of system to study is arbitrary. What is a system for one purpose might be an element in a larger system for another purpose or several systems for still a different purpose.[32] An element in the context of a system is merely a part which is not to be divided further.

Some systems can be studied and controlled by persons who use only their normal sense organs. Other systems are too small for the relevant detail to be perceived without the use of sensory aids such as a microscope. Still others are too large to be approached by a single individual in any situation.

Klir and Valach use the helpful expression, "resolution level," to refer to the degree of detail to be studied in a system.[33] Generally, as the system grows smaller, the level of resolution required to study it rises. Cyberneticists usually content themselves with the lowest resolution level that will permit them to perceive the relations among the elements in the system, assuming that the relations can be perceived at all.

Systems can be arbitrarily classified in numerous ways. One dichotomy is physical and abstract. (The former could be an airplane; the latter an equation.) An especially interesting classification that we consider later is animate and inanimate. (The former could be a human being; the latter, a clock.)

Several terms must be defined in the context of cybernetics. "Stimuli" is defined as all effects of the environment on the system and "responses" as all effects of the system on the environment. The "behavior" of a system is thought of as the response produced

---

[32]In the light of our earlier discussion of minimum and maximum dimensions we cannot help but wonder about the limits on the size of existing systems. Presumably, the largest is the cosmos itself, and the smallest is the combination of two quarks or whatever the smallest denomination of matter may be.

[33]Klir and Valach, *Cybernetic Modelling*, p. 25.

by a given stimulus. Finally, the "structure" of a system refers to the arrangements of the elements within the system.

Wiener emphasizes that cybernetics is based on information; that is, the control of the behavior of the system is accomplished through exchanges of information between the system and its environment. He regards cybernetics as being mainly the theory of messages, or information theory. The quantity of information in a system relative to its size is a function of its degree of organization. The higher the quantity, the higher the degree of organization and the lower the degree of confusion.

Wiener says that confusion is the archenemy of scientists in general and cyberneticists in particular. He points to the tendency in nature for the degree of organization in any system to decrease over time. He recognizes, particularly, the loss of information that occurs in communications. The content of a message received is seldom as large as the content of the message sent. A principal concern of the cyberneticist is to minimize the tendency toward loss of information.

Wiener likens the tendency toward increasing confusion to the generally increasing entropy as indicated by the second law of thermodynamics. This idea stipulates that heat will not pass from a cooler to a warmer object. As the heat passes from a warmer to a cooler element in a system, the potential energy remaining in the system is reduced. Thus, the system tends to run down. In general terms, entropy refers to the tendency of an isolated system to achieve a uniform distribution of energy throughout its elements, resulting in the cessation of all activity. Curiously, entropy increases as uniformity is approached; at maximum entropy, uniformity (and thus stagnation) is achieved.

The universe or at least the solar system is generally subject to increasing entropy. Ultimately all earthlings are likely to be the victims of heat-death as the sun's energy is more evenly distributed. Even so, there are now what Wiener calls "enclaves" of decreasing entropy in the larger environment of increasing entropy. A system whose information (degree of organizing) is expanding is an example. The work of the cyberneticist is to maximize the antientropic character of various systems.

The heart of cybernetics is the concept of feedback. This concept distinguishes cybernetics from our traditional concept of automation. The central idea of feedback is that a machine, which can be thought of as any purposive system, be able to adapt its performance to accommodate itself to a change in its environment. The classic and simple example is the old Watt governor to control the speed of a machine. The governor works in this fashion: Weighted arms are attached to an engine. As the engine turns at increasing speed, the arms also turn faster. Mounted on pivots, the arms rise by centrifugal force as they turn more rapidly. A valve allows power to enter and cause the engine to turn. As the arms rise with increasing speed of the engine, they reduce the size of the valve opening. The resulting reduction in the intake of power causes the engine to turn more slowly. If the engine slows too much, the arms fall to the extent of allowing extra power to come through the valve to speed the engine. Thus, the engine is allowed to maintain the stipulated speed but is prevented from exceeding it. The stipulated speed is attained by self-regulation after the input and output are balanced.[34]

A more modern example of feedback is found in the operation of a guided missile pursuing a target that is taking evasive action. The missile adjusts its course to correspond to changes in the course of the object being pursued. Input into the missile system includes information having to do with earlier performance of the missile and changes in the missile's environment, namely the moving target. Using information that it generates about itself and its environment, the missile can *adapt*. This adaptation is the essence of feedback and the distinctive feature of cybernetics.

Adaptation distinguishes a cybernetic system from what we popularly regard as automation. An automated machine is one capable of repetitively performing a given task, even a highly complicated one. A cybernetic system is one capable not only of performing this task but also of learning how to improve its performance on the basis of its earlier mistakes or how to alter its performance as necessitated by a change in its environment.

In discussing feedback Wiener contrasts a cybernetic system with a mere mechanical system where little figures dance on a music box. The dancing figures perform their programmed routine on signal. They cannot omit any of it, add to it, or otherwise change it. The stimulus-response pattern is set. The system is closed. On the other hand, a cybernetic system includes "sense organs" to alter the input

---

[34]A more detailed description is found in Beer, *Cybernetics and Management*, p. 29. It could be said that the governor regulates the homeostasis of the engine's behavior. See Chapter 3 for a discussion of homeostasis.

and the output. The function of monitoring is also included. As Wiener explains:

This control of a machine on the basis of its *actual* performance rather than its *expected* performance is known as *feedback*, and involves sensory members which are actuated by motor members and perform the function of *tell-tales* or monitors. . . . It is the function of these mechanisms to control the mechanical tendency toward disorganization; in other words, to produce a temporary and local reversal of the normal direction of entropy.[35]

The simple but yet remarkable phenomenon of feedback has led to the development of systems referred to as learning machines. A system of this type has the capacity to measure its performance against a specified goal and alter its performance continuously in order to maximize attainment of the goal.

In complex systems the learning and thus the control rest in a digital computer (or a group of linked computers) coupled with a performing machine (or group of performing machines). The computer accepts information about earlier performance and about the environment as input, processes the information in accordance with instructions given to it, prepares output in the form of instructions to the performing machine(s) that it controls, and monitors the activity of the machine(s). Simultaneously it makes adjustments to maximize the goal-seeking potential of the system.

Cybernetics can use feedback in a simple, deterministic type of system where a given stimulus leads to a known or determinable response. More importantly, a cybernetic system can operate in the face of considerable uncertainty. In fact, Wiener stresses that a cybernetics model can operate on a probabilistic basis in a contingent universe. The computer accepts the data about earlier performances and the environment as input. It stores the information and uses it as necessary in computation of the probability that each of numerous courses of action will lead to the desired goal. On the basis of the probability computations it then chooses the course of action most likely to achieve the goal.

To illustrate the concept Wiener comments on the possibility of developing a machine to play a reasonably inspired game of chess. At each move the machine actually calculates at very high speed all

---

[35]Wiener, *The Human Use of Human Beings*, pp. 24-25, used by permission.

its own admissible moves and takes into account in each case all the opponent's admissible ripostes for two or three moves ahead. It then selects the move with the highest probability of checkmating the opponent in due course. With each move, it reassesses the situation and alters its selections accordingly, even learning from its own mistakes and from the style of game displayed by its opponent. Wiener refers also to a learning machine that is a checker-playing apparatus. The machine in the course of 10 to 20 operating hours learns to defeat in a fairly consistent way the person who programmed it.[36] Wiener insists that these machines are anything but trivial in their import. Their refinement since the time of his writing bears out his point.

Let us look briefly at one more illustration. Stafford Beer describes one example of a remarkable family of cybernetic machines developed by Gordon Pask. One variant of the Pask machines can, itself, be used to help a human being learn. This learning machine then also becomes a teaching machine. The particular machine described by Beer is programmed to teach a person how to operate a key punch machine used to prepare punch cards. The keyboard has 12 keys. Beer's description of its operation (which really is an account of his own experience) is highly informative. Beer related his experience as follows:

> You are confronted with a punch: it has blank keys, for this is a "touch typing" skill. Before you, connected to the punch, is Pask's machine. Visible on it is a little window, and an array of red lights arranged like the punch's keyboard. The figure "7" appears in the window. This is an instruction to you to press the "7" key. But you do not know which it is. Look at the array of lights. One is shining brightly: it gives you the position of the "7" key, which you now find and press. Another number appears in the window, another red light shines and so on. Gradually you become aware of the positions of the figures on the keyboard, and therefore you become faster in your reactions. Meanwhile, the machine is measuring your responses, and building its own probabilistic model of your learning process. That "7", for instance, you now go to straight away. But "3", for some obscure reason, always seems to elude you. The machine has detected this, and has built the facts into its model. And now, the outcome is being fed back to you. Numbers with which you have difficulty come up with increasing frequency in the otherwise random presentation of digits. They come up more slowly, too, as if to say: "now take your time." The numbers you find easy, on the contrary, come up much faster: the speed with which each number is

[36]Wiener, *Cybernetics or Control and Communication* . . . , pp. 169-73.

thrown at you is a function of the state of your learning. So also is the red-light system. For as you learn where the "7" is, so does the red-light clue gradually fade. The teacher gives you less and less prompting. Before long, if you continue to improve on "7", the clue light for "7" will not come on at all. It was getting fainter on "5", for you were getting to know that position. But now you have had a relapse: "5" is eluding you altogether. Your teacher notes these fresh mistakes. "5" is put before you with renewed deliberation, slowly; and the red light comes back again, brightly.

So the teaching continues. You pay little intellectual attention: you relax. The information circuit of this system of you-plus-machine flows through the diodes and condensers of the machine, through the punch, through your sensory nerves and back through your motor nerves, the punch, the machine. Feedback is constantly adjusting all the variables to reach a desired goal. In short, you are being conditioned. Soon the machine will abandon single digits as the target, and substitute short runs of digits, then longer runs. You know where all the keys are now; what you have to learn next are the patterns of successive keys, the rhythms of your own fingers.[37]

Exceedingly complex systems have now been built to do a variety of tasks, each task contributing to the goal programmed into the system. The science and technology of cybernetics are proceeding so rapidly that even the distinction between living systems and inanimate systems is not so clear-cut as it once was. We traditionally think of a living system as having progenitors, as having the ability to exchange matter and energy with its environment, as having the ability to anticipate the future, as being excitable, as being able to organize information within itself and thus improve itself, and as being able to reproduce itself.[38] With the exception, perhaps, of excitability, certain inanimate systems now exhibit the characteristics we have traditionally associated with living systems. As we have observed, they can take information from the environment and improve themselves in terms of their programmed goals. They can compute probabilities. In theory at least, a cybernetic computer-manufacturing machine also can be programmed so as to reproduce itself. In fact, a whole cybernetic factory theoretically can be programmed to reproduce itself.

In the final chapter of their *Cybernetic Modelling* Klir and Valach speculate on the question: Can an inanimate system live? They point out that traditional criteria for ascertaining life have been (1) the behavior of the system and (2) the structure of the

---

[37]Beer, *Cybernetics and Management*, pp. 124-25. used by permission.
[38]Klir and Valach, *Cybernetic Modelling*, pp. 406, 411-13.

elements of the system, that is, the way the elements are related to one another. Given the complexity and sophistication of many modern systems, these authors despair of applying the old criteria to distinguish between living and inanimate systems. They leave the matter unsettled.

Wiener argues that such words as life and living are vague and that we might as well avoid them. He suggests that the really pertinent issue is the extent to which certain systems can simulate behavior of other systems, particularly human behavior. He says that these life imitators simply resemble human beings in representing pockets of decreasing entropy in a general environment where entropy usually tends to increase.[39]

We would be remiss in concluding our discussion of the nature of cybernetics without commenting on the concept of the "black box." Cybernetics is not limited to the control of systems whose operations are thoroughly understood. Let us visualize a system with numerous inputs and one or more outputs. The cyberneticist may fully understand what inputs are necessary to obtain a desired output and what occurs within the system to cause the stimuli to produce the desired response. A situation so understood is referred to as a "white box." Suppose, in respect to another system, that the cyberneticist has little or no understanding of the structure of the system. Using a probability-statistical approach, he may still be able over time to observe that a given pattern of inputs will produce the desired output. Thus, he may be able to exercise considerable control over the system without actually having the faintest understanding of how or why the particular input leads to the particular output. This situation is referred to as a "black box." The black box concept has been used for centuries in medical practice. Since it also applies to cybernetics, it adds another dimension to the potential of this powerful science.[40]

Second Industrial Revolution

Wiener envisioned that cybernetics would soon create a second industrial revolution fully as important as the first.[41] Kenneth Boulding

---

[39]Wiener, *The Human Use of Human Beings,* pp. 32-33.
[40]For more details see Beer, *Cybernetics and Management,* pp. 49-57.
[41]Chapter 9 of *The Human Use of Human Beings* is entitled "The First and The Second Industrial Revolution."

seems to have been thinking in a similar vein when he wrote that this nation and others are entering a postcivilized stage of maturity.[42] Herman Kahn and Anthony Wiener use the term "post-industrial society" to refer to much the same kind of transition.[43] Clearly, machines are rapidly assuming a growing burden of the work in our society. Whereas they formerly provided merely the power for extracting materials from the earth, processing the materials, and distributing the products, they now do more by exercising much of the control over these activities.

The development of cybernetics is bound to continue, probably at an increasing rate. Wiener has observed that not even the cyberneticists have the power to undo what they have done. For better or worse, the growing knowledge is at the disposal of man to make of it what he will.[44] We can reasonably expect that by the turn of the century the cybernetic revolution will be far advanced. Factories without workers, unmanned transports, self-operated entertainment facilities, schools without human teachers, and cybernetically monitored self-service retail establishments may be more nearly the rule than the exception. Cybernetic treatment of business and personal finance may mean that money as a medium of exchange will be outmoded and that financial institutions may be of quite a different character. Medical technology and health care are likely to be highly cybernetic.

Although the details are quite speculative, the trends seem to be reasonably clear. Cybernetic systems will become a major means of production in the United States and perhaps in other highly advanced societies. Probably few people are aware of just how profound and dramatic the changes over a 30-year period are likely to be!

The greatest uncertainty lies in the question of the power of cybernetics to circumvent or at least forestall the consequences of population overgrowth discussed in earlier chapters. Population pressures may be so great as to swamp the productivity benefits that cybernetics, coupled with low-cost energy, may bring. If world

[42]Kenneth E. Boulding, *The Meaning of the Twentieth Century* (New York: Harper & Row, Publishers, 1964). Chapter 1 is devoted to a discussion of the "Great Transition."

[43]Herman Kahn and Anthony Wiener, *The Year 2000* (New York: The Macmillan Company, 1967), pp. 185-220.

[44]Wiener, *Cybernetics or Control and Communication . . .* , p. 28.

population continues to grow indefinitely at an average annual compound rate of 2 percent or more, it is hard to see how mankind can live comfortably even in a cybernetic society.

We would do well to recall here Sir Julian Huxley's warning that we err in viewing mankind as being caught in a race between population and production of life-sustaining goods and services. He reminds us that there is no hope of ultimately winning a race against a indefinitely increasing population. Rather, for the sake of the human species, population must be stabilized. Whether the maturation of cybernetics proves to be a turning phase in the economic affairs of the human race or merely a delaying gambit in the human drift toward disaster remains to be seen.

Ethical and Moral Implications

Regardless of whether the next few decades are characterized by feast or famine, we can see several long-run ethical and moral implications of cybernetics. Moreover, they seem to work at cross purposes. On the one hand, the prospect is highly reassuring. As the title of Wiener's popular book implies, the idea of a machine doing work so as to free a human being for activities befitting his human status is exciting indeed. Relief from tasks that a nonhuman system can perform is potentially a great boon to humanity. The opportunities for a general upgrading of all human effort are almost utopian in character.

On the other hand, as Wiener warns, cybernetics brings with it the prospects for disaster. He was not concerned that the machine-systems would assume control of worldly affairs or seize control in any sense.[45] He did, however, see a danger in cybernetic systems being used by unscrupulous men to pursue socially reprehensible goals.[46] This prospect, however, as dangerous as it is, was not Wiener's major concern. He feared even more the consequences of human beings having the slave labor that cybernetic systems someday could provide. As Wiener put it, cybernetics

. . . gives the human race a new and most effective collection of mechanical slaves to perform its labor. Such mechanical labor has most of the economic

---

[45]In fact, he objects in *The Human Use of Human Beings*, pp. 182-83, to the ideas in Samuel Butler's *Erewhon*, where machines conquer mankind by using men as subordinate agents.

[46]Wiener, *Cybernetics or Control and Communication* . . . , p. 27.

properties of slave labor, although, unlike slave labor, it does not involve the direct demoralizing effects of human cruelty. However, any labor that accepts the conditions of competition with slave labor accepts the conditions of slave labor, and is essentially slave labor. The key word of this statement is *competition*. It may very well be a good thing for humanity to have the machine remove from it the need of menial and disagreeable tasks, or it may not. I do not know. . . .

Perhaps I may clarify the historical background of the present situation if I say that the first industrial revolution, the revolution of the "dark satanic mills" was the devaluation of the human arm by the competition of machinery. There is no rate of pay at which a United States pick-and-shovel laborer can live which is low enough to compete with the work of a steam shovel as an excavator.[47] The modern industrial revolution is similarly bound to devalue the human brain, at least in its simpler and more routine decisions. Of course, just as the skilled carpenter, the skilled mechanic, the skilled dressmaker have in some degree survived the first industrial revolution, so the skilled scientist and the skilled administrator may survive the second. However, taking the second revolution as accomplished, the average human being of mediocre attainments or less has nothing to sell that it is worth anyone's money to buy.[48]

How sad the last sentence of the quotation really is. Since most human beings may be "of mediocre attainments or less," the full flowering of the cybernetic revolution may mean that computer-machine systems may be able to do virtually any repetitive productive task better than most human beings. The experience is bound to be humiliating. The fact that these marvelous machines were themselves designed by and remain generally subservient to highly intelligent men may be of little comfort to the large masses of people who understand neither their more intelligent peers nor the machines designed by their peers.

The ramifications of cybernetics for insurance are by no means clear. If population is controlled and large numbers of people are freed from the necessity of working as much as they work now, the leisure-related problems discussed in Chapter 6 will be real. If, as may well be the case, population overgrowth brings growing scarcities despite the development of cybernetics, the growing aware-

---

[47]Wiener originally wrote this in 1947. Now, even the steam shovel has grown obsolete.

[48]Wiener, *Cybernetics or Control and Communication* . . . , pp. 27-28, used by permission.

ness of the machines' numerous superiorities may simply compound some of the problems discussed in earlier chapters. In either situation—growing abundance or growing scarcity—a widespread realization on the part of adults and young people that machines can simulate and even improve upon many aspects of human behavior may prove to be degrading. Such a realization may provide another loss of the general sense of human dignity. If so, the effect on the ethical pillars of insurance and on moral behavior may be extreme.

8

ETHICAL RELATIVISM
AND INSURANCE

Thus far we have considered the long-range influence on ethical thought and moral behavior, as related to insurance, of several major changes that may occur in the next few decades. We have speculated about population overgrowth, inflation, the possibility of increased leisure, certain concepts in physics and astronomy, three areas of likely advancement in biology, and probable further sophisticated developments in cybernetics. We have been interested in the possible difficulty each phenomenon might create for insurance through a change in ethical thought or moral behavior.

We recall that in Chapter 1 ethics was defined as what men ought to do and morality as what they actually do as measured against their ethics. Ethical *thought*, therefore, would relate to what men *think* they ought to do. What they ought to do and what they think they ought to do, however, are not necessarily the same. The disparity, if any, would result from a flaw in men's ethical thinking.

Our foregoing discussions have evaluated how the several phenomena may alter men's thinking about what they ought to do, but we have not really considered the underlying question of what, indeed, they *ought* to do. Even our discussion in Chapter 2 about the ethical foundation of insurance relates only to the behavioral prerequisites of insurance. The discussion does not extend to whether insurance or anything else really "ought to be." Such an extension would take us far away from the main theme of this book, namely, possible difficulty for insurance because of changes in ethical thought or moral behavior. The selection of this topic in the first place, however, is sufficient evidence that in the author's ethical thought insurance ought to be.

Whether the phenomena selected for study in the earlier chapters are the ones that will have primary influence on future ethical thought and moral behavior remains to be seen. Their selection for discussion in this book is, itself, a value judgment. Perhaps other major developments affecting nations or the community of nations should have been selected instead. Only time will reveal the vision or lack of vision in the choice. Wisely or unwisely, we have proceeded on the assumption that ethical thought and moral behavior are strongly influenced by the state of affairs in which human beings find themselves. We have undertaken to show that their ideas about ethics and their morality may be influenced by a number of fundamental phenomena in the world in which they live. In this view ethical thought and moral behavior are partly dependent variables; they are regarded as being dependent to some extent on major features of the physical environment.

In the present chapter we consider a different point of view in which ethical thought and moral behavior are not wholly derived from the physical universe but, rather, seem to be capable of changing in and of themselves. Such changes, according to this view, may occur apart from causal changes in the physical environment and, in fact, may actually produce changes in the physical environment. We consider briefly one major trend in ethical thought which, if not totally independent of the phenomena discussed in earlier chapters, may at least go far beyond what these phenomena would require. The trend appears to be stronger than necessary to have been generated by the phenomena we have studied. It appears to be feeding upon its own momentum or upon other causes we have not identified. The trend is toward relativism in ethical thought.

RELATIVISM VERSUS ABSOLUTISM

Relativism in ethics and morality is not a simple thing to understand. For centuries it has been the subject of discussion and disagreement. Currently, it goes by many names: ethical pluralism, moral skepticism, contextualism, situationism, or the "new morality," to mention a few. Each label carries its own peculiar conceptual connotations and nuances.

Unless we are careful to distinguish between relativism and absolutism in ethics and morality, we could easily become confused. We can draw the distinction that is central to our purpose by posing for ourselves the following question: Are there one or more objective, absolute, universal, permanent rules to guide all men in all times and all places, without exception as to circumstances, in what they ought to do?

We should recognize, by the way, that the answer to this question does not depend on our knowing what the rules are. We must confess, however, that one would be hard pressed to know that such rules exist without knowing what they are. Still, such knowledge is possible. For the purpose of this chapter we need only recognize at this point that an affirmative answer implies absolutism in ethics and a negative answer implies relativism. We are not attempting to identify any rules or to say whether or not they are absolutely binding.

Apart from the matter of offering a substantive answer to the question, we find ourselves confronted with a bewildering residue of other related questions. For example, if the answer is affirmative and one or more permanent, absolute, universal rules do exist to permit man to make ethical judgments, how did such rules come into being? Some ethicists may choose to answer this question in metaphysical and theological terms and say that the rules were created by God. They may also say that God promulgated the rules.[1] H. Richard Niebuhr seemed to have been thinking in this vein in writing that any ethical system not based on a monotheist faith was strictly relativistic.[2] On the other hand, Immanuel Kant seemed to say that absolute moral rules exist apart from God but that they have God's blessing since they are perfectly consistent with God's purpose for man.[3]

---

[1]While "promulgated" sounds suspiciously like property-liability insurance jargon, it is also a handy term for ethicists, who use it freely.

[2]H. Richard Niebuhr, "The Center of Value," in Ruth Anshen, ed., *Moral Principles of Action* (New York: Harper & Brothers, 1952), pp. 162-75.

[3]W. T. Jones and others, eds., *Approaches to Ethics* (New York: McGraw-Hill Book Company, Inc., 1962), p. 255. As we see later in this chapter, Kant took the position that the absolute moral law is discernible by the use of reason and not dependent on specific revelation by God to man. See the discussion of Kant's *Religion Within the Bounds of Reason Alone* in A. D. Lindsay, *Kant* (London: Oxford University Press, 1934), pp. 203-14. See also pp. 45-49 of Lewis White Beck's translation of Kant's *Critique of Practical Reason* (Chicago: The University of Chicago Press, 1949). The passage is in Beck's introduction.

If the answer to our central question is negative, numerous residual questions, apart from the matter of *how* ethical judgments are to be made, remain. For example, are there any rules at all? If at any given time there are one or more rules that are not immutable, on what basis do changes in the rules occur and to what are the rules relative? If one or more rules permitting ethical judgments are subject to exception, what additional rule or rules, if any, expose and regulate the exception?

One approach to relativism, as illustrated by Shia Moser, professor of philosophy at the State University of New York at Buffalo, is that of "necessary evil." The view is that something normally ethically undesirable may have to be done or tolerated as the price of achieving a greater good or avoiding a greater evil.[4] He cites the case of patricide among certain warring Indian tribes as the means of saving oldsters from a much more horrible death at the hands of victorious and vengeful enemy tribes. In a related situation, a certain action may be wrong, but those performing it are not blameworthy. Moser's example of this is the practice of the ancient Moabites in sacrificing children to Moloch in the belief that the sacrifices were required to placate Moloch who could strike the whole people with disaster.[5]

A second approach to relativism is suggested by Howard Selsam. Selsam says that a society's ethics is created by the difference between individuals' circumstances and their aspirations—by the spread, as it were, between their reality and their vision. In this view "the ought" in ethical judgments apparently is relative to the possible, and it changes as technology or another causative agent changes what is possible. The rules for ethical judgments are the products of the geography and the state of technology in question. The exceptions appear—and ultimately change the rules—as man's knowledge increases and his aspirations expand. Changes in the rules occur because man, and only man, becomes discontent with his life and his fate and wants to improve them.[6]

A third—and the extreme—approach to relativism is found in pure moral skepticism. Here the point of view is that cases requiring

---

[4]Shia Moser, *Absolutism and Relativism in Ethics* (Springfield, Ill.: Charles C Thomas, Publisher, 1968), pp. 25-26.

[5]Moser, *Absolutism and Relativism in Ethics*, pp. 21, 23.

[6]Howard Selsam, *Ethics and Progress: New Values in a Revolutionary World* (New York: International Publishers, 1965), pp. 13-18.

ethical judgment vary so widely as to be virtually unique. Generalities become practically useless, and each judgment has to be made in "standardless moments" for which there are no applicable rules. Few ethicists seem to go so far as to insist that no generalizations of any sort can be applied to any ethical judgments. The case for moral skepticism, but not necessarily pure moral skepticism, is found in Mortimer Adler's *A Dialectic of Morals*. Adler as the teacher argues for a moral law applicable in the same objective way to all men, while the student argues that there is no such moral law but rather that morals are subjective and relative to the time and place. In the dialogue Adler is forced to stop short of proving the operation of any objective rules for ethical judgments, equally binding on all men at all times and all places.[7]

While additional comments could be made about absolutism and relativism, perhaps enough has been said to clarify the distinction and to suggest the complexity of both concepts. Let us look very briefly, then, at the attention paid to these concepts by some of the famous ethicists of the past and the present.

TWO STREAMS OF THOUGHT

Generalizations about ethical thought are difficult to draw. Seldom, if at all, have any two ethicists arrived at precisely the same idea of what is good or at precisely the same method for making ethical judgments. Even within the numerous schools of thought the differences between master and disciple and the differences among disciples are pronounced. Virtually every treatment that has been preserved over the years, decades, and centuries is unique in some important respect. Perhaps this very uniqueness has been a factor in the preservation of the treatment.

Despite the diversity and the discontinuity that characterize ethical thought, one can see that the issue of absolutism versus relativism has been recognized in many of the writings. It is too much of a simplification to say that every ethicist identifies himself as an absolutist or a relativist on the matter of ethical judgments. Some of the writings—at least to a layman—are so obscure as to defy con-

---

[7]Mortimer J. Adler, *A Dialetic of Morals* (Notre Dame, Ind.: University of Notre Dame, 1941).

fident classification. Others suggest that the writer wanted to occupy both sides of the issue simultaneously or to ignore the matter
altogether.

No oversimplification is involved, however, in one's saying that
the works of numerous famous ethicists seem to fit more comfortably on one side than on the other of this great and continuing
debate.[8] We might profit from even a crude attempt to place the
two streams of thought in juxtaposition. Granted the use of huge
tolerances and highly purposive sampling, we are in a position to
proceed, provided we recognize that brevity and misunderstanding
may do an injustice to those whose writings we consider. Let
us discuss, first, the ethical thought that seems to fit under the
general heading of absolutism, beginning with the early Greek
ethicists.

One of Socrates' principal doctrines is that virtue is knowledge.
This doctrine apparently was formulated in rebuttal of the moral
skepticism of the Sophists. Socrates held that evil arises out of
ignorance and that knowledge would show the error of evil ways.
With knowledge applicable and available to all in full measure,
virtue becomes absolute, being based on objective knowledge.[9]

Plato, a pupil of Socrates, uses the dialogues in the *Republic*
and *Philebus* to set forth Socrates' position. Also concerned with
showing the error in Sophist thought, Plato wrote in the *Republic*
about Absolute Good or the Idea of the Good. This good, he said,
manifests itself in four cardinal virtues: justice, wisdom, fortitude
(courage), and temperance. He believed that knowledge of the
Absolute Good is achievable by only a few persons, who should be
the rulers. The knowledge comes, he felt, only through study and
contemplation. His description of the ideal republic was an effort to
show that there is only one ideal system of moral conduct based on
knowledge of the Absolute Good.[10]

---

[8]Since ethicists characteristically address themselves to the strengths or weaknesses in the positions taken by other ethicists, use of the word "debate" may be
permissible.

[9]Summarized from Reginald A. P. Rogers, *A Short History of Ethics* (London:
Macmillan and Co., Ltd., 1937), pp. 34-36. Readers will notice that heavy reliance
in the following paragraphs is placed on Rogers's crisp and lucid treatment of the
history of ethics. Acknowledgment is gratefully made of this source.

[10]Rogers, *A Short History of Ethics*, pp. 32, 52-59.

Evidence of a belief in absolutism is found also in the dogma of the Stoics. Stoicism is doubtless the product of many minds and perhaps varies from one source to another. Some of the tenets, in fact, came from the earlier Cynics, including Antithenes. Central to Stoicism, however, is the idea of accepting and acting rationally in accordance with the eternal and immutable laws of the universe, abjuring discontent, accepting pain, controlling emotions, and resigning oneself to the larger Nature of which man is but so small a part. In Stoicism, virtue is the chief good and requires recognition of the authoritativeness of duty and the cultivation of indifference to misfortune. Many facets of Stoicism were accepted by the early Christians and also were used by Spinoza, Kant, and others.[11]

Several variations of the ethical thought of the Middle Ages were clearly related to Christian or Hebrew theology and, naturally, emphasized the absolute, as revealed by God through faith. Philo, Plotinus, and Augustine were among the ethicists who wrote on the subject in the first 500 years or so following the crucifixion of Christ. Of the Scholastic philosophers who were active from the ninth to the fifteenth century, Thomas of Aquinas (1225-1274) is perhaps the best remembered writer. St. Thomas held fast to the absolutism in

---

[11]Rogers, *A Short History of Ethics*, pp. 95-102; Gerald H. Rendall, *Marcus Aurelius Antoninus to Himself: An English Translation with Introductory Study on Stoicism and the Last of the Stoics* (2nd ed.; London: Macmillan and Co., Ltd., 1898). Because of the influence of the Stoics on Kant and because of the attention given later to Kant's ethical thought, a passage is quoted in this footnote to give us a bit of the flavor of Marcus Aurelius' brand of Stoicism: "When you awake, say to yourself—To-day I shall encounter meddling, ingratitude, violence, cunning, malice, self-seeking; all of them the results of men not knowing what is good and what is evil. But seeing that I have beheld the nature and nobility of good, and the nature and meanness of evil, and the nature of the sinner, who is my brother, participating not indeed in the same flesh and blood, but in the same mind and partnership with the divine, I cannot be injured by any of them; for no man can involve me in what demeans. Neither can I be angry with my brother, or quarrel with him. . . . Every hour staunchly, as a Roman and a man, resolve to do the work in hand, with scrupulous and unaffected dignity, affectionately, freely, justly; securing respite for yourself from all other intruding regards. And this you will secure, if you perform each task as though it were your last, free from all waywardness, from passions adverse to the dictates of reason, from insincerity, self-love, and discontent with destiny. . . . Ever bear in mind what nature is at large, what my own nature is, how this stands to that, how small a portion of how great a whole, and further, that no man can prevent you from keeping act and word always accordant with that nature of which you are a part" [pp. 12, 14, 15].

Christian theology and to the thought that faith aids reason in discernment of the truth. He believed that Aristotle's intellectual system provides the best description of natural reason, that knowledge of God is the highest good, and that this knowledge leads to proper ethical judgments.[12]

Baruch (Benedict) Spinoza, who lived from 1623 to 1677, displayed in his principal work, *Ethica*, a sentiment akin to Stoicism. In this sense Spinoza was an absolutist, believing that peace of mind comes with recognition that the laws of nature are unalterable. He regarded reality as perfect and evil as being caused by ignorance of reality. In the latter respect he was like Socrates. He linked personal well-being to the exercise of virtue and believed, like Socrates and Plato, that knowledge is intrinsically good. These precepts suggest a thought system that presupposes unalterable rules for making ethical judgments.

A large body of ethical thought is known as intuitionism. Ralph C. Cudworth, who lived in seventeenth century England, was an early intuitionist. Some of the modern ethicists who are currently publishing also might be classified as intuitionists. A large group stands between Cudworth and the present-day ethicists. While intuitionists differ widely one from another in their thinking, most of them have argued that rules for ethical judgments can be discerned intuitively. The implication is that the discernment can be made because the rules are consistent and objective, applying to all. Some intuitionists, such as Shaftesbury, have insisted that the discernment comes through a special faculty, a "moral sense."[13] Others, such as Butler, have regarded conscience as having a supremacy of authority and as permitting one to intuit right from wrong. Still others, especially Kant, have argued that, while the discernment is intuitive, it comes as the result of the use of the intellect rather than through a special moral sense or conscience. Whatever their particular beliefs, intuitionists have generally taken the position that good is absolute, that moral conduct is subject to inviolate laws, and that an act good or evil for one person is similarly good or evil for another.

[12]Rogers, *A Short History of Ethics*, pp. 113-15.

[13]See, for example, James Bonar, *Moral Sense* (New York: The Macmillan Company, 1930).

Perhaps the principal message this brief review holds for us is that quite a sizable body of ethical thought down through the centuries indicates that what one ought to do is determined by definite, unchangeable, nonexceptional rules that are consistently and universally applicable. This body of literature further emphasizes that, while one may act in ignorance of the rules, he cannot escape their immutable consequences.

The history of the opposing stream of ethical thought, that of relativism in ethical decisions, is long and varied. A convenient starting point is found in the pronouncements of the Sophists in the fifth century B.C. Protagoras is reported to have said, "Man is the measure of all things." Another way of putting the thought might be that good is entirely subjective and that for any person, what appears to him to be good *is* good. Further, he need worry about no one but himself. This emphasis on self is often termed "exclusive egoism." Gorgias, who might have been the particular Sophist whom Socrates and Plato were rebutting, reduced the concept to pure moral skepticism in denying any objectivity whatsoever to moral behavior.[14]

Led by Aristippus of Cyrene, who was born about 435 B.C., the Cyrenaics turned the concept as expounded by Gorgias from negative to positive by arguing that immediate pleasure is the only good. They advocated basing all ethical judgments on the pleasures of the moment. An act or a quality is virtuous, they held, only if it yields immediate pleasure. The Cyrenaics were the first Greek hedonists.[15] Hedonism is the general name of the doctrine that pleasure is the only, or at least the chief, good.

Epicurus, born about 341 B.C., refined the Cyrenaic type of hedonism into an ethical system whose chief end is the maximizing of long-run pleasure, not merely the pleasures of the moment. In his view knowledge is only the means of efficiently pursuing the well-being that comes in pleasures of long duration; it is not a virtue or an end in and of itself. Among the pleasures he personally valued were rest, freedom from disturbance, contemplation, and friends. He thought of justice as a mere convention, a compact, by

---

[14]Rogers, *A Short History of Ethics*, pp. 31-34.
[15]Rogers, *A Short History of Ethics*, pp. 39-40.

which individuals mutually agree not to injure each other. He recognized that reason and experience remind us that not all potentially pleasurable activities should be pursued without restraint. Some control over one's emotions and impulses would be necessary to achieve the goal of maximum long-run pleasure. He pointed to pleasure during a whole life as the highest good and deemed temperance to be an important means of attaining that good.

Unlike the Stoics, the Epicureans—or at least some of them—advocated avoiding unpleasantness at all cost.[16] Given their exclusive emphasis on pleasure, one might argue that the Epicureans are absolutists, with pleasure being the only absolute. Such an argument is weakened, however, by the fact that the sources of pleasure need have no consistency from one person to another or even for a given person from one period to the next. The answers to questions of "ought," therefore, are not based on immutable laws governing moral behavior but rather on one's anticipation of pleasure in alternative courses of action.

Aristotle would seem to have been somewhat ambivalent in his ethical concepts as they apply to absolutism and relativism. His ideas do not fit neatly into either stream of thought, although in some respects they fit better into the relativistic than the absolutistic stream. As we noticed in Chapter 6, Aristotle regarded contemplation of the good as the final goal of human activity and thus as something pursued for its own sake. He discussed well-being as the ultimate good but implied that its substance is far from being exact.[17] One is left with the feeling that Aristotle was primarily a relativist on matters pertaining to ethical decisions.

After the Middle Ages, relativistic ethical thought flowered again. In 1651 Thomas Hobbes published his *Leviathan*. Hobbes's thought is closely linked to that of Epicurus. Hobbes can be classified as being in the school of "egoistic naturalism." His view, in brief, is that each individual is a center of desires and aversions and that political organization is the means for providing maximum satisfaction for all individuals. He believed that the organization had to be extremely powerful in order to create the harmony conducive to the satisfaction of individual desires. His choice of the word

---

[16]Rogers, *A Short History of Ethics*, pp. 85-92.
[17]Rogers, *A Short History of Ethics*, pp. 64-81.

"Leviathan" (a sea creature of huge size mentioned in the forty-first chapter of Job) is a clue to his thinking in this regard. In Hobbes's view the good of the state becomes intermediate and primary to the good of the individual, but, at the same time, the state exists only to permit the interests of the individual to be served. Like Epicurus, Hobbes held that justice is a conventional necessity, not a natural virtue. He believed that a powerful political organization is the best means for providing the necessary mutual respect for personal desires and aversions. The implication in Hobbes's pattern of thought is that ethical decision making is based on relativities, depending on what best serves the immediate interests of the particular organization and thereby the interests of individuals in the aggregate.[18]

David Hume also deserves attention in this survey. He is considered to have been a naturalist. In his *Treatise of Human Value* (1739) he asserted that moral distinctions are derived from feelings, not from reasons or any mysterious intuitive perception. He held that virtue is that which is pleasing and vice is that which is painful.[19] This view is similar to that of Epicurus; yet the contextual difference between Hume's "pleasing" and Epicurus' "pleasure" seems to be significant. Perhaps Hume allowed more room than did Epicurus for the pleasant feeling that could come from a kindness or other favor done for another. Hume wrote in his *Enquiry Concerning the Principle of Morals* (1748) that from society's point of view, ethical judgments should be based on public utility. In this thinking he anticipated the utilitarians.

Jeremy Bentham and John Stuart Mill were the prominent utilitarians. The essence of utilitarianism is that ethical judgments should be made to provide the greatest happiness to the greatest number of human beings. An action demanded in one case is not necessarily demanded in another. Bentham formulated the basic principle of utility, which, he felt, pointed to what men ought to do. In his *Introduction to the Principles of Morals and Legislation* (1789) he said that any action could be approved or disapproved according to its tendency to increase or decrease the sum total of human happiness. He argued that all other ethical standards are of

---

[18]Rogers, *A Short History of Ethics*, pp. 126-43.
[19]Jones and others, *Approaches to Ethics*, pp. 232-38.

no consequence. This principle of utility is relative in the sense that no given action necessarily ought to be performed at all times in all places and circumstances; that is, what ought to be done is relative to the time, place, and circumstance. Bentham contrived a calculus by which to measure pleasure on the hedonistic scale.

Mill modified Bentham's ideas in several respects, especially in stating that pleasure needs to be considered in qualitative as well as quantitative fashion. In his *Utilitarianism* (1863) he wrote that a sense of dignity makes a man choose to be Socrates unhappy rather than a pig satisfied.[20]

Several recent types of ethical thought reveal distinct relativistic qualities. The pragmatism associated with William James and John Dewey is an example. Pragmatism has been characterized in this manner: "If I state that something is red, or if I state that it is good, what I say will be allowed to be true if regarding it as red or regarding it as good are [sic] conducive to the satisfaction of desires of different kinds."[21] In the extreme, that which is good—and thus that which ought to be—is that which is useful in the satisfaction of a want, presumably any want.

Logical positivism is akin to pragmatism in its practical orientation. According to Moritz Schlick, a logical positivist, many ethicists forget that ethics is a matter of fact. He states that we have to ascertain what is good by observing what has been good, that we learn what we ought to do by observing the results of what has been done. He implies that what is good in one situation need not be good in all others, although it is likely to be good in many others. He recommends the establishment and testing of successively higher norms until the highest-level generalization is reached that can be justified by observation.[22] In logical positivism ethics is strictly a

---

[20]This summary of the ethical thinking of Bentham and Mill is based largely on Rogers, *A Short History of Ethics*, pp. 234-56.

[21]Mary Warnock, *Ethics Since 1900* (2nd ed.; London: Oxford University Press, 1966), p. 76. Used by permission of the Clarendon Press, Oxford. Warnock cites James's "Philosophical Conceptions and Practical Results." See William James, *Collected Essays and Reviews* (New York: Longman's, Green & Co., 1920), pp. 406-37. James credits Charles S. Pierce with introducing him to the principle of practicalism.

[22]Moritz Schlick, "What Is the Aim of Ethics?" in A. J. Ayer, ed., *Logical Positivism* (New York: The Free Press, 1959), pp. 247-63.

matter of understanding. Logical positivists, as such, are not interested in encouraging one type of moral behavior over another. Existentialism, as identified for example with Jean-Paul Sartre, embodies rather extreme relativism. An existentialist may believe that existence precedes being and that no human is conceived for any purpose whose pattern of activity is determined in advance. Rather, human beings in a most frustrating sense are free. A person's essence comes after and grows out of his existence. The frustration stems from the belief that nothing is common to all human beings or essential to all human nature. In this view there are no guidelines as to what ought to be and most people may seek to escape their freedom and its accompanying nausea by using bad faith to delude themselves in the pretense that they have no choice.[23]

Currently, much attention is given to ethical situationism, still another variation of relativism in ethical decision making. Situationism, a type of moral skepticism, is not totally dissimilar from some aspects of the teachings of the Sophists. It is a logical development of the concept of ethical relativism and within itself takes numerous forms, none of which is as extremely relativistic as the type of existentialism just discussed. Somewhat detailed attention is given to Christian situation ethics later in this chapter.

This tracing of relativism in ethical thought is crude and incomplete. Nietzsche, Schopenhauer, and others could be mentioned. Still the account here is sufficient to show that many ethicists over the centuries have concluded that practical moral behavior cannot be based on any discernible absolute rule or rules. These ethicists have differed grossly in their concepts of how the choices ought to be made and on the extent to which generalizations can be applied to cover normal moral behavior.

In the absolutism-relativism issue we find a dichotomy that runs with many turns and twists through much of ethical thought. Even the customary contrasts between paired schools of thought seem to be based partly on this dichotomy. Thus, we find that the subjectivists are primarily relativists and the objectivists are primarily absolutists. Similarly, the same rough division might be applicable to

[23]Warnock, *Ethics Since 1900*, pp. 115-39.

the hedonists and the Stoics, the naturalists and the intuitionists, the egoists and the universalists, and the extrinsicalists and the intrinsicalists.

The issue is by no means settled and perhaps will not be on this side of eternity. It remains highly relevant to ethical thought and moral behavior, and as such it is also highly relevant to the future of insurance. Because of this relevance let us now examine in greater detail one example of absolutism and one example of relativism in ethical thought.

Immanuel Kant was one of the most notable absolutists of Western civilization. While his ideas were formulated almost 200 years ago, they packaged much of the ethical thought that has guided and described the actions of many people over the centuries. Many of his ideas pertain to the traditional and the familiar in the absolutism found in ethical judgment making in many parts of the world today. Perhaps millions of people who never heard of either Immanuel Kant or his categorical imperative have nevertheless based their own ethical judgments and moral behavior to some extent on the concepts that Kant articulated.

In contrast, the writings of Joseph F. Fletcher, capsuling as they do situational ethical thought, are highly relativistic and fundamentally different from the writings of Immanuel Kant. Fletcher's work is especially pertinent as a possible harbinger of things to come. The ethical thought that Fletcher espouses may become increasingly accepted in the decades ahead. If so, the consequences for insurance could be quite important.

ETHICAL THOUGHT OF IMMANUEL KANT

Kant was born in 1724 and died in 1804. He lived in Königsberg, East Prussia, where he taught philosophy as a university professor. His *Critique of Pure Reason* is dated 1781; his *Critique of Practical Reason* was published in 1788; and his *Eternal Peace* was published in 1795 when he was 71.

Kant's books are difficult to read because of his heavy, formal style. His lectures, which also have been published, afford a less formidable source for many of his basic thoughts. Three of the excerpts from Kant included in this section come from his lectures on ethics. While the following summary fails to do justice to the order and beauty in Kant's thinking, hopefully it captures some of the substance.

Kant is perhaps most famous for his categorical imperative. The need for a definite rule to use in making ethical judgments is made clear by a statement from one of his lectures:

But as we all need a basis for our moral judgments, a principle by which to judge with unanimity what is morally good and what bad, we apprehend that there must exist a single principle having its source in our will. We must therefore set ourselves to discover this principle, upon which we establish morality, and through which we are able to discriminate between what is moral and what immoral.[24]

Kant concluded that this single principle could be expressed as an imperative in categorical manner. He stated the principle as follows: "Act only on that maxim whereby thou canst at the same time will that it should become a universal law."[25] A paraphrase might be: Act only on the motive you would want everyone else to follow universally.

The principle can be illustrated by asking whether one, motivated by self-love, should make a promise with the intent of breaking it. Kant says that if everybody did this sort of thing, promises would lose their utility. Furthermore, even if everyone did not follow this course of action, the promisee would want the promisor to keep his promise. Thus, whether there be one or many outcomes of this sort, Kant says that self-love comes into opposition with itself. Rogers paraphrases the categorical imperative by saying: "If the maxim of your action cannot be given universal validity without coming into opposition with itself, then it is not moral."[26]

Kant's ethical thought lays great stress on reason as the means for discerning how to act in accordance with the moral command in the categorical imperative. He argues in effect that knowledge for ethical decisions comes not from feelings (as Hume asserted) or from any special moral sense (as Shaftesbury asserted) but rather from pure reasoning.

---

[24]Jones and others, *Approaches to Ethics*, pp. 250-51. Copyright © 1962 by McGraw-Hill Book Company. Used with permission of McGraw-Hill Book Company. Jones and others cite Immanuel Kant, *Lectures on Ethics* (London: Methuen & Co., Ltd., 1930) as the source of this passage; they do not show by ellipses the omissions they have made from the full text in Kant.

[25]As found in Rogers, *A Short History of Ethics*, pp. 194-95.

[26]Rogers, *A Short History of Ethics*, p. 195.

He also insisted that any two rational beings in exercising their reasoning capacities on any matter of moral behavior would come to the same conclusion. Thus, in the framework of the categorical imperative the two persons would be under a duty to make the same ethical judgment; their ethical judgment would not be dependent on the peculiarities of the situation or their individual biases. As revealed by reason, then, the moral law is unconditional and absolute. It is equally discernible by all rational beings and applies to all in exactly the same way. The absolute moral law, in Kant's thinking, is to be obeyed absolutely.

Kant called the freedom of rational beings the source of all value. In his words:

The inherent value of the world, the *summum bonum*, is freedom in accordance with a will which is not necessitated to action. Freedom is thus the inner value of the world. But on the other hand, freedom unrestrained by rules of its conditional employment is the most terrible of all things. The actions of animals are regular; they are performing in accordance with rules which necessitate them subjectively. Mankind apart, nature is not free; through it all there runs a subjectively necessitating principle in accordance with which everything happens regularly. Man alone is free; his actions are not regulated by any such subjectively necessitating principle; if they were, he would not be free. And what then? If the freedom of man were not kept within bounds by objective rules, the result would be the completest savage disorder. There could then be no certainty that man might not use his powers to destroy himself, his fellows, and the whole of nature. I can conceive freedom as the complete absence of orderliness, if it is not subject to an objective determination. The grounds of this objective determination must lie in the understanding, and constitute the restrictions to freedom. Therefore the proper use of freedom is the supreme rule.[27]

The highest duty of man, Kant implied, is to use his freedom to contribute to the moral perfection of the human race. Man is to use his freedom by exercising his reason in order to follow the categorical imperative. Obedience to this imperative is the means for achieving the goal of the human race. Freedom used in any other manner is self-defeating. The result of the proper use of freedom is

---

[27] Jones and others, *Approaches to Ethics*, pp. 258-59. Used with permission of McGraw-Hill Book Company. The italics are those of Jones and his coeditors. If Kant is correct that only man is free, any hope—such as we speculated about in Chapter 3—that man might possess some sort of homeostatic system for controlling the size of human population may be utterly groundless.

goodwill, and this goodwill is the fundamental good. It derives from (1) using reason to ascertain the action required by the imperative and (2) acting out of the sense of duty that reason dictates. The results, Kant maintained, will be perfectly consistent with one another and will lead to moral perfection in the human race.

On the other hand, violation of the categorical imperative, Kant said, is a source of discord. In his lectures he used truthfulness to illustrate the point by saying that truthfulness "is in accord with every purpose; it is in harmony with the will of others, and every one can guide his conduct by it; one truth is consistent with another."[28] He said that lies, by contrast, contradict each other and therefore are inconsistent not only with the purposes of others but also with the purpose of the one who lies. He argued that an inclination to lie eventually comes into opposition with itself and in so doing creates a breach in the categorical imperative. He adds that even a lie told with the intention of preventing a murder is wrong. The presumed effects of a lie, in his view, have nothing to do with its morality.

Kant's system of thought embodies the premise that happiness is distributed in proportion to the goodwill one possesses and uses in adhering to the categorical imperative. For the distribution of happiness to be proportionate to virtue, three conditions are required. The first is the existence of God. The distribution of happiness could not occur without the hand of God, who alone is capable of measuring virtue and the commensurate happiness. The second postulate is the freedom of will. As we have already noticed, man would not be free in the absence of freedom from a necessitating motive. He would neither deserve nor fail to deserve the happiness that might come to him, if, indeed, he were capable in the absence of freedom of experiencing happiness at all. The third postulate is immortality of the soul. Since compensating happiness does not necessarily follow quickly upon the possession of goodwill, no time scale would necessarily be adequate for this relationship. Hence, eternity is necessary to permit the relationship to hold. The lag may be such, Kant implied, that the happiness does not show itself until after the death of the body.

---

[28] Jones and others, *Approaches to Ethics*, p. 252. Used with permission of McGraw-Hill Book Company.

In summary, Kant's categorical imperative expresses a unity in moral law in that all rational beings come to the same ethical judgments through exercising reason. The imperative also expresses a plurality in that every human being is treated as having absolute worth, as being an end in himself. Finally, it also expresses a totality in the sense that there cannot be any contradiction, and thus all are bound by the same absolute, universalized, immutable moral authority.

We need only add that Kant's system is based on duty, not love. In his view love, while commendable, is a matter of impulse and as such is undependable. It cannot necessarily be successfully commanded. Duty, by contrast, is reliable and is a sufficient motive. Kant said that one who acts out of duty does enough and that generosity is superfluous. Duty, as revealed by reason, was for Immanuel Kant the sufficient motive for the moral perfection of the human race.

ETHICAL THOUGHT OF JOSEPH F. FLETCHER

The relativism of numerous theologian ethicists is a striking contrast to the absolutism of Immanuel Kant. Prominent among them is Joseph F. Fletcher, the Robert Treat Paine Professor of Social Ethics, Episcopal Theological School, Cambridge, Massachusetts. Fletcher's books include *Morals and Medicine, Situation Ethics: The New Morality,* and *Moral Responsibility: Situation Ethics at Work.*[29] The first pertains to certain moral issues in the practice of medicine, especially the patient's right to know serious things. The second book succinctly summarizes Fletcher's situational ethical thought, and all of Fletcher's quotations and writings presented in this chapter are taken from it. The third book is a collection of papers prepared by Fletcher in recent years and previously published in periodicals or other media.

The expression "new morality" is quite fashionable at the time of this writing. However, the term has received many diverse interpretations and thus is quite ambiguous. A brief look at several of

---

[29]The first book was published in 1954 by Princeton University Press. The second and third were published in Philadelphia by Westminster Press in 1966 and 1967, respectively.

the treatments given it in recent decades will indicate the extent of this diversity.

1. Durant Drake's *The New Morality*, published in 1928, attacked authoritarian and supernaturalistic ethics. He used "new morality" to refer to his belief that no god or universal authority existed.

2. G. E. Newsome's *The New Morality*, published in 1933, is primarily a protest against the libertine ethics recommended by Bertrand Russell.

3. A papal encyclical, *Humani Generis,* in 1950 called existentialism a type of situationism and a "philosophy of error." In 1952 the Sacred Congregation of the Holy Office used the expression "the new morality" in referring to and condemning pure situationism in ethical thinking.

4. In 1963 John A. T. Robinson, British Bishop of Woolwich, set forth in his book *Honest to God* his concept of God who, he felt, was not a being and did not intervene in the affairs of man. He referred to his beliefs as the new morality.

5. Fletcher used the term in a 1966 article and also (as we have seen) in the title of a book in reference to situation ethics.[30]

Since 1967 the expression has been heavily used in the popular press to the point of faddism. Often it is related to the subject of sex by users who apparently know little of its history and dimensions. In our discussion here, "new morality" is identified with Fletcher's situation ethics.[31]

Fletcher places situationism in the middle ground between legalism and antinomianism, the polar extremes of ethical decision making. He explains that a situationist cannot find a position in either extreme.

---

[30]Edward LeRoy Long, Jr., "The History and Literature of 'The New Morality'," in Harvey Cox, ed., *The Situation Ethics Debate* (Philadelphia: The Westminster Press, 1968), pp. 102-7. Additional works not referred to here include William Dunphy, ed., *The New Morality* (New York: Herder and Herder, Inc., 1967); Arnold Lunn and Garth Lean, *The New Morality* (London: Blandford Press, 1964); Douglas A. Rhymes, *No New Morality* (London: Constable & Cox, Ltd., 1964); and Frederick C. Wood, Jr., *Sex and the New Morality* (New York: Association Press, 1968).

[31]Some scholars have written about situationism without referring to it as the new morality. These include Emil Brunner, Dietrich Bonhoeffer, Paul Lehmann, Joseph Sittler, and H. Richard Niebuhr. In the main these scholars argue that they were asserting not a new mode of thinking but rather reasserting an old one found both in the letter and the spirit of the Reformation. In any case, their ethical thought is relativistic and emphatic on the point that situations transcend principles. See Long, "The History and Literature of the 'The New Morality'," pp. 105-7.

In Fletcher's view legalism of natural, scriptural, or any other origin is cumbersome and self-defeating. It eventually becomes a massive and inconsistent prefabrication of rules and regulations. As ethical decisions are made by the letter of the law, the law must continually expand to provide the clarification needed to cover the tremendous variety in men's affairs. The ponderous but still growing body of law grows ever more complex. Casuistry, or the effort to deal sensibly with diverse and individual cases of moral behavior, is commendable, he says, but ultimately impossible in the face of the growing and tangled web of the law. Fletcher argues that the literalness and the ultimate authority of legalism have to be broken before ethical judgments can be made properly. He regards Immanuel Kant as the archpriest of legalism.

Fletcher says that antinomianism is the polar extreme of legalism. Instead of everything being spelled out, nothing is elaborated. Antinomianism is the doctrine that through faith and by the saving grace of God a Christian is freed not only from the Old Testament ecclesiastical legalism but also from the generally accepted and generally prevailing standards of ordinary morality. Fletcher says that the Apostle Paul had much difficulty in combating the rise of antinomianism in the early churches at Corinth and Ephesus. Antinomianists may consider themselves very special persons who are above the law and free to do as they please.

In his discussion of the subject, Fletcher seems to depart somewhat from the rather narrow meaning of antinomianism and to use it in the sense that we have been using pure moral skepticism, as a complete discarding of all rules for making ethical decisions. He cites the existentialists and the moral rearmament advocates in his discussion. Existentialism does seem to embody pure moral skepticism, but moral rearmament does not. As Fletcher illustrates, the moral rearmament movement insists on absolute moral purity. The "hero morality" as opposed to the "herd morality" distinguished by Frederick Nietzsche might fit except that Fletcher seems to say that the polar extreme of legalism is simply no rules at all.

Fletcher sees situationism as the reasonable compromise between the literalness of legalism and the total unprincipledness of antinomianism.

The situationist enters into every decision-making situation fully armed with the ethical maxims of his community and its heritage, and he treats them with respect as illuminators of his problems. Just the same he is prepared in any situation to compromise them or set them aside *in the situation* if love seems better served by doing so.[32]

Laws, principles, maxims, and other generalizations are to be used fully by the situationist as he appraises ethical problems and contemplates ethical decisions. Unlike the ethical legalist, however, the situationist is free to set the generalizations aside whenever the situation warrants.

Fletcher's concept of ethics is based on four presuppositions and six propositions. The presuppositions are that situation ethics is pragmatic, relative, positive, and personal. Discussion of the six propositions takes up almost two-thirds of his book, but a brief summary of them here should give us a reasonably clear idea of the essence of his thinking on the subject. The summary, however, does not capture the vitality and interest-holding quality of his writing style.

Proposition I: Only Love is Intrinsically Good. Fletcher says that love is the only intrinsic value and that the worthiness of everything else is extrinsic and dependent on the situation. Only love is necessarily and always good. Furthermore, love, according to his concept, is not something one has. It is something one does. Fletcher makes much of the fact that love is a verb.

In Fletcher's situation ethics love is the only regulator of behavior, the only source of value. It is the only scriptural revelation held inviolate. Conceivably, another situation ethicist could have a source of value, some intrinsic good, other than love. Fletcher stresses that situationists are chary of any generalizations. Some source of value is needed to measure the extrinsic relativities; otherwise the results could be chaotic. His base of comparison is love.

We should be careful to understand that the use of the word "Christian" in the Fletcher context is meant only to connote the type of love brought out in Proposition II. It does not necessarily embrace the personal salvation doctrines of the immaculate conception, the atoning death, and the victorious resurrection of Jesus Christ. Thus, there could be many "Christian" situation ethicists

---

[32]Joseph F. Fletcher, *Situation Ethics: The New Morality* (Philadelphia: The Westminster Press, 1966), p. 26. Copyright © MCMLXVI by W. L. Jenkins, The Westminster Press; used by permission.

who are not Christians in the sense of believing in Jesus Christ as the source of eternal life. Being a Christian situation ethicist simply means considering love as the only norm. Fletcher states that other situationists could use pleasure, happiness, self-realization, or something else in place of love.

The opposite of love, according to Fletcher, is not hate but indifference. Aside from love and its negative counterpart, nothing is intrinsically good or bad. There are no universals save that love is good and indifference is bad. He illustrates by saying that a lie told in love is good. He says that Kant's insistence that a lie is always wrong is legalism at its worst. According to the situationist, whether one should tell the truth or lie in a given situation depends on which would be the more loving act, all things considered. If to lie is more loving, the lie is not merely an excusable and forgivable evil; it is positively good![33] This point is of essential importance in situational ethical thought.

Proposition II: Agape-Love is the Ruling Norm. Agape-love, Fletcher says, is nonreciprocal. It is not romantic love *(eros)* or friendship love *(philia)*. It is love of neighbor where neighbor is anybody and everybody—good samaritanism practiced to the fullest. It is goodwill guided by reason and genuine concern for the needs of others.

In Fletcher's view no universal moral laws exist to stand in the way of love. For that matter, neither, he says, should any civil or criminal law interfere with love. Laws are to be respected and obeyed when they serve love. In cases of conflict between love and law, Fletcher opts for love, saying that the law must be subservient to love and never in a partnership status with it. Fletcher even argues that the Ten Commandments are not really commandments but are more in the nature of general admonitions, normally but not necessarily reliable as rules of conduct.

---

[33]A candid and slightly different treatment of lying is found in Arnold M. Ludwig, *The Importance of Lying* (Springfield, Ill.: Charles C Thomas, Publisher, 1965). In one passage Ludwig has written: "To advocate that man behave honestly and truthfully regardless of the consequences would be to fall into the same moralistic trap that has long prevented any real understanding of the phenomenon of lying and also prevented man from modifying his behavior in more reasonable, realistic and beneficial ways. Truth and honesty may be worthwhile goals in some situations, but it would be sheer nonsense to claim that they are worthwhile and useful in all situations and under all circumstances," p. 231. Courtesy of Charles C Thomas, Publisher, Springfield, Illinois.

Fletcher's point about agape-love is not simply that it can and should transgress the law in certain situations; at times it will even send the situationist far beyond the law in helping neighbors in danger or distress. Fletcher cites the common example of going to the aid of a person in distress when Anglo-American law recognizes no such duty. He also cites the agape-love requirement of a motorist to warn, even at his own peril, another motorist ahead of the critical danger evidenced by a wobbling wheel. Agape-love in Fletcher's view is aggressive, not merely prudent.

Proposition III: Love Equals Justice. Fletcher says that love is justice distributed. This proposition carries him into utilitarianism because, as we have seen, utilitarians are concerned about the greatest good for the greatest number.

Agape-love is not necessarily doing for a neighbor what the neighbor wants done. Rather, as Fletcher illustrates, it is doing for the neighbor what is best for him in the honest judgment of the situationist, who is obliged to become informed about the possible consequences of alternative courses of action. Presumably, the situationist is also obliged to gain some appreciation of the probabilities of the respective possible outcomes. Since in a given decision situation many others besides the particular neighbor may feel the consequences, the situationist must weigh the relative interests. Fletcher does not define precisely how the weighing should take place in order to serve the interests of love in a complicated situation. He does say that love, with its one-to-many correspondence, is not sentiment but is rather a calculating, cunning, prudent exercise in best serving the interests—possibly the conflicting interests—of all. Fletcher says that love "figures the angles." The result, he says, is justice distributed, for justice is merely love "working out its problems." In the Fletcher view this love is not the work of the Holy Spirit but rather *is* the Holy Spirit.

Fletcher says that we have a moral obligation to obey civil law to the extent possible in doing acts of love. If and when civil law and the work of love conflict, he recommends, as we have already observed, that the situationist follow the dictates of love—even to the extent of disobeying the law. He makes his position quite clear in the following passage:

In this connection we should note that the strategy of civil disobedience poses the problem neatly. We ought not to hesitate to break a law that is in all conscience unjust, that is to say, unloving. Perhaps also we should before or *pari passu* do what we can to get it reinterpreted in the courts or thrown out on some ground such as constitutionality, using legislative machinery to correct it. But neither the state nor its law is boss for the situationist; when there is a conflict, he decides for the higher law of love. He has to weigh immediate and remote consequences as well as local and broader interests, but if the scales go against the law, so does he.[34]

Proposition IV: Love Even Without Liking. Fletcher in this proposition sounds a bit like Kant in saying that Christian love, stripped to its essence, is benevolence or goodwill. Fletcher brings out that it is goodwill toward all, including the persons who from the point of view of the situationist are thoroughly unlikable. Agape-love goes to the undeserving, to the ugly, to the offensive, following the example set by Jesus.

Being justice distributed, as brought out in Proposition III, agape-love is not an emotion but rather an attitude. It weighs the odds and dictates the action most likely to be in the best interests of the neighbor—or of neighbors in the aggregate when more than one is involved. It extends beyond friends to the stranger and even to the enemy.

Fletcher's examples are dramatic. Faced with the choice of saving from a burning building one's father (an ordinary person) or a medical genius, one saves the medical genius out of love for those whom the genius might be able to help. Faced similarly with saving the Mona Lisa or an ordinary baby, one saves the baby, a life instead of a thing.

Proposition V: Only the End Justifies the Means. Fletcher's situation ethics (and he emphasizes that others may have a different view) breaks with classical Christian ethics and moral theology, which assert that some acts are intrinsically and always wrong. (We recall Kant's assertion that a lie is always wrong because it springs from self-love and ultimately comes into opposition with itself.) Fletcher avers that there is no act that is necessarily always right and no act that is necessarily always wrong. He says that the new morality (situation ethics) judges all things right or wrong according to the situation, and that therein lies the revolution in morals.

He cites the hypothetical case of a pioneer woman going along Wilderness Road into Kentucky. He poses the question of what she

---

[34]Fletcher, *Situation Ethics: The New Morality*, p. 101, used by permission.

should have done when her sick baby was about to cry and betray the whole party to a band of murder-bent Indians who were close by and in search of the pioneer party. If the mother had clung to her baby with the result that its crying brought the Indians who discovered and killed all the settlers in the party, including the baby, would the mother have done right? If the mother had killed her baby to prevent its revealing the hiding place of the party, would she have done wrong? Fletcher implies that the answer to both questions could be no. Actions, he says, must be weighed in the light of the ends, the means to achieve such ends, the motives, and the foreseeable consequences. Although a given action may usually be right or wrong, no action, Fletcher holds, is right or wrong in and of itself.

Proposition VI: Love Works Situationally, Not Prescriptively. This proposition appears to be primarily a reemphasis of points already made. It does, however, show precisely the opposition of situationism to the classical tradition of following the moral law without thought of the consequences. An old classical maxim goes like this: Do good though the heavens fall. Fletcher takes a dim view of such advice. A passage from his writing may be useful in suggesting the intensity of his distaste:

> The metaphysical moralist of the classical tradition, with his intrinsic values and moral universals and code apparatus, says in effect, "Do what is right and let the chips fall where they may." The situational decision maker says right back at his metaphysical rival: "Ha! Whether what you are doing is right or not depends precisely upon where the chips fall." Only the unwary will be taken in by the pseudobravery and bogus prophetic courage of those who drive ahead to an ideal regardless of the pain or price involved. It is right or wrong to follow a principle only according to who gets hurt, and how much.[35]

In this frame of thought Fletcher says that extramarital sex can be good instead of evil unless someone is hurt. He hastens to add that the "unless" is a very big one. He also says that an unchaste act done in love could outweigh technical and malicious chastity.

In summary, the situation ethics of Joseph Fletcher shies from the absolute or, as he puts it, the "tablets of stone." Agape-love is

---

[35]Fletcher, *Situation Ethics: The New Morality*, p. 144, used by permission.

the only norm. Rules are useful to the situationist as guides but not as commands. In lovingly serving the needs (but not necessarily the desires) of his neighbors, the situationist does what love requires, be it a transcension or even a transgression of the law. When viewed in the framework of situation ethics, no act is always right or wrong. Only love is good; everything else is situational.

SPECULATION ABOUT FUTURE ETHICAL THOUGHT

Our purpose in the remainder of this chapter is not to indicate a preference or to argue for absolutism or relativism in ethical thought. Articulation of the kind of "ought" we really ought to think, feel, and profess now and in the years to come is beyond the scope of our treatment. The remaining tasks in this chapter are to offer a speculation about the direction ethical thought may go in this country over the next 30 years or so and on the basis of this speculation to discuss some of the possible consequences for insurance.

While cause and effect can never be proved in matters of ethics and morality, one could argue that the new morality is already exerting an influence. The widespread use of organized and disruptive protest, the large-scale civil disobedience, the increased openness of the subject of sex, the widespread questioning of authority and tradition, the cynicism toward and criticism of patriotism, the spiraling crime and divorce rates,[36] and the increasing bitterness concerning the economic and political systems in this country may

---

[36]We must never forget the possibility of new situations creating the occasion for new types of insurance. A bizarre example turned up in a report of the meeting of the European Society of Jurists. The jurists were told that a number of European countries, including West Germany and Sweden "are preparing legislation which would make it mandatory for the bridegroom to insure the bride against divorce in advance of the wedding ceremony." "Divorce Insurance Studied," *Indianapolis Star* (November 10, 1968), sec. 6, p. 12. The insurance is based on the premise that a large number of marriages will not last and that the divorced wife should be provided with appropriate financial security. The mandatory feature in the proposed insurance might well be unfair to those couples who intend to make their marriage last and who manage to do so. Incidentally, according to the July 28, 1969, *Population Profile* of the Population Reference Bureau, Inc., pp. 1 and 2, divorce rates in the United States per 1,000 married women (age 15 or older) increased from 9.2 in 1960 to 11.2 in 1967. The number of children affected by divorce decrees also increased sharply.

be attributable partly to relativism in ethical thought. The idea that the end justifies the means and that the traditional belief in absolutes was mistaken in the first place certainly fits the mold of situation ethics and other types of ethical relativism.

Doubtless many, and perhaps most, of those currently flouting traditional behavioral patterns have never heard about situation ethics and are unfamiliar with the historical controversy pertaining to relativism and absolutism in ethical thought. Nevertheless, their behavior may have been and in the future may be strongly influenced by leaders who are informed about relativism. We should be careful not to underrate the extent to which a few people can influence the behavior of many.

Several types of thought leaders seem to have been particularly active during the last decade. One important group, perhaps more influential than in other recent decades, has been the clergy. Highly publicized examples of ministers or priests leading civil rights marches, encouraging student protests, burning draft board records, counseling draft evasion, sanctioning pre- and extramarital sex, and otherwise challenging established authority and patterns of social conduct can have an immense effect on people of all ages, especially on those who are young. Ironically, one of the effects may have been to undermine respect for the authority of the organized church.

While theology is generally beyond the scope of this book, we should note at this point that members of the clergy have undoubtedly influenced ethical thought by the positions they have taken on theological issues. Widespread denial of absolutes in theology has accompanied, or perhaps encouraged, relativism in ethical thought. Numerous theologians have made strong and prominent efforts to "deliteralize" and demythologize religious dogma. They have attempted to substitute a remote deism for a highly personal theism, to bend and broaden doctrine to accommodate widely divergent groups of adherents, and to secularize religion in order to appeal, in Harvey Cox's words, "to men come of age."[37] The result over the long-range future could be a weak, debilitating theology that requires little from its believers and offers little to them. If so, mem-

[37]See Harvey Cox, *The Secular City* (rev. ed.; New York: The Macmillan Company, 1966).

bers of the clergy who espouse such views might actually be under-cutting the sense of personal responsibility and the belief in per-sonal accountability—in this life or the next—that religion has engendered in people over the ages. The substitution in popular thought of a vague "God-ness" or "Life-Principle" or "Ground-of-Being" in place of a personal God who holds each one of His crea-tures accountable for his life could produce a drastic long-range deterioration in human behavior. In the Christian context the denial of traditionally accepted dogma is so extreme as to leave little theo-logical substance to Christianity as a religion.

Teachers at all levels of education form another strongly influen-tial group of ethical thought leaders. The standards conveyed by the teacher through his ideas, speech, dress, manners, and priorities and the desire of students to emulate the teacher have always been a reliable—perhaps the most effective—means of education. Teachers are also in a most influential position because some of the most critical ethical issues to confront society are aired first in high school and college classrooms. In responding to these issues, many teachers have strongly encouraged adoption of the precepts of relativistic ethics.

Undoubtedly, another tremendously powerful type of leadership in ethical thought has been and continues to be generated by stu-dents and other young political activists of all persuasions. By num-ber, vigor, and success of the activists, the principal influence prob-ably has come from the political left. Political activists are skilled at seeking political ends by using ethical arguments to influence be-havior. When, for example, political ends can be gained by an in-sistence that a given end justifies a particular means, political strategy calls for all-out ethical offensives. The result may be that customs are condemned, laws defied, and institutions attacked, all in the name of moral behavior. Doubtless, many of the individuals participating in the activity never see beyond the ethical to the po-litical implications of what is being done. The observation applies especially to organized campus protests. Similarly, when and as the agape-love of situation ethics is appropriate to the political aims of the activists, as for example in matters of race, such love is preached, even if with a hollow ring. The new morality is used by political activists to attack at the most vulnerable points the eco-nomic, educational, religious, and other institutions of this country. The fact that much of the support enjoyed by the political activists is ethical rather than political does not make it any less useful to the activists.[38]

Those who control television programming constitute another and perhaps currently the most important group of ethical thought leaders. The types of programs, the content and style of advertising, the fashions used in clothing and furniture, the hair styles, the vocabulary, the tones and idioms of conversation, the treatment of the news, the timing and the manner of presentation of documentaries, and a host of other innuendos are all fundamentally important in conveying ethical thought and in influencing moral behavior. Commenting about electric informational media in general, and television in particular, Marshall McLuhan and Quentin Fiore wrote recently:

> All media work us over completely. They are so persuasive in their personal, political, economic, aesthetic, psychological, moral, ethical, and social consequences that they leave no part of us untouched, unaffected, unaltered. The medium is the massage. Any understanding of social and cultural change is impossible without a knowledge of the way media work as environments.[39]

Ethical thought leaders may be even more effective in the future than they have been in the past, largely because of television. (At least, they may be able to work faster.) The result may be that ethical thought and moral behavior may change more rapidly in the future than they have in the past. Given the historical pace of change in ethical thought, a period of a few decades, such as we are using in this discussion to frame our speculations, would be much too short to justify any serious expectation of substantial change in ethics or morality. Historically, centuries rather than decades have been needed to accommodate the changes that have occurred. The lead time needed by ethical thought leaders may be much shorter in the future.

---

[38]A refreshingly candid statement by Carl Oglesby, a former president of the Students for a Democratic Society, emphasizes the political content and aims of the new left and illustrates, at least by implication, the use of the new morality in achieving those ends. See his article, "Break Down the System?" in *The General Electric Forum*, vol. 12 (Spring, 1969), pp. 8, 10, 12, 14.

[39]Marshall McLuhan and Quentin Fiore, *The Medium is the Massage*, coordinated by Jerome Agel (New York: Bantam Books, Inc., 1967), p. 26. Copyright © 1967 by Marshall McLuhan, Quentin Fiore, and Jerome Agel. By permission of Bantam Books, Inc.

The new behavior that seems to be growing out of the new morality displays some discernible characteristics. Since these characteristics are pertinent to insurance, we might notice briefly a few of them.

First, the new behavior is distinctly antiauthoritarian. While it attracts a wide variety of individuals, including believers and atheists, blacks and whites, sophisticates and innocents, young and old, all of these individuals seem to share a common distaste for authority, especially ethical authority. For example, urban rioters, campus protesters, and civil rights militants seem to be united in condemning and defying authority. We must be careful not to imply that all such civil protesters are ethical relativists. Many may be motivated only by racial or economic motives. On the other hand, many are relativists who adopted their ethics either consciously or unconsciously and who have convinced themselves that the ends justify the means. The authority of school administrators, employers, parents, athletic coaches, public officials, religious leaders, and even government itself may be questioned. The assaults on authority, in part politically inspired as we have observed, are strengthened by what appears to be a denial of—even a revulsion against—absolutism in any form. As far as many of the antiauthoritarians are concerned, nothing apparently is sacred, not family, church, the arts, country, or even self.[40] Disrespect for the national anthem, as a case in point, may be symbolic of something far more than racial problems, youthful arrogance, or economic stress. Public rudeness and intolerance may imply more than poor manners.

A second characteristic of much of the new behavior is impatience. The impatience may have many explanations. One of these explanations could be found in the abandonment of the traditional ethical concept that happiness is distributed by God according to the virtue of the individual. Another traditional concept that is losing force is that work is honorable and progress in one's calling is indicative of a sound relationship with God. If people come to be-

---

[40]One newspaper columnist, for example, recently reported astonishment at Johann Sebastian Bach's being referred to as an "old dead punk" who typified middle-class values. See William F. Buckley, Jr., "Strange Idea of What Makes 'Middle Class Values'," *Bloomington* (Ind.) *Daily Herald-Telephone* (March 27, 1969), p. 29.

lieve that happiness is unrelated to virtue or work, time preferences change, and desires become more immediate. Given ends are seen to necessitate increasingly drastic means.

Still a third characteristic of the new behavior seems to be a growing willingness to compromise. If one believes that nothing in ethics is absolute (save, perhaps, the command of agape-love), he is hard-pressed to demarcate any behavior as not being negotiable and eligible for change. Lying, cheating, stealing, reneging, coercing, disappointing, betraying, and undermining become mere means to an end. If the end rather than the means is paramount and if no other generality necessarily applies, compromise of virtually any sort can be viewed more easily as a tactic than as a sin.

Fourth, the new behavior can be highly irresponsible in the sense of being misinformed. Challenge of an existing order, whether or not justified, presumes a considerable knowledge of the consequences of alternative courses of action. The new behavior is vulnerable to becoming more aggressive than intelligent. Agape-love or any other situational ethics demands extensive effort to get the facts. The discipline needed in situation ethics is strict. The new behavioralists may succumb to the temptation of acting without learning as much as they need to know about the situation.

Finally, we should recognize that the new behavior is intense. Whether or not it is politically inspired, it often springs from deep convictions, unbridled energy, and powerful motives. Whether it is based on love or hate, hope or despair, knowledge or ignorance, it is likely to be intense. Ideas are power. Ethical ideas are no exception.

No one knows what ethical ideas will prevail by the turn of the century. An ethical and theological backlash may have restored absolutism in prevailing thought. Immanuel Kant's categorical imperative may have become indisputably recognized as a universal ethical command. Adherents to Christianity, Judaism, and other religions of the world may have come to reaffirm the old absolutes or to accept new ones. As our discussion has indicated, however, the trend in ethical thought clearly seems to be in the other direction—that is, toward relativism.

Whether the relativism of the early twenty-first century is to be the agape-love type of situationism or some other type of relativism is unknowable at this point in time. Perhaps the answer is unimportant since by its very nature relativism in ethics is not static. Its most important characteristic is its denial of immutable, universal, nonexceptional laws to govern moral behavior.

In any case, and for better or for worse, the probable growing acceptance of ethical pluralism and the accompanying retreat from absolutism seem to have progressed so far already as to be irreversible within this century. The odds are that the institution of insurance will be called upon to operate in an increasingly relativistic ethical climate. Let us speculate about the possible difficulties this probable increase in ethical relativism may present to the long-range availability and use of insurance.

POSSIBLE CONSEQUENCES FOR INSURANCE

Even if our speculation proves to be correct and people generally become more relativistic in ethical thought and moral behavior, insurance will not necessarily be adversely affected by such a change. Only if loss ratios or expense ratios increase, investment yield declines, tax rates increase, or demand for insurance fails to grow commensurately with the economy will the trend toward relativism spell trouble for insurance. However, considerations of the size of insurers' investment yields and the level of the taxes levied against insurers are so roundabout as to be beyond our speculation. In practical terms, therefore, our speculation will be concerned with a consideration of the effect of ethical relativism on insurance loss ratios and expense ratios and on the demand for insurance.

Relativism is a difficult premise for ethical thought because of the demands it makes upon the ethical decision maker. It may require more of him than he is inclined or able to deliver. We must recognize that many forms of relativistic ethics are difficult disciplines without the softness and looseness often attributed to them. For example, Fletcher's concept of agape-love situationism certainly is a stern and rigorous ethical taskmaster. Difficulty arises, however, in putting the concept to work. How in the thick of situations are we able to know which of two alternative courses of action better serves the cause of love? We may not really know what this love is or how it is to be measured over a span of time. Without this knowledge we can err in presuming to know in a crowded world what the needs of our neighbors really are and what is best for each of them. Decisions on our part, even though made with the purest of agape-love motives, could still have tragic consequences when they are made with insufficient knowledge. Situationists are sometimes—perhaps unfairly—accused of "playing God" in presuming to decide in complex cases and with scanty information what is best for others.

When our ethical decisions might affect several or many in conflicting ways, we have to make the interpersonal comparisons that have proved so difficult to welfare economists. These comparisons are no less difficult in ethics. Fletcher offers us little help in using the agape-love criterion that he has so eloquently presented to us. Similarly, John Robinson, a situationist also, leaves it strictly to intuition. He has written: "Love alone, because, as it were, it has a built-in moral compass, enabling it to 'home' intuitively upon the deepest need of the other, can allow itself to be directed completely by the situation."[41] Robinson does not go into detail as to how love's "homing" device operates. Perhaps his saying that love works intuitively is all that is necessary.

Unless we possess a special moral sense of the type that Shaftesbury described or a conscience with the authority Butler imputed to it, we seem to be left only with our intellect to use in discerning the path agape-love would have us follow in a complex maze of human relations. When the ethical absolutes of do's and don'ts are removed, we could be left with few ethical tools. George Woods, professor of divinity at the University of London, has made the point in an interesting way with the following observation: "It [situation ethics] looks like an attempt to fill a wage packet with nothing but deductions."[42]

Whether or not Woods's analogy is overdone, situationism or any other ethical relativism requires rather sophisticated decision making. Human nature being what it is, one can easily delude himself into thinking that what his neighbor needs is the very thing that he (the decision maker) wanted to do in the first place. Situationism is often confronted with the temptation of making a rather easy truce with the way of the world. Edward L. Long, Jr. observed that situation ethics aims toward "relaxing the tensions" between faith and

---

[41]John A. T. Robinson, *Honest to God* (Philadelphia: The Westminster Press, 1963) p. 115. Copyright © by SCM Press, Ltd., 1963. Used by permission.
[42]George Woods, "Situational Ethics," in Ian T. Ramsey, ed., *Christian Ethics and Contemporary Philosophy* (New York: The Macmillan Company, 1966), p. 338. Copyright © 1966 by The Macmillan Company. Used by permission.

culture by "a congenial acceptance" of whatever is new in the culture. A feature of this ethical thought, he says, seems to be a type of compromise that makes heroes of the "culturally avant garde," whatever the substance of their conduct.[43]

Perhaps the principal problem for insurance in a situationist environment is that the decision maker may rationalize his motives in order to do what he pleases rather than what agape-love actually requires. The rationalization may be quite shallow and transparent to others or may be so subtle as to escape identification completely. Whatever its variety, it is a shoal on which many of us can flounder.

Without the immutable absolutes, one can think, as relativists do, that it is not always and necessarily wrong to cheat, steal, burn, wreck, malinger, waste, lie, injure, or even kill. In such a frame of thought one can perhaps find the occasion that constitutes for him the exception to the maxim that such activity is generally immoral. The fact that it might be illegal would not be compelling to him because of his belief that love stands above the law. He would judge the situation exceptional only in the belief that the noble end could be achieved in no other way. Having found the exception once, he might be prone to resort to it again and again. The possibility exists that the exception could become commonplace. If so, cheating, lying, stealing, burning, and the like would increase.

Thus, rationalization could be the Achilles heel of situation ethics. In the absence of strong, clear ethical prohibitions and equally strong and clear positive imperatives, human beings in the main simply may not be morally strong enough to meet the demands of agape-love situationism in a crowded world. If they are not, the institution of insurance may be hard pressed to continue to make insurance available to a society in which some or all of the members believe that causing insured losses or cheating the insurer in settling claims can occasionally be a commendable act of agape-love.

A further point is worth stressing in this regard. Our highly technical, cybernetic economy of the long-range future may be comprised of parts so interrelated and interdependent as to be highly vulnerable to disruption by a small number of individuals. Consequently, insurer loss and expense ratios, already sensitive to the actions of a few, may become increasingly so as the years go by.

[43]Long, "The History and Literature of . . .," pp. 109-10.

One only need think about the physical damage and loss of earnings one arsonist can cause to appreciate the sensitivity of these ratios. A small change in behavior can play havoc with the insuring process.

Of course, no certainty exists that relativism in ethics must produce such a result. However, since our principal concern is to alert ourselves to possible difficulties, we are justified in looking for the worst that could occur over the long run as a means of being ready for it. The most telling indictment seems to be that, after a few generations of people have been reared on increasingly strong ethical relativism, rationalization may become the nemesis of situationism, whatever norm the situational ethicist uses.

The other side of the figurative coin is related to the demand for insurance over the long-range future. Conceivably, the progression of ethical relativism could significantly dampen the enthusiasm of society for insurance. This case does not appear to be nearly as substantial, however, as that for an upturn in the loss ratios and expense ratios.

The reasoning about the possibility of dampened demand for insurance is fairly direct. It has to do with the sense of personal responsibility that is one of the ethical pillars of insurance. If the absolutism in our ethical thought tends to disappear over the decades, some people will decide (as indeed a few have already) that apprehending the future and being personally responsible for one's self and one's own are not necessarily always right. Such individuals may not use insurance to provide for themselves and their dependents. Depending on how widespread this sort of ethical thinking might become, the demand for insurance, particularly personal coverages, could be substantially lower than it would be otherwise.

We might notice that those who disavowed personal responsibility probably would do so not merely in respect to insurance but also in respect to other aspects of living. They might tend to be unproductive. If so, they would tend to become wards of society and beneficiaries of public charity, private charity, or both. Insurance, then, could not function as the means for the redistribution of the wealth necessary to sustain them.

No implication is made that relativism in ethical thought necessarily engenders indolence. The point is simply that this possibility exists in respect to an undetermined number of people. If it should come about, its consequences for insurance would be important.

Again, we should remember that a small swing in terms of numbers could make a perceptible difference in the terms under which insurance could be offered to those who still wanted it.

If and as the ethical relativism we have discussed becomes increasingly prominent, it may bring a new concept of change. Instead of change being regarded as primarily a transition from one stable state to another, it may be viewed commonly as a process that has no fixed points for making sightings and comparisons. Donald A. Schon, former director of the Institute for Applied Technology in the National Bureau of Standards, has commented on this quite clearly.

All in all there has been a gradual deterioration of reference points for personal identity and for sense of self. It is less and less possible to explain who I am in terms of the job I do, the profession I represent, the region of the country in which I live, the institution to which I belong or the class or race from which I come. This newly experienced difficulty in saying who I am goes hand in hand with an increasing confusion about where I am going.[44]

Increased confusion about who we are and where we are going does not encourage routine in the institution of insurance. Let us hope that future change in the environment insurance serves also brings an increasing adaptability in the phenomenon of insurance itself.

[44]Donald A. Schon, *Technology and Change* (New York: A Seymour Lawrence Book/Delacorte Press, 1967), pp. 196-97, used by permission. His full discussion about the change in the concept of change and about our reaction to it is found in his concluding chapter, "An Ethic of Change," pp. 189-218.

9

PROGRAM OF
PERSUASION

In the preceding chapters we studied the ethical precepts upon which a healthy and long-lasting system of insurance depends. We speculated about several fundamental forces within our society that over the long-range future could influence ethical thought and moral behavior and thus seriously affect insurance. We speculated also about the possibility that ethical thought may undergo a self-generating change that could further disturb the future availability and use of insurance in this country.

Several questions remain. They relate to what can and should be done by whom to lessen the danger that insurance may fail to serve as a major device for redistributing loss in our society over the decades ahead. We consider these questions in this chapter.

WHAT CAN BE DONE?

One of the questions has to do with what can be done. This question is answerable in two parts. First, an effort can be made to thwart the particular developments that, according to our speculations, could place insurance in jeopardy. Worldwide overgrowth of population can be opposed. Inflation, particularly that above 2 percent per year, can be combatted. Misuse of free time can be reduced (here we refer to the additional time freed from occupational demands that could become available to many if energy costs are drastically reduced). The loss of the sense of human dignity that might grow out of technological advances in physics, astronomy, biology, cybernetics, and other fields can be overcome. Finally, the drift toward relativism in ethical thought and moral behavior can be resisted.

Second, an effort can be made to reinforce directly the ethical thought that is compatible with the long-range availability and use of insurance. An effort can be made to strengthen each of the ethical pillars of insurance as described in Chapter 2.

Both of these approaches would require large-scale programs of persuasion. Part of the persuasion could be directed toward influencing the actions of government, as, for example, in the strengthening of family planning programs around the world or in the controlling of inflation. Other persuasive efforts would have to be directed to the public at large, for example, in motivating people to want to use free time constructively or in educating them to take in stride the technological advances that are to come. Further, the reinforcement of the ethical pillars would have to be directed to the public at large or to broad segments of it. The persuasion would have to embrace a giant-scale selling effort that utilized public information media and other interpersonal contacts of virtually every available type. It would have to be a program to influence ethical thought on individual, group, national, and international levels.

WHO CAN TAKE THE ACTION?

The second question that arises has to do with who can undertake the necessary persuasion. The answer is that the insurers can do so as they act individually, in concert with one another, or, for some purposes, in league with other organizations.

One might wonder why insureds might not be able to conduct the program of persuasion. Individually, they might do so according to their inclinations. Many insureds doubtless would be interested in persuading other people to endorse and live by the ethical precepts we have discussed. To the extent that insureds as a whole exhibit the requisite values in their own lives, the difficulties that have been anticipated will not arise in the first place. To the extent that they do not, some or all of the difficulties may arise. Organized persuasion by the collective body of insureds, however, will not be forth-coming; the collective body of insureds is too large for such activity. To refer in our society to insureds is tantamount to referring to the public at large. We cannot expect the public as such to do anything about urging itself to avoid possible ethical undermining of insurance. If the prevailing ethical thought or moral behavior turns awry, we cannot expect the general public to undertake to persuade itself to avoid doing what it generally is disposed to do. The public would be acting in opposition to itself.

As we cannot expect the public to urge itself not to abandon the ethical precepts requisite to insurance, neither can we expect the preventive action to be taken by any level of government. To the extent that a government is democratic, it expresses the wishes of the constituent public. To expect a freely elected government to move in the long run against the wishes of the majority of those exercising the franchise is unjustified. Hence, the government over the long-range future cannot be expected to urge the populace to hold fast to any ethics the populace is disposed to abandon. In a free society the government does not have the responsibility for preserving the ethical foundation of insurance.

The persuasion, if it is to be done at all, must be initiated by a segment of the public, not by the public as a whole. The segment to exert this persuasion must be composed of individuals who, in the main, are interested in the continued availability and use of insurance over the long-range future. Presumably, those associated with insurers generally meet this criterion. The fact that their principal motive may be livelihood does not detract from their eligibility to serve as persuaders, assuming, to begin with, that insurance has been and will continue to be useful to society.

The expression, "those associated with insurers," as used here is vague and in need of clarification. Specifically, the expression covers members of boards of directors, managers, and other employees of insurance companies and insurance trade associations; insurance company stockholders; agents and brokers plus their employees; loss adjusters and their employees; and others involved in the insuring process except the insureds. Whether the expression extends to educators and government officials who serve as insurance regulators is debatable. The expression does not include policyholders, not even mutual insurance policyholders, for the reason already explained.

Numerous other segments of society and numerous other organizations also may be interested in reinforcing the same ethical precepts that insurers should be interested in reinforcing and in avoiding the same changes in behavior that insurers should be interested in avoiding. What would threaten the availability and use of insurance might also threaten numerous other types of economic activity. For this reason insurers, individually or in concert, may be able to make alliances with many organizations and individuals as opportunities arise. Since abandonment of the ethics necessary to support insurance might be almost the same as abandonment of ethics necessary to support private property and capitalism, it is reasonable to think that numerous alliances might be made.

An important point, however, is that insurance as a social institution is likely to feel the effects of change sooner than most other social institutions. This early sensitivity makes the insurance industry more vulnerable than most other industries to major shifts in ethical thought or moral behavior. Because of this particular vulnerability, those associated with insurers have a compelling reason to take the initiative if such efforts are to be pursued at all.

SHOULD INSURERS ACT?

A more difficult question than "what" or "who" is whether or not insurers, individually and collectively, should engage in efforts to influence prevailing patterns of ethical thought and moral behavior. Several strong arguments counsel against insurers attempting to influence large-scale social patterns. The first argument has to do with the possibility that use of insurance company assets for such purposes may be unfair. Insurance company stockholders and policyholders are not of a single mind about the ethical precepts discussed in Chapter 2. Doubtless these precepts are an anathema to some. The use of funds on which they may have some type of claim for ends to which they object raises the question of equity. Furthermore, the insurance trade press publications and other insurance literature leave no doubt that insurance company managers are conspicuous in the diversity of their ethical thought. Opinions about ethics and moral behavior run the gamut even within the insurance community. To force all of these people into the same thought mold might be awkward to say the least. If the insurance industry should take a strong position on birth control or urge a particular value system upon the public, the reaction among stockholders, policyholders, and others could be violent. Some would respond because of disagreement with the precepts advocated, others because of general objection to ethical meddling by insurers. Some stockholders probably would vote for removal of the offending management and some policyholders would be deterred from buying new coverages or retaining present coverages with offending companies. If the offending efforts at ethical persuasion came from the industry as a whole, policyholders might bear ill will toward the whole institution of insurance.

A second reason for being highly skeptical about insurers attempting to deal with major social forces is that the effort would have to be frightfully expensive to be effective. Since the public is so large and since public opinion on ethical matters may move so cumbersomely, the effort would have to be massive to be perceptible. Worse yet, even the most gigantic effort conceivable may appear minuscule in comparison to the magnitude of the task of significantly influencing ethical thought. The results might be analogous to the waves created by dropping a small pebble into a very large lake. The effort on any significant scale would be certain to increase the cost of insurance at a time when cost is already at a crisis level for several types of insurance. The question of the legitimacy of including in the insurance premium the cost of fostering particular ethical thought would surely be raised by the many groups of insurance cost-watchers.

A third reason for skepticism is that the benefits, if any, would likely fall quite unevenly on the many insurers in the industry without regard to the contribution of each to the effort. Any cost-benefit analysis on a company-by-company basis would almost surely fail to match benefits to costs. Moreover, at best a very long lag would likely characterize the cost-benefit relationship.

A final reason is that this study has not proved conclusively that a healthy system of insurance depends on the ethics described in Chapter 2. The relationship between insurance and ethics was more nearly postulated than demonstrated. The relationship may not exist. Even if it existed in the past, it may not exist in the future. Any heavy financing of such an effort would have many of the aspects of gambling. The money, so to speak, might easily be put on the wrong horse.

We can see that arguments against insurers attempting to influence social forces and reinforce ethical thought are formidable.

Certainly, precedent is on the side of insurers remaining aloof from such activity. Aside from taking a position against inflation, insurers generally have not pursued the activities described earlier in this chapter. Even the anti-inflation gestures have usually been made only halfheartedly.

The argument on the other side of the issue, however, is simple. It is that the survival of the institution of insurance may be at stake over the next few decades. The ethical pillars of insurance described here have been the prevailing ethics in all societies where insurance has flourished. This long concommitance strongly suggests that the relationship is more than coincidental. It must have some causality about it. If so, maintenance of the precepts is perhaps the best possible means of maintaining a healthy system of insurance over the long-run future. Similarly, loss of the precepts may be the quickest route to disaster. Unless a massive countering effort is undertaken, adverse change in ethical thought in this country in the years ahead could be unprecedented in magnitude.

Over the next few decades expenditure of effort on preserving the ethical foundation of insurance could prove to be much more important and far-reaching than much of the persuasive effort currently being expended. Campaigns to urge people to lock cars, drive safely, eat properly, avoid infection, practice industrial safety, guard against fire, package carefully for shipment, be alert against embezzlement, and the like, as important as they are to loss prevention, may not be of the highest priority. Urging people to be honest, abhor waste, accept responsibility, feel proud of achievement, obey the law, and the like may be even more important in terms of slightly longer-run loss prevention. Working for a noninflationary fiscal policy or for increased family planning programs in Asia, Africa, or South America might be more important than making investments in ghetto areas or endowing highway safety programs.

In short, there is an unsettling probability that the persuasion program pertaining to ethics may involve nothing less than the long-range survival of the institution of insurance and ultimately the survival of our economic and social systems. In such a circumstance the normal decision rules pertaining to expenses, to cost-benefit analysis, to equity among constituent members of an organization and to the probability of the success necessary to justify undertaking a new program become secondary. Since a major shift in ethical thought and moral behavior could severely interfere with the insuring process, insurers should attempt to forestall the possibility of such a development. Otherwise, the future might reveal that not doing so was a fundamental and an irreversible error.

A PROGRAM OF PERSUASION

These considerations, despite whatever problems they entail, support the view that insurers, individually and in concert, should conduct a large-scale program of persuasion during the next several decades. Money, manpower, and other industry resources should be used in advertising, lobbying, and many other types of interpersonal contacts to influence legislative and public opinion.

Assuming it is interested in encouraging the availability and use of insurance over the long-range future, the insurance industry should begin at once to:

1.　　Promote among governments and the public at large an awareness of the critical danger of population overgrowth and the imperative need for family planning in every country of the world, including our own.

2.　　Go strongly on record about the dangers of inflation and urge all governments to avoid practices that are inflationary.

3.　　Encourage people to educate themselves in the cultivation of leisure.

4.　　Educate the general population to the idea that past and future advances in technology glorify man.

5.　　Urge the public at large to believe in and to recognize ethical absolutes in the form of one or more immutable, universal, moral laws.

6.　　Remind the public that people ought:

    a.　to achieve;

    b.　to acquire;

    c.　to abhor waste;

    d.　to be apprehensive about the future;

    e.　to obey the law;

    f.　to exhibit honesty;

    g.　to respect tradition;

    h.　to accept personal responsibility and accountability;

    i.　to show charity.

The investment in such a program of persuasion by the turn of the century could mean the difference between order and chaos in insurance or even in society as a whole. Who is more expert in persuasion than insurers?

APPENDIX

APPENDIX

Consumer Price Index Numbers for
64 Countries and Territories, Selected Years, 1953-1966*

	1953	1957	1958	1959	1960	1961	1962	1964	1965	1966
Barbados	—	90	92	94	95	97	98	101	104	—
British Honduras	96	96	97	99	98	97	99	100	102	107
Burma	94	105	101	90	101	105	103	102	—	—
Cambodia	57	72	77	80	86	92	94	102	106	105
Cameroon	—	—	—	—	—	88	90	106	108	110
Cape Verdi Islands	75	83	86	81	83	84	91	101	102	99
Central African Republic	—	—	—	—	86	91	95	107	—	—
Chad	65	68	76	82	88	93	95	108	114	121
Congo, Democratic Republic of	—	—	—	—	—	—	—	137	134	155
Cyprus	72	92	96	98	99	98	98	100	100	100
El Salvador	92	96	102	101	101	98	99	102	102	101
Falkland Islands	81	85	84	85	89	93	95	105	107	111
Fiji Islands	—	—	—	—	96	97	99	103	111	111
French Polynesia	—	—	—	84	90	96	99	106	118	135
Gabon	—	—	—	—	—	—	93	103	106	109
Gibralter	77	87	88	89	92	93	95	103	107	110
Greenland	74	82	84	86	87	88	96	106	111	117
Grenada (1964)	—	—	—	—	—	—	—	100	100	104
Guatemala	95	99	100	100	98	98	100	100	99	100
Guyana (1964)	82	90	90	93	93	94	97	100	103	105
Honduras	86	93	95	96	94	96	97	105	108	110
Hong Kong	99	97	95	102	98	99	98	103	—	—

	1953	1957	1958	1959	1960	1961	1962	1964	1965	1966
Iraq	—	—	—	—	—	—	—	99	98	99
Ivory Coast	—	—	—	—	92	102	100	101	104	108
Jamaica	—	81	85	88	91	97	99	102	105	107
Kenya	—	—	92	93	94	96	99	99	104	108
Laos	—	—	—	39	45	45	52	198	233	254
Liberia (1965)	—	—	—	—	—	—	—	98	100	103
Libya (1964)	—	—	—	—	—	—	—	100	106	114
Luxembourg	89	94	95	95	96	96	97	103	107	—
Madagascar (1964)	—	—	—	—	—	—	—	100	104	108
Malawi	—	—	—	—	93	95	98	102	—	—
Malaysia	—	—	—	97	97	97	97	100	100	101
Malta	83	87	88	90	94	98	98	102	104	104
Mauritania	—	—	—	—	—	89	91	108	107	112
Mauritius	—	—	—	—	—	—	101	102	104	106
Mozambique	—	—	—	—	—	96	99	102	104	107
Netherland Antilles	88	95	96	97	98	99	99	101	102	103
New Caledonia	71	78	83	92	96	98	99	105	108	110
Nicaragua	—	99	104	101	99	99	99	105	108	111
Niger (1964)	—	—	—	—	—	—	99	100	104	115
Panama	—	—	—	—	—	—	100	102	103	103
Paraguay (1964)	—	—	—	—	—	—	—	100	104	107
Puerto Rico	81	87	89	91	94	96	98	102	105	108
Rhodesia, Southern	—	—	94	—	96	98	99	105	107	—
Ryukyu Islands	99	91	91	92	93	95	97	103	104	110
St. Lucia (1965)	—	—	—	—	—	—	—	97	100	102
Senegal	63	69	83	88	90	93	97	104	106	109
Sierra Leone	—	97	94	94	96	100	99	112	117	122
Singapore	—	—	—	—	97	97	98	102	102	104
Somalia	72	73	80	87	89	98	97	113	128	124
Southern Yemen	—	—	90	89	92	91	93	103	104	106
Sudan	75	81	87	86	86	94	96	104	101	103
Surinam	81	91	92	92	94	96	98	104	106	111
Syria	—	—	—	—	—	—	98	106	102	108
Tanzania	101	99	103	101	102	103	103	102	108	114
Thailand	—	—	—	—	96	97	99	102	103	107
Trinidad and Tobago	77	84	88	90	92	94	96	101	103	107
Tunisia	—	—	—	—	—	—	97	104	111	115
Uganda-Ouganda	—	101	103	104	98	114	98	109	127	122
Vietnam, Republic of	65	86	84	86	85	90	93	103	120	194
Zambia	—	94	96	98	99	99	100	103	112	123

*1963 = 100 except where different base year entered by name of country.
Source: *Statistical Yearbook United Nations, 1967* (New York: United Nations, Department of Economic and Social Affairs, 1968), pp. 535-41. Table 177 in the *Statistical Yearbook* indicates that for certain countries or other entities the index numbers apply only to a certain city or other limited area.

BIBLIOGRAPHY

BIBLIOGRAPHY

Books

Abbott, Lawrence. *Economics and the Modern World*. 2nd ed. New York: Harcourt, Brace & World, Inc., 1967.

Ackley, Gardner. *Macroeconomic Theory*. New York: The Macmillan Company, 1961.

Adler, Mortimer J. *A Dialectic of Morals*. Notre Dame, Ind.: University of Notre Dame, 1941.

Allee, Warder C. *Animal Life and Social Growth*. Baltimore: The Williams & Wilkins Company, 1932.

_____; Emerson, Alfred E.; Park, Orlando; Park, Thomas; and Schmidt, Karl P. *Principles of Animal Ecology*. Philadelphia: W. B. Saunders Company, 1949.

Annual Abstract of Statistics, 1967. London: Central Statistical Office.

Appleman, Philip. *The Silent Explosion*. Boston: Beacon Press, 1965.

Athearn, James L. *Risk and Insurance*. New York: Appleton-Century-Crofts, Educational Division, Meredith Corporation, 1962.

Baade, Fritz. *The Race to the Year 2000*. Garden City, N.Y.: Doubleday & Company, Inc., 1962.

Barker, Ernest, trans. *The Politics of Aristotle*. Oxford: Oxford University Press, 1961.

Beckwith, Burnham Putnam. *The Next 500 Years*. New York: Exposition Press, 1967.

Beer, Stafford. *Cybernetics and Management*. New York: John Wiley & Sons, Inc., 1959.

Best's Aggregates and Averages. 30th ed. Morristown, N.J.: Alfred M. Best Company, Inc., 1969.

Best's Insurance Reports, Fire and Casualty, 1965. New York: Alfred M. Best Company, Inc., 1965.

Blum, Walter J., and Kalven, Harry, Jr. *Public Law Perspectives on a Private Law Problem*. Boston: Little, Brown and Company, 1965.

Bonar, James. *Moral Sense*. New York: The Macmillan Company, 1930.

Boner, Harold A. *Hungry Generations*. New York: King's Crown Press, Columbia University, 1955.

Boulding, Kenneth E. *The Meaning of the Twentieth Century.* New York: Harper & Row, Publishers, 1964.

Boyd-Orr, John. *The White Man's Dilemma: Food and the Future.* London: George Allen and Unwin Ltd., 1953.

Brightman, Edgar Sheffield. *Moral Laws.* New York: The Abingdon Press, 1933.

Bronfenbrenner, Martin. "Some Neglected Implications of Secular Inflation." In *Post Keynesian Economics,* edited by Kenneth K. Kurihara. New Brunswick, N.J.: Rutgers University Press, 1954.

Brown, Harrison; Bonner, James; and Weir, John. *The Next Hundred Years.* New York: The Viking Press, 1957.

Brunner, Heinrich Emil. *The Divine Imperative: A Study in Christian Ethics.* Philadelphia: The Westminster Press, 1947.

Burnet, F. MacFarlane. *2000 A.D.—A Biologist's Thoughts on the Next Forty Years.* Sir John Morris Memorial Institute Lecture. Melbourne: The Adult Education Board of Tasmania in association with Melbourne University Press, 1959.

Burns Annotated Indiana Statutes. 1968 Cummulative Pocket Supplement to 1965 Replacement Volume. Vol. 8, Part 1, Section 39-5239. Indianapolis: The Bobbs-Merrill Company, Inc.

Burns, Arthur F. *Prosperity Without Inflation.* New York: Fordham University Press, 1957.

Cahill, James M. "Ratemaking in Liability Insurance and Related Lines." In *Property and Liability Insurance Handbook,* edited by John D. Long and Davis W. Gregg. Homewood, Ill.: Richard D. Irwin, Inc., 1965.

Chase, Stuart. *The Most Probable World.* New York: Harper & Row, Publishers, 1968.

Cloudsley-Thompson, J. L. *Animal Conflict and Adaptation.* Chester Springs, Pa.: Dufour Editions, Inc., 1965.

Conard, Alfred E.; Morgan, James N.; Pratt, Robert W., Jr.; Voltz, Charles E.; and Bombaugh, Robert L. *Automobile Accidents Costs and Payments—Studies in the Economics of Injury Reparation.* Ann Arbor: The University of Michigan Press, 1964.

Cox, Harvey. *The Secular City.* Rev. ed. New York: The Macmillan Company, 1966.

Crick, F. H. C. "Ethical Considerations." In *Man and His Future,* edited by Gordon Wolstenholme. Boston: Little, Brown and Company, 1963.

Crow, James F. "Heredity and Evolution." In *Scientific Progress and Human Values,* edited by Edward and Elizabeth Hutchings. New York: American Elsevier Publishing Company, Inc., 1967.

Darwin, Charles Galton. *The Next Million Years.* Garden City, N.Y.: Doubleday & Company, Inc., 1953.

Davis, Kingsley, "Urbanization—Changing Patterns of Living." In *The Changing American Population,* edited by Hoke S. Simpson. New York: Institute of Life Insurance, 1962.

De Castro, Josue. *The Geography of Hunger.* Boston: Little, Brown and Company, 1952.

De Grazia, Sebastian. *Of Time, Work, and Leisure.* New York: The Twentieth Century Fund, 1962.

De Jouvenel, Bertrand. *The Art of Conjecture,* translated by Nikita Lary. New York: Basic Books, Inc., 1967.

Denenberg, Herbert S.; Eilers, Robert D.; Hoffman, G. Wright; Kline, Chester A.; Melone, Joseph J.; and Snider, H. Wayne. *Risk and Insurance.* Englewood Cliffs, N.J.: Prentice-Hall, Inc., 1964.

Dickerson, O. D. *Health Insurance.* Rev. ed. Homewood, Ill.: Richard D. Irwin, Inc., 1963.

Dunphy, William, ed. *The New Morality.* New York: Herder and Herder, 1967.

Durand, J. D., "Comments on Macura." In *World Population—The View Ahead,* edited by Richard N. Farmer; John D. Long; and George J. Stolnitz. Bloomington, Ind.: Bureau of Business Research, Graduate School of Business, Indiana University, 1968.

Eaton, Joseph W., and Mayer, Albert J. *Man's Capacity to Reproduce.* Glencoe, Ill.: The Free Press, 1954.

Ettinger, Robert C. W. *The Prospect of Immortality.* Rev. ed. New York: MacFadden-Bartell Corporation, 1966.

Faulkner, Edwin J. *Health Insurance.* Rev. ed. New York: McGraw-Hill Book Company, Inc., 1960.

Ferenczi, Imre. *The Synthetic Optimum of Population: An Outline of an International Demographic Policy.* International Studies Conference. Paris: International Institute of Intellectual Co-operation (League of Nations), 1938.

Finniston, H. M. "Gadgets, Games, and Gambles." In *The World in 1984,* edited by Nigel Calder. Vol. 2. Baltimore: Penguin Books, 1965.

Fisher, Joseph L., and Potter, Neal. *World Prospects for Natural Resources.* Baltimore: The Johns Hopkins Press, 1964.

Fletcher, Joseph F. *Moral Responsibility: Situation Ethics at Work.* Philadelphia: The Westminster Press, 1967.

_____. *Morals and Medicine.* Princeton, N.J.: Princeton University Press, 1954.

_____. *Situation Ethics: The New Morality.* Philadelphia: The Westminster Press, 1966.

Gabor, Dennis. "Inventing the Future." In *Automation: Implications for the Future,* edited by Morris Philipson. New York: Vintage Books, 1962.

Galbraith, John K. "Administered Prices and Monetary-Fiscal Policy." In *Money and Economic Activity,* edited by Lawrence S. Ritter. 3rd ed. Boston: Houghton Mifflin Company, 1967.

_____. *The Affluent Society.* Boston: Houghton Mifflin Company, 1958.

Gell-Mann, Murray. "The Elementary Particles of Matter." In *Scientific Progress and Human Values,* edited by Edward and Elizabeth Hutchings. New York: American Elsevier Publishing Company, Inc., 1967.

Gibbon, Edward. *The History of the Decline and Fall of the Roman Empire.* Vol. 2. New York: The Heritage Press, 1946.

Godwin, William. *Of Population: An Enquiry Concerning the Power of Increase in the Numbers of Mankind, Being an Answer to Mr. Malthus' Essay on That Subject.* London: Longman, Hurst, Rees, Orme and Brown, Paternoster Row, 1820.

Green, Leon. *Traffic Victims: Tort Law and Insurance.* Evanston, Ill.: Northwestern University Press, 1958.

Greene, Mark R. *Risk and Insurance.* 2nd ed. Cincinnati: South-Western Publishing Company, 1968.

Greenstein, Jesse L. "The Speculations of Science About the Universe." In *Scientific Progress and Human Values,* edited by Edward and Elizabeth Hutchings. New York: American Elsevier Publishing Company, Inc., 1967.

Haberler, Gottfried. *Inflation, Its Causes and Cures.* Rev. and enl. ed. Washington, D.C.: American Enterprise Institute for Public Policy Research, 1966.

Halacy, D. S., Jr. *Cyborg: Evolution of the Superman.* New York: Harper & Row, Publishers, 1965.

Haldane, J. B. S. "Future of the Mind." In *Man and His Future,* edited by Gordon Wolstenholme. Boston: Little, Brown and Company, 1963.

Hammond, J. D., ed. *Essays in the Theory of Risk and Insurance.* Glenview, Ill.: Scott, Foresman and Company, 1968.

Hansen, Alvin H. *Economic Issues of the 1960's.* New York: McGraw-Hill Book Company, Inc., 1960.

Hauser, Philip M. "Urbanization—Problems of High Density Living." In *World Population—The View Ahead,* edited by Richard N. Farmer; John D. Long; and George J. Stolnitz. Bloomington, Ind.: Bureau of Business Research, Graduate School of Business, Indiana University, 1968.

Hazlitt, Henry. *What You Should Know About Inflation.* Princeton, N.J.: D. Van Nostrand Company, Inc., 1965.

Himmelfarb, Gertrude, ed. *On Population—Thomas Robert Malthus.* New York: The Modern Library, 1960.

Hoagland, Hudson. "Potentialities in the Control of Behaviour." In *Man and His Future,* edited by Gordon Wolstenholme. Boston: Little, Brown and Company, 1963.

Hoyle, Fred. *The Nature of the Universe.* Rev. ed. New York: Harper & Row, Publishers, Inc., 1960.

Huebner, S. S.; Black, Kenneth, Jr.; and Cline, Robert S. *Property and Liability Insurance.* New York: Appleton-Century-Crofts, 1968.

Hutton, Graham. *Inflation and Society.* London: George Allen and Unwin Ltd., 1960.

Huxley, Julian. *The Human Crisis.* Seattle: University of Washington Press, 1963.

Insurance Facts. New York: Insurance Information Institute, 1969.

Insurance Markets of the World. Zurich: Swiss Reinsurance Company, 1964.

James, William. *Collected Essays and Reviews.* New York: Longmans, Green & Co., 1920.

Jones, W. T.; Sontag, Frederick; Beckner, Morton O.; and Fogelin, Robert J., eds. *Approaches to Ethics.* New York: McGraw-Hill Book Company, Inc., 1962.

Kahn, Herman, and Wiener, Anthony J. *The Year 2000: A Framework for Speculation on the Next Thirty-Three Years.* New York: The Macmillan Company, 1967.

Kant, Immanuel. *Critique of Practical Reason.* Translated by Lewis White Beck. Chicago: The University of Chicago Press, 1949.

Katona, George. *Psychological Analysis of Economic Behavior.* New York: McGraw-Hill Book Company, Inc., 1951.

Keeton, Robert E., and O'Connell, Jeffrey. *Basic Protection for the Traffic Victim: A Blueprint for Reforming Automobile Insurance.* Boston: Little, Brown and Company, 1965.

Keynes, John Maynard. *The General Theory of Employment Interest and Money.* New York: Harcourt, Brace and Company, n.d. (preface dated 1935).

Klir, Jiri, and Valach, Miroslav. *Cybernetic Modelling.* Translated by Pavel Dolan. London: Iliffe Books Ltd., 1967.

Krebs, Charles J. *The Lemming Cycle at Baker Lake, Northwest Territories, During 1959-62.* Montreal: The Arctic Institute of North America, 1964.

Kulp, C. A., and Hall, John W. *Casualty Insurance.* 4th ed. New York: The Ronald Press Company, 1968.

Landsberg, Hans H.; Fischman, Leonard L.; and Fisher, Joseph L. *Resources in America's Future.* Baltimore: The Johns Hopkins Press, 1963.

Lederberg, Joshua. "Biological Future of Man." In *Man and His Future,* edited by Gordon Wolstenholme. Boston: Little, Brown and Company, 1963.

Lenkers, John Nicholas, trans. *Luther's Epistle Sermons.* Vol. 2. Minneapolis: The Luther Press, 1909.

Life Insurance Fact Book. New York: Institute of of Life Insurance, 1969.

Lindsay, A. D. *Kant.* London: Oxford University Press, 1934.

Long, Edward LeRoy, Jr., "The History and Literature of 'The New Morality'." In *The Situation Ethics Debate,* edited by Harvey Cox. Philadelphia: The Westminster Press, 1968.

Lorimer, Frank. "Issues of Population Policy." In The American Assembly, *The Population Dilemma.* Englewood Cliffs, N.J.: Prentice-Hall, Inc., 1963.

Ludwig, Arnold M. *The Importance of Lying.* Springfield, Ill.: Charles C Thomas, Publisher, 1965.

Lunn, Arnold, and Lean, Garth. *The New Morality.* London: Blandford Press, 1964.

Macura, Milos. "The Long-Range Outlook—Summary of Current Estimates." In *World Population—The View Ahead,* edited by Richard N. Farmer; John D. Long; and George J. Stolnitz. Bloomington, Ind.: Bureau of Business Research, Graduate School of Business, Indiana University, 1968.

Magee, John H., and Bickelhaupt, David L. *General Insurance.* 7th ed. Homewood, Ill.: Richard D. Irwin, Inc., 1964.

Malthus, Thomas Robert. *An Essay on the Principle of Population.* Volumes 1-3. 5th ed. London: John Murray, 1817.

_____. *Principles of Political Economy.* 2nd ed. New York: Augustus M. Kelly, Inc., 1951.

Markowitz, Harry. *Portfolio Selection.* New York: John Wiley & Sons, Inc., 1959.

Mayerson, Allen L. *Introduction to Insurance.* New York: The Macmillan Company, 1962.

McCann, Edson. *Preferred Risk.* New York: Dell Publishing Company, 1955.

McGill, Dan M. *Life Insurance.* Rev. ed. Homewood, Ill.: Richard D. Irwin, Inc., 1967.

McLuhan, Marshall, and Fiore, Quentin. *The Medium is the Massage,* coordinated by Jerome Agel. New York: Bantam Books, Inc., 1967.

Medewar, P. B. *The Future of Man.* New York: Basic Books, Inc., 1960.

Mehr, Robert I., and Cammack, Emerson. *Principles of Insurance.* 4th ed. Homewood Ill.: Richard D. Irwin, Inc., 1966.

Meyers, Albert L. *Elements of Modern Economics.* 4th ed. Englewood Cliffs, N.J.: Prentice-Hall, Inc., 1956.

Michael, Donald N. "Free Time—The New Imperative in Our Society." In *Automation, Education, and Human Values,* edited by William W. Brickman and Stanley Lehrer. New York: School & Society Books, 1966.

Michelbacher, G. F. *Multiple-line Insurance.* New York: McGraw-Hill Book Company, Inc., 1957.

Moser, Shia. *Absolutism and Relativism in Ethics.* Springfield, Ill.: Charles C Thomas, Publisher, 1968.

Mowbray, Albert H., and Blanchard, Ralph H. *Insurance—Its Theory and Practice in the United States.* 5th ed. New York: McGraw-Hill Book Company, Inc., 1961.

New Zealand Official Yearbook, 1968. 73rd ed. Wellington: Department of Statistics.

Niebuhr, H. Richard. "The Center of Value." In *Moral Principles of Action,* edited by Ruth Anshen. New York: Harper & Brothers, 1952.

Paddock, William, and Paddock, Paul. *Famine 1975! America's Decision: Who Will Survive?* Boston: Little, Brown and Company, 1967.

Palyi, Melchior. *An Inflation Primer.* Chicago: Henry Regnery Company, 1961.

Patterson, Edwin W. *Essentials of Insurance Law.* New York: McGraw-Hill Book Company, Inc., 1935.

Pearl, Raymond. *The Biology of Population Growth.* New York: Alfred A. Knopf, 1925.

Penney, William. "The Future of Nuclear Power as Seen From the United Kingdom." In *Scientific Progress and Human Values,* edited by Edward and Elizabeth Hutchings. New York: American Elsevier Publishing Company, 1967.

Pfeffer, Irving. *Insurance and Economic Theory.* Homewood, Ill.: Richard D. Irwin, Inc., for the S. S. Huebner Foundation for Insurance Education, 1956.

Piddington, R. A. *The Limits of Mankind: A Philosophy of Population.* Bristol: John Wright and Sons Ltd., 1956.

Pollard, Spencer D. *How Capitalism Can Succeed.* Harrisburg, Pa.: The Stackpole Company, 1966.

Prehoda, Robert W. *Designing the Future.* Philadelphia: Chilton Book Company, 1967.

Products Liability—Brief Opposing Strict Liability in Tort. Milwaukee: The Defense Research Institute, Inc., 1966.

Rendall, Gerald H. *Marcus Aurelius Antoninus to Himself: An English Translation with Introductory Study on Stoicism and the Last of the Stoics.* 2nd ed. London: Macmillan and Co., Ltd., 1898.

Rhymes, Douglas A. *No New Morality.* London: Constable & Cox, Ltd., 1964.

Riegel, Robert, and Miller, Jerome S. *Insurance Principles and Practices.* 5th ed. Englewood Cliffs, N.J.: Prentice-Hall, Inc., 1966.

Robinson, John A. T. *Honest to God.* Philadelphia: The Westminster Press, 1963.

Rodda, William H. *Property and Liability Insurance.* Englewood Cliffs, N.J.: Prentice-Hall, Inc., 1966.

Rogers, Reginald A. P. *A Short History of Ethics.* London: Macmillan and Co., Ltd., 1937.

Samuelson, Paul A. *Economics: An Introductory Analysis.* 7th ed. New York: McGraw-Hill Book Company, 1967.

Sauvain, Harry C. *Investment Management.* 3rd ed. Englewood Cliffs, N.J.: Prentice-Hall, Inc., 1967.

Scarlott, Charles A. "Energy." In Foreign Policy Association, *Toward the Year 2018.* New York: Cowles Education Corporation, 1968.

Schlick, Moritz. "What is the Aim of Ethics?" In *Logical Positivism,* edited by A. J. Ayer. New York: The Free Press, 1959.

Schon, Donald A. *Technology and Change.* New York: A Seymour Lawrence Book/ Delacorte Press, 1967.

Schurr, Sam H.; Netschert, Bruce C.; Eliasberg, Vera F.; Lerner, Joseph; and Landsberg, Hans H. *Energy in the American Economy, 1850-1975.* Baltimore: The Johns Hopkins Press, 1960.

Selsam, Howard. *Ethics and Progress: New Values in a Revolutionary World.* New York: International Publishers, 1965.

Shannon, Claude E., and Weaver, Warren. *The Mathematical Theory of Communication.* Urbana: University of Illinois Press, 1949.

Sidgwick, Henry. *The Method of Ethics.* 7th ed. Chicago: The University of Chicago Press, 1907.

Slichter, Sumner H. *Economic Growth in the United States.* Baton Rouge: Louisiana State University Press, 1961.

Source Book of Health Insurance Data. New York: Health Insurance Institute, 1969.

Statistical Abstract of Sweden. Stockholm: Central Bureau of Statistics, 1967.

Statistical Abstract, 1963. Dar Es Salaam: Republic of Tanganyika, Central Statistical Bureau, Directorate of Development Planning, 1964.

Statistical Yearbook United Nations, 1967. New York: United Nations, Department of Economic and Social Affairs, 1968.

Taeuber, Conrad, and Taeuber, Irene B. *The Changing Population of the United States.* Census Monograph Series. New York: John Wiley & Sons, Inc., 1958.

Taylor, Gordon Rattray. *The Biological Time Bomb.* New York: The World Publishing Company, 1968.

Thorp, Willard L., and Quandt, Richard E. *The New Inflation.* New York: McGraw-Hill Book Company, Inc., 1959.

U.S. Department of Commerce. *Business Statistics, 1967—A Supplement to the Survey of Current Business.* 16th biennial ed. Washington, D.C.: U.S. Govt. Printing Office, 1967.

_____. Bureau of the Census. *Historical Statistics of the United States—Colonial Times to 1957.* Washington, D.C.: U.S. Govt. Printing Office, 1960.

_____. Bureau of the Census. *Statistical Abstract of the United States, 1967.* 88th ed. Washington, D.C.: U.S. Govt. Printing Office, 1967.

_____. Bureau of the Census. *Statistical Abstract of the United States, 1968.* 89th ed. Washington, D.C.: U.S. Govt. Printing Office, 1968.

_____. Bureau of the Census. *Statistical Abstract of the United States, 1969.* 90th ed. Washington, D.C.: U.S. Govt. Printing Office, 1969.

U.S. Department of Labor. *Handbook of Labor Statistics—1968.* Washington, D.C.: U.S. Govt. Printing Office, 1968.

Vance, William R. *Handbook on the Law of Insurance.* 3rd ed. (Prepared by Buist M. Anderson.) St. Paul: West Publishing Company, 1951.

Warnock, Mary. *Ethics Since 1900.* 2nd ed. London: Oxford University Press, 1966.

Weber, Max. *The Protestant Ethic and the Spirit of Capitalism.* Translated by Talcott Parsons. New York: Charles Scribner's Sons, 1958.

Wiener, Norbert. *Cybernetics or Control and Communication in the Animal and the Machine.* 2nd ed. New York: The M.I.T. Press and John Wiley & Sons, Inc., 1961.

_____. *The Human Use of Human Beings.* Boston: Houghton Mifflin Company, 1954.

Wilde, Frazar B. "Introduction." In *Managing A Full Employment Economy.* New York: Committee for Economic Development, 1966.

Williams, C. Arthur, Jr., and Heins, Richard M. *Risk Management and Insurance.* New York: McGraw-Hill Book Company, 1964.

Winter, William D. *Marine Insurance—Its Principles and Practices.* 3rd. ed. New York: McGraw-Hill Book Company, 1952.

Wood, Frederick C., Jr. *Sex and the New Morality.* New York: Association Press, 1968.

Woods, George. "Situational Ethics." In *Christian Ethics and Contemporary Philosophy,* edited by Ian T. Ramsey. New York: The Macmillan Company, 1966.

1970 World Population Data Sheet (Washington, D.C.: Population Reference Bureau, Inc.).

Wynne-Edwards, V. C. *Animal Dispersion in Relation to Social Behaviour.* New York: Hafner Publishing Company, 1962.

Wythenshawe, Lord Simon of. *Some Aspects of World Population and Food Resources.* Occasional Papers on Eugenics, no. 9. London: Cassell and Company Ltd. and The Eugenics Society, 1955.

Young, Louise B., ed. *Population in Perspective.* New York: Oxford University Press, 1968.

Periodicals

"Ark. Denies Riot Charge." *Business Insurance,* vol. 72 (May 20, 1968).

Buckley, William F., Jr. "Strange Idea of What Makes 'Middle Class Values'." *Bloomington* (Ind.) *Daily Herald-Telephone* (March 27. 1969).

Burck, Gilbert. "Must Full Employment Mean Inflation?" *Fortune,* vol. 74 (October, 1966).

Blake, Judith Ann. "Income and Reproductive Motivation." *Population Index,* vol. 33 (July-August, 1967).

Berkner, Lloyd V. "Man Versus Technology." *Population Bulletin,* vol. 22 (November, 1966).

Bridgman, Percy W. "The New Vision of Science." *Harper's Magazine,* vol. 158 (March, 1929).

Calabresi, Guido. "Views and Overviews." *The University of Illinois Law Forum* (Fall, 1967).

"Charges Developed by Three Bureaus for Civil Disorders." *National Underwriter*, vol. 72 (March 29, 1968).

Calhoun, J. B. "Population Density and Social Pathology." *Scientific American*, vol. 206 (February, 1962).

Cole, Lamont C. "Population Phenomena and Common Knowledge." *The Scientific Monthly*, vol. 67 (November, 1948).

Cook, Robert C. "Soviet Population Theory from Marx to Kosygin." *Population Bulletin*, vol. 23 (October, 1967).

Davis, Kingsley. "The Urbanization of the Human Population." *Scientific American*, vol. 213 (September, 1965).

Dickerson, O. D. "The Problem of Overutilization in Health Insurance." *Journal of Insurance*, vol. 26 (Spring, 1959).

"Divorce Insurance Studied." *Indianapolis Star*, (December 15, 1968).

Elliott-Jones, M. F. "Population Growth and Fertility Behavior." *Conference Board Record*, vol. 5 (September, 1968).

Experiodica, vol. 3, no. 4 (no date).

Farmer, Richard N. "The Ethical Dilemma of American Capitalism." *California Management Review*, vol. 6 (Summer, 1964).

Friedman, Milton, and Savage, L. J. "The Utility Analysis of Choices Involving Risk." *Journal of Political Economy*, vol. 56 (August, 1948).

Gainsbrugh, Martin R. "Inflation and the New Economics." *Conference Board Record*, vol. 4 (August, 1967).

Harriss, C. Lowell. "Inflation's Hidden Effects." *Tax Review*, vol. 28 (July, 1967).

"Higher Birth Rate Sought by De Gaulle." *Indianapolis Star* (November 10, 1968).

Hoagland, Hudson. "Cybernetics of Population Control." *Bulletin of the Atomic Scientists*, vol. 20 (February, 1964).

"Industry's Responsibility in a Young Society," moderated by R. L. Cutler. *General Electric Forum*, vol. 12 (Spring, 1969).

Kimball, Spencer L. "Automobile Accident Compensation Systems—Objectives and Perspectives." *The University of Illinois Law Forum* (Fall, 1967).

"Law Institute Hit for Urging Concept of Strict Liability." *National Underwriter*, vol. 70 (September 16, 1966).

"Lawyers Look to Social Reform, Not Law to Cure Crime Problem." *National Observer* (August 12, 1968).

"Leisure in America." Chase Manhattan Bank *Business in Brief*, no. 57 (July-August, 1964).

Levy, Michael E. "Full Employment and Inflation: A 'Trade-off' Analysis." *Conference Board Record*, vol. 3 (December, 1966).

Mann, E. J. "Inflation and Accounting in Brazil." *Journal of Accountancy*, vol. 124 (November, 1967).

Martin, William McChesney, Jr. "Statement to Congress." *Federal Reserve Bulletin*, vol. 53 (December, 1967).

Monthly Labor Review, current issues.

Morris, Judy K. "Professor Malthus and His Essay," in "Malthus in Retrospect." *Population Bulletin*, vol. 22 (February, 1966).

Oglesby, Carl. "Break Down the System?" *The General Electric Forum*, vol. 12 (Spring, 1969).

Picone, Alexander. "1968: The Year of Truth." *Journal of Insurance Information*, vol. 30 (January-February, 1969).

Rinfret, Pierre A. "Inflation Hedges." *The Institutional Investor*, vol. 2 (June and July, 1968).

_____. "Inflation—So What?" *The Institutional Investor*, part 1, vol. 2 (August and September, 1968).

Schmidt, Richard F. "Does a Deductible Curb Moral Hazard?" *Journal of Insurance*, vol. 28 (September, 1961).

Shaw, Milton, and Whitman, Merrill. "Nuclear Power: Suddenly Here." *Science and Technology*, no. 75 (March, 1968).

Smith, Delos. "Pure Antibody Structure 'Spelled Out'." *Bloomington* (Ind.) *Daily Herald-Telephone* (April 14, 1969).

"Soviet Population Theory From Marx to Kosygin." *Population Bulletin*, vol. 23 (October, 1967).

"Soviets Stride in Tapping H-Power." *Bloomington* (Ind.) *Daily Herald-Telephone* (April 11, 1969).

Steinmetz, R. C. "Arson Developments." *Best's Insurance News*, Fire and Casualty Edition, vol. 67 (February, 1967).

Strecker, Robert L. "Populations of House Mice." *Scientific American*, vol. 193 (December, 1955).

Survey of Current Business, current issues.

Taeuber, Irene B. "The Changing Population." *Urban Land*, vol. 26 (July-August, 1967).

Thompson, Arthur A. "The Control of Demand-Pull Inflation: A Policy Suggestion." *Quarterly Review of Economics and Business*, vol. 8 (Spring, 1968).

Tracy, Myles A. "Insurance and Theology: The Background and the Issues." *Journal of Risk and Insurance*, vol. 33 (March, 1966).

Vila, George R. "The Wages of Leisure." *Conference Board Record*, vol. 5 (March, 1968).

Wynne-Edwards, V. C. "Population Control in Animals." *Scientific American*, vol. 211 (August, 1964).

Miscellaneous

Annual Report of the American Bar Association Including Proceedings of the Ninety-second Annual Meeting. Chicago: American Bar Association, 1969.

Bogue, Donald J. "The Prospects for World Population Control." Mimeographed. Chicago: University of Chicago, 1966.

Boyarsky, A. Y. "A Contribution to the Problem of World Population in the Year 2000." *Proceedings of the World Population Conference—Belgrade, August 30-September 10, 1965.* Vol. 3. Sales no. 66XIII.6. New York: United Nations, 1967.

Durand, John D. "World Population Estimates." *Proceedings of the World Population Conference—Belgrade, August 30-September 10, 1965.* Vol. 2. Sales no. 66XIII.6. New York: United Nations, 1967.

Employment Act of 1946. United States Code Annotated (1963), Title 15, Section 1021.

"FAIR Plan Status at a Glance." A chart developed by the American Mutual Insurance Alliance, December 10, 1968, and updated by "General Bulletin 69-10," January 29, 1969.

Greene, Mark R. "A Sociological View of Insurance." Presented at the 1965 Risk Theory Seminar of the American Risk and Insurance Association, Chicago, Illinois.

Mehr, Robert I., and Neumann, Seev. "Inflation, Technology and Growth: Possible Implications for Insurance." Manuscript to be published by the Bureau of Business Research, Graduate School of Business, Indiana University, Bloomington, Indiana.

National Economic Projections to 1975/76. Washington, D.C.: National Planning Association, 1965.

Report of the Administrative Board of the Judicial Conference of the State of New York for the Judicial Year July 1, 1966 through June 30, 1967. Legislative document no. 90. Albany: State of New York, 1968.

Report of the Special Committee on Insurance Holding Companies. New York: State of New York, Insurance Department, 1968.

Swadener, Paul. "Fire Insurance Rate Level Revision Procedures." Unpublished doctoral dissertation, Graduate School of Business, Indiana University, 1968.

Taeuber, Irene B. "Future Population Trends and Prospects: Statement by the Moderator," *Proceedings of the World Population Conference—Belgrade, August 30-September 10, 1965.* Vol. 1. Sales no. 66XIII.6. New York: United Nations, 1966.

Urban Property Protection and Reinsurance Act of 1968. United States Code Annotated (1969), Title 12, Subchapter IX-C, Sec. 1749 bbb.

U.S. Department of Commerce. Bureau of the Census. *America at Mid-Decade.* Washington, D.C.: U.S. Govt. Printing Office, 1966.

———. Bureau of the Census. *Heads of Families at the First Census of the United States in the Year 1790.* Washington, D.C.: U.S. Govt. Printing Office, 1907.

———. Bureau of the Census. *Population Estimates, Current Population Reports.* Series P-25, no. 443 (February 1, 1970).

———. Bureau of the Census. *Population Trends in the United States 1900 to 1960,* by Irene B. Taeuber. Bureau of the Census Technical Paper no. 10. Washington, D.C.: U.S. Govt. Printing Office, 1964.

———. Bureau of the Census. "Summary of Demographic Projections." *Current Population Reports.* Series P-25, no. 388 (March 14, 1968).

U.S. Department of Justice. Federal Bureau of Investigation. *Crime in the United States—Uniform Crime Reports—1968.* Washington, D.C.: U.S. Govt. Printing Office, 1968.

———. Immigration and Naturalization Service. *1967 Annual Report of the Immigration and Naturalization Service.* Washington, D.C.: U.S. Govt. Printing Office, 1968.

———. Immigration and Naturalization Service. *1968 Annual Report of the Immigration and Naturalization Service.* Washington, D.C.: U.S. Govt. Printing Office, 1969.

U.S. National Commission on Technology, Automation, and Economic Progress. *Technology and the American Economy.* Vol. 1. Washington, D.C.: U.S. Govt. Printing Office, 1966.

U.S. President's National Advisory Panel on Insurance in Riot-Affected Areas. *Hearings Before the President's National Advisory Panel on Insurance in Riot-Affected Areas,* November 8-9, 1967.

———. *Meeting the Insurance Crisis of our Cities.* Washington, D.C.: U.S. Govt. Printing Office, January, 1968.

Wagner, Peter. *The Scope and Financing of Urban Renewal and Development.* NPA Planning Pamphlet 119. Washington, D.C.: National Planning Association, 1963.

World Population Prospects As Assessed in 1963. Population Studies no. 41. New York: United Nations, 1966.

INDEX

Index of Authors

Index of Subjects

A

Absolute Good, 244, 248

Abundance, 85, 177-78, 193-96, 199, 237

Achievement as ethical pillar of insurance, 26-27, 43, 125, 138-41, 170, 196-98, 201, 203, 235-37, 239-40, 270-74, 276, 280-81

Acquisitiveness as ethical pillar of insurance, 27-29, 43, 125, 170, 196-98, 201, 203, 235-37, 239-40, 270-74, 276, 280-81

Additional living expense insurance, 33

Adverse selection, 34

Advertising, 280-81

Agape-love, 260-62, 266, 269-72

American Bar Association, 96

Amish, 38-39

Animal behavior, 76-78, 94-95, 223-24

Antiauthoritarianism, 268

Antinomianism, 257-58

Apprehension as ethical pillar of insurance, 31-32, 43, 125, 201, 203, 208, 235-37, 239-40, 270-74, 276, 280-81

Arguments for continuing inflation, 151-70

Arson, 103-7, 133, 272-73; civil disobedience, 106-7; fraud, 104-5; fun, 105; juvenile, 105; mobster, 105; public buildings, 105-7

Astronomy, 205-8, 276

Athens, 188

Atomic fission, 183-87

Atomic fusion, 183-87

Automation, 228-29

Automobile insurance, 98, 113, 117, 119-20

Automobile thefts, 97-98

Averaging of insured losses, 107-19

Aversion to loss, 29, 197

B

Balanced budget, 161-62

Bank deposits, 164-68

Barter, 20-21, 24

Biology, 208-25, 276

Bionics, 216

Bird behavior, 77-78

Black box, 233

Body organs, 211-14

Breeder reactors, 185-86

Building blocks of universe, 203-5

Bureau of the Census. See U.S. Bureau of the Census

Business interruption insurance, 33

C

Calvinist ethic, 189

Campus unrest, 193-96, 268

Capitalism, 26, 49, 56, 133, 278

Categorical imperative, 252-56, 269

Charity as ethical pillar of insurance, 39-40, 43, 125, 201, 235-37, 239-40, 270-74, 276, 280-81

Cheating, 133-38, 170, 269, 272

Chimera, 215

Christianity, 194, 207, 245-46, 251, 258-60, 266, 269

Civil disorders, 1, 106-8, 113-17, 261-62, 264

Clergy as ethical thought leaders, 265-66

Cloning, 220

Coal, 178, 180-81

Coinsurance, 196

Collectivism and insurance, 112

Committee for Economic Development, 161

Computer, 209, 230-32, 234, 236

Conglomerates, 124

Consequential insurance, 33, 36

Consumer prices, 140, 143-45, 147-54, 169, appendix

Contemplation of the good, 188-89, 194, 247-48

Controlled thermonuclear fusion, 183-84, 186

Cost of energy, 171, 177-79, 186-87

Crime, 1, 27, 86-108, 133, 261-62, 269, 272; auto thefts, 97-98; civil disorders, 1, 106-8, 261-62, 264; crime index, 88-90; FBI data, 87-93; implications for insurance, 97-107; outlook, 95-96; population density, 93-96; rates in U.S., 86-96; rates elsewhere, 87; repetition, 90-92; situationism, 261-62, 264, 272

Cryogenics, 123, 212

Curve of gentility, 11

Cybernetics, 94, 215, 225-37, 272

Cyborg, 214-17

Cynics, 245

Cyrenaics, 247